HUNTINGTON BEACH
The Gem of the South Coast
By Diann Marsh

ISBN: 1-886483-20-5

Library of Congress Card Catalog Number: 97-078260

Author and Photo Editor: Diann Marsh

Publisher: C.E. Parks

Editor-in-Chief: Lori M. Parks

VP/National Sales Manager: Ray Spagnuolo

VP/Corporate Development: Bart Barica

Regional Manager: Kathee Finn

Project Coordinators: Marci Potter, Victoria Coles

Production Manager: Deborah Sherwood

Project Art Director: Gina Mancini

Production Staff: Sean Gates, Brad Hartman, David Hermstead, Jay Kennedy, John Leyva, Paul Scates, Steve Trainor, Ray Williams

Operations Manager: Marla Eckhoff

Editorial Manager: Betsy Blondin

Editorial Coordinators: Lesley Abrams, Susan Ikeda, Renee Kim, Betsy Lelja, Molly O'Connor, Sara Rufner

Administration: Cory Graham, Scott Reid, Ellen Ruby, Juan Diaz

Profile Writers: Barbara Barclay, Betty Lougaris, Marilyn Marcus, Trudie Mitschang, Cynthia Pinsky, Chris Trela,

Jody Marquez Wood, Sharon Wurth, Toby Young

Produced in cooperation with the Huntington Beach Historical Society

19820 Beach Boulevard

Huntington Beach, CA 92648

(714) 969-9108

Published by

Heritage Media Corp.

6354 Corte del Abeto, Suite B

Carlsbad, California 92009

www.heritagemedia.com

Printed by Heritage Media Corp. in the United States of America

Dedication Robert Marsh

This book is dedicated to Robert Marsh, my wonderful husband of 45 years. We share a love of history, antiques and historic buildings.

Photo by Debbie Stock

Photo by Debbie Stock

Contents

Foreword

From Surf to Space...we have it all. Huntington Beach is a wonderful place to live, to work and to raise families. We are proud of our eight and a half miles of beaches, over 2,000 acres of wetlands and more than 600 acres of parks. We are a beautiful city because we are blessed with a perfect environment. Both our residents and our visitors enjoy our parks and beaches. It was through the efforts of the citizens of Huntington Beach that we were able to save thousands of acres, which are now in parks throughout the city. At the heart of this City is our library which is located in Central Park. The Huntington Beach Public Library is considered one of the finest in the nation, and has the largest children's wings west of the Mississippi. Our Community Theater is located in the library, and every summer concerts take place in the park. Downtown is the home of our Art Center, which receives ongoing rave reviews for its innovative and experimental approach to art. Huntington Beach is the home of the Golden West Community College.

This beautiful environment is amazing since Huntington Beach was once an oil town having the second largest oil field in the state. Before that we were home to many Native Americans who lived a simple, but successful life using the coastal resources, the entire area was a Spanish land grant, and then a very productive agricultural area, before oil was discovered.

Huntington Beach is a city of beautiful homes, from homes in Huntington Harbor to the unique living in downtown and the new homes built on Edwards Hill. We also know the importance of industry and commercial development if a city is to provide services to its citizens. We are the home of Boeing's Space Division, with surrounding industrial parks. Currently a new resort is being built adjacent to the beautiful Waterfront Hilton. Major improvements are being made in the downtown area, and we recently dedicated our Pier Plaza at the head of the pier. Two fine restaurants have opened at the pier, which add to the excellent restaurants already in Huntington Beach.

What makes Huntington Beach the great city it is? The answer is the people of our city make Huntington Beach what it is. They are tireless in their efforts to make this the best place to live and visit. Our citizens have fought to save wetlands and parks, they have raised thousands of dollars to build a library, they support our Art Center, our schools, and are represented on boards and commissions. Citizens serve on the Planning Commission, Library Board, Public Works, Allied Arts Board, and many others. We see senior citizens volunteering with our Police and Fire Departments; our residents make sure our city is ready for any emergency by volunteering their time to prepare for disasters. The list goes on and on. Citizens are the heart and strength of the city. Their efforts make this a city we are all proud to call our hometown, Huntington Beach, California.

Shirley Dettlof
Mayor, Huntington Beach

Introduction

In February 1999, the City of Huntington Beach celebrates the 90th year of its incorporation. In 1909, when the community decided to incorporate, it's very possible that no one dreamed of the many directions in which the community would blossom and grow. The fascinating story tells about the city's successful ventures in agriculture, the oil fields, tourism and the beach, industry, and the remarkable housing growth of the 1960s, 70s and 80s.

In 1986, I worked for Thirtieth Street Architects on the Historic Resources Survey of the historic section of the city. I met a large group of enthusiastic and hardworking Huntington Beach residents who spent hundreds of hours helping with the windshield survey, research, writing and photography that resulted in a successful document.

The Huntington Beach Historical Society has been instrumental in the preservation, restoration and maintenance of the Queen Anne Victorian Newland House. It sits, clean and shining with fresh white paint, on the top of a knoll next to the Newland Center. The park lands behind the house slope down to the same tree-filled ravine that was present when the Newlands built the house in 1898. Although the lowlands beyond are covered with modern houses instead of a swamp and willows, one can get the sense of the topography as the family saw it so long ago.

I remember the first time I saw the Newland House. Ramps led across the large dirt squares where the Pacific Coast Archaeological Society was conducting digs in an effort to discover artifacts left behind by the Indians hundreds of years ago. I was impressed by the house's perfect setting on a knoll high above a meandering tree-filled ravine. It was easy to picture how the place must have looked to the Newland family when they moved into their new house in 1898. Keeping the house open so that its special beauty can be shared by others is a big task that has been undertaken by the Historical Society for the past 25 years. Members of the organization, especially Maureen Rivers and Carl Clink, aided in the writing of this book by opening the archives on the second floor of the Newland barn and generously loaning many important photos to me.

There is a lot about Huntington Beach to enjoy. Wandering along the paths of the Bolsa Chica E

The First American Title Insurance Company, where curator Barbara Blankman cares for a repository of thousands of historic photos, allowed me to select items from their collection that helped bring the history of Huntington Beach alive. Photos from the 1950s and 60s were obtained from Marshall Duell, curator of the Geivet Collection of the Old Courthouse Museum in the Old Orange County Courthouse.

Arline Huff Howard, who is so proud of her heritage and her community, lent many materials and photographs to me, spending a couple of afternoons telling me about the Huff and Gallienne families.

City Historian Alicia Wentworth is a veritable storehouse of historical information. We spent an afternoon together in her office in City Hall discussing her first-hand experiences. She lent me the sets of Sanborn map slides for 1909, 1922 and 1930 and the book she compiled about Huntington Beach history. I also had a chance to meet City Clerk Connie Brockway and read her interesting publication of notes taken from old city council minutes.

Jerry Person, who has written many interesting historical articles for the newspaper, clearly loves Huntington Beach history and the people who have made it special. His personal style of writing brings his characters to life.

Dr. Barbara Milkovitch, who spent long hours setting up the Historical Society Archives, has written many articles and pamphlets about the Newland House and city history. Historian friends Keith Dixon, Jim and Nola Sleeper, Don Dobmeier, Phil Brigandi, Carol Jordan, Esther Cramer, Steve Donaldson and Ellen Lee possess an amazing amount of information about the history of every part of Orange County and can always be called upon to help.

There is a lot about Huntington Beach to enjoy. Wandering along the paths of the Bolsa Chica Ecological Preserve just as the Indians had done hundreds of years ago can bring a sense of peace. On a hill in the distance are the trees that mark the site of the old Bolsa Chica Gun Club. Traveling the streets between Orange and Lake you will come upon many charming beach cottages and historic houses. The Boy Scout Cabin, built of logs in 1924, sits under the tall trees at Lake Park. Huntington Beach history is there to see, if you seek it out.

Diann Marsh

February 1999

Chapter One

NATURAL WONDER

For almost 50 years after Columbus discovered the east coast of America, the west coast slumbered in undisturbed splendor. The only inhabitants of the west were the Indians who roamed freely over the valleys, foothills and mountains. They gathered the seeds of wild grasses, fruit and berries and feasted on any wild animals they could snare. In the summer, they made camp on the beaches, catching fish and consuming large amounts of clams.

THE BOLSA CHICA WETLANDS

Where the rivers meet the sea are shallow coastal bays, a unique mixture of both salt and fresh water. Rich with nutrients, the estuaries are nature's nurseries, teeming with an abundance of wildlife and plants.

In the early spring, the wetlands are alive with terns, gulls and other birds displaying courtship behavior. Soon, the birds are tending nests on the sandy islands. Purple sand verbena, sea lavender frankenia and telegraph weed bloom at water's edge.

Summer brings five different species of terns and black skimmers, deftly diving for fish to feed their young. Sea hares, some as large as 15 inches long, and round stingrays populate the shallow bays. Predators such as coyotes, prowl the nesting sites. Snowy plovers congregate in flocks on the bare islands, while brown pelicans soar overhead. Avocets, phalaropes, sanderlings, yellowlegs and stilts move quickly along the the water's edge, looking for food. Green algae provide essential nutrients for the birds and fish.

In the fall, migrating birds such as pintail ducks and geese stop on their way south. White Pelicans, sandpipers, widgeons, great blue herons and shorelers occupy the bays and islands.

In the winter, a variety of birds can be seen feeding along the shoreline. White herons are easy to spot as they walk slowly among the weeds along the shoreline. Small smooth-mouthed sharks, grey millets and stingrays can be seen as they move silently through the water.

Each season brings a treasury of animals, birds, plants and fish to the Bolsa Chica Wetlands.

CALIFORNIA

The very name — California — makes us think of sunny days, sandy beaches, and exotic and romantic scenes. In *Ranchos of California*, Robert Cowan puts forth the theory that the name California comes from the Garcia Ordonez de Montalvo book entitled *Las Sergas De Explanadian*. Published in 1510 in Seville, Spain, the novel describes a place called California as being close to the imaginary Terrestrial Paradize, "to the right of the Indies." Powerful black amazons and griffiths, ruled by Queen Califia, inhabited the mythical land which was described as rich with precious stones and gold. When the Spanish and Mexican pioneers settled in the region, they were called "Californios."

From the ancient Hokan-speaking Indian tribes which roamed the west coast over 2,000 years ago, to the rush of thousands of cars on a 12-lane freeway,

A LAND OF NATURAL WONDERS

Courtesy Arline Huff Howard

the virgin land called California has changed beyond our wildest dreams.

THE INDIANS OF THE COASTAL LANDS

The stone age tribes which first occupied the hills, plains, beaches and valleys of Southern California could have arrived as early as 6000 B. C. They are believed to have been members of the Hokan-speaking language group. The cause of their disappearance is a mystery. Archaeologists continue to search for physical evidence of these early aboriginal tribes.

The early pioneers called the coastal region between the present cities of Huntington Beach and Long Beach by the descriptive name of Shell Beach because of the hundreds of thousands of empty shells left along the beaches and bluffs by the Indians.

THE SHOSHONEANS

Over 1,500 years ago, members of the Shoshonean linguistic group drifted across the Great Basin, walked through the mountain passes, and began to occupy the arid and unspoiled coastal lands, valleys, foothills and

Huntington Beach: The Gem of the South Coast

(Far left) This view of the interior of a thatched hut features a bed made of tree branches and covered with animal skins. *Courtesy First American Title Insurance Co.*

The Gabrielino, Juaneno and Luiseño Indians lived in thatched huts made of tule grasses over frames made of bent willow branches. These houses were sometimes called wickiups. *Courtesy First American Title Insurance Co.*

mountains of what we now call Southern California. The Shoshoneans were related to the Indian tribes of the western desert, such as the Hopis, Comanches and Utes.

Although the Shoshoneans often moved around to find available food sources, they also lived in semi-permanent villages. An article in the *Santa Ana Independent* (August 15, 1951) surmises that the Indians camped near the ocean in the summer to take advantage of the cool ocean breezes, and moved back into the hills and canyons when winter came. They gave musical-sounding names to their villages such as Pavuunga, Tibaha and Lukupa. Some archaeologists think that Lukupa, sometimes called Lukup, was located on the knoll where the Newland family built their home in 1898. The site is one of the few knolls in that area that rises above the Santa Ana River floodplain. Other experts believe that the location was just across the gully from where the Serrano adobe is now located.

The Indian tribal names of Gabrielino, Juaneno, and Luiseño were not in use until the arrival of the mission fathers, and it is not known whether the Indians themselves used them. The names reflect the mission territory in which the Indians lived. For example, the Indians attached to the San Gabriel Mission were called Gabrielinos. Those who lived on the lands given to the Mission San Juan Capistrano were called Juanenos. Mission San Luis Rey was the home of the Luiseños. The Gabrielino tribe occupied the area from the ocean to as far east as the Prado area near Corona.

The Shoshoneans, having no written language, have passed their knowledge and rich traditions down through the ages, providing a unique background of songs, ceremonies, petroglyphs, pictographs, dances and story-telling.

THE RELIGION CALLED CHINIGCHINICH

There is little written material available which describes the everyday lives of the Gabrielino Indians. A handful of early scholars made significant efforts to describe the life of the Indians living in Southern California. One of the earliest and most detailed descriptions was written by Father Geronimo Boscana, who served at the Mission San Juan Capistrano for several years. When he died at the Mission San Gabriel in 1831, his observations, written in Spanish, were discovered in his room. It was not until 1846 that Alfred Robinson, realizing the importance of the manuscript, translated it into English. In modern times the manuscript has been printed under the name of *Chinigchinich*.

More than 1,500 years ago, the Shoshonean-speaking Indians crossed the mountain passes from Arizona and occupied the plains, valleys, foothills, mountains and beaches of Southern California. The territory in which they settled was called the Shoshonean Wedge. They lived on wild game, seeds, wild fruits, frogs, water birds, shellfish and whatever edible food they could find. *Courtesy Pacific Coast Archaeological Society*

This illustration of a cogged stone, usually made from basalt or granite, are found in only two places in the world: Southern California and Las Salinas, Chile. The stones had varied shapes and number of cogs. No one knows what they were used for or why they were made. *Courtesy Pacific Coast Archaeological Society*

14

The discoidal and pestles shown here were found by Arline Howard at her grandfather's farm on Huff's Hill, northeast of Huntington Beach. Some archaeologists think the discoidals, which are shaped like round wheels, were used in games and contests. *Courtesy Arline Howard Collection*

Religious beliefs, customs and superstitions played a strong role in the everyday life of the average Indian. Chinigchinich, first worshiped by the Gabrielinos, was the name of a supreme deity who later became the key figure in the religion practiced by the Luiseños and the Juanenos. Each community made its own Chinigchinich god out of a coyote skin, with the hair, feet and head still attached. The skin was stuffed with the feathers of specific kinds of birds, deer horns, mountain lion claws, bird beaks, talons and crow parts. When finished, the deity looked like a coyote with arrows projecting from its mouth, and wore a skirt of special hawk feathers. The god had his own oval-shaped temple made of bent poles covered in rushes. The center of the roof was open to the sky. Ritual sand paintings, in deep colors, were spread on the ground in front of the special temple, which was surrounded by a fence.

According to Father Boscana, Chinigchinich was not particular in whom he protected. He could shield the evildoer as well as the believer who worshiped him. The chief and council members were shown a certain respect; however, there were no written laws and the people lived much as they pleased. There were a few laws that everyone was expected to follow: only certain people could enter the temple, hunters could not eat animals that they themselves had killed, and fasting was mandatory during the puberty ceremony. If a person broke a taboo or angered the chief, he could lose his life.

As with most Indian cultures, the puberty ceremony represented a significant rite of passage. A young girl was allowed to marry only if she had completed her ritual. Lying on a bed of hot coals in a shallow pit, she was the center of attention as the women of the tribe danced around her and prayed to Chinigchinich to make her the mother of many children. Both males and females were required to fast for three days as part of this important ceremony.

In hopes of making the young male fierce in battle, he was branded on the upper arm, whipped with nettles and covered with ants. After he had survived these trials he surely felt worthy to take his place among the men of the tribe.

THE EVERYDAY LIFE OF THE GABRIELINOS

Father Boscana said of the Indians, "they neither cultivated the ground or planted any kind of grain, but lived upon the abundance of the game."

Before modern times, rabbits, quail, deer, squirrels, bears and other animals were plentiful in the foothills and valleys. Hunting, cooking and eating these animals not only helped meet nutritional needs, but also clothing needs. The resourceful Indians put to good use any kind of animal they were able to obtain. In addition, there were fish, water birds and frogs in the river, and, if they journeyed to the ocean, they could find shellfish and ocean creatures.

Acorns provided the major food for the Indian's sustenance. Gathered from oak trees in the hills, they were dried and stored in large baskets. In order to make them edible, the acorns had to be leached with hot water to remove the strong tannin. The meal which resulted after the acorns were ground in a metate was most often cooked as a mush. In addition, wild grapes, manzanita berries, wild plums, gooseberries, cactus fruits, and other seasonal fruits and berries added important vitamins to their diet.

According to Father Zephyrin Englehardt, the women wore skirts or cloaks made of rabbit skins. They wore their hair long and loved to wear jewelry made from shells or feathers. The children usually wore nothing. The men sometimes wore one or more animal pelts about their shoulders, and, in cold weather sometimes plastered themselves with mud in an effort to ward off the cold.

Because of the mild climate in Southern California, the Indians could wear clothing made of grasses, rushes

and feathers. According to Margaret L. Class, an expert on weaving, the Indians used the basic technique of fingerweaving. Resembling modern macramé, the process produced head bands and belts decorated with shell beads or feathers. Knotted skirts of twisted cedar strips, featuring an open lacy pattern, were especially prized. The fur of the many rabbits who lived in the region was often woven into a warm blanket.

A mystery that has never been solved is the use of the cogged stones left behind on the Bolsa Chica Wetlands by the Indians. They are thought by some to have some obscure religious significance. Carved from hard stone, the cogged stones had a varying number of cogs. They have been found in only two places in the world — Southern California and Las Salinas, Chile.

Each community had its share of small semi-circular sweathouses, used primarily by men, either for hygiene or ritual purposes. These semi-subterranean sweathouses had roofs supported by wooden poles set into the ground and covered with soil. A fire, built near the doorway, was used to heat the interior to high temperatures. A nearby pool was used for rinsing.

The Gabrielinos, Luiseños and Juanenos made beautiful baskets and pottery that were useful while performing the chores of their everyday living. Hugo Reid wrote that the Gabrielino baskets were "so well known as to require no description." Both coiled and twisted baskets were made for a variety of uses. For example, special large cone-shaped baskets were made so that acorn harvests could be brought into the village on the backs of the women. Woven water baskets, with

asphalt-coated necks and flat bottoms, served as early canteens. Among the most intricate and beautiful baskets were the ceremonial ones, usually made by the most skilled of village artisans. In the 1880s and 1890s, the baskets became very popular and were collected by the local residents. They are now considered priceless.

"Nothing is forever," is certainly an appropriate saying in regard to the massive changes that were to take place in the future of the Indians. They did not know that the simple life they led among the hills and rivers would someday be gone forever. Change was inevitable. As the small band of Spanish padres and their accompanying soldiers marched into Alta California, heading resolutely toward the future site of the mission at San Diego, the Indians had no clue that the only way of life that they had known was about to disappear forever.

THE FIRST EXPLORERS

Setting sail from Mexico on June 27, 1542, Juan Rodriguez Cabrillo and his two small ships, the *San Salvador* and *La Victoria*, headed north along the uncharted coast of Alta California. Cabrillo is credited with being the first white man to ever set foot on Southern California soil. On September 28, 1542, after three long and difficult months, Cabrillo and his men sailed into the magnificent bay they christened San Miguel. Later renamed San Diego Bay, the port was to become, in 1769, the starting point for the establishment of the chain of California missions. Cabrillo and his men must have been in awe as they entered the beautiful San Diego Bay, glimpsed snow-crowned mountains, and sailed around the wind-swept off-shore islands.

Sadly, Cabrillo died and was buried on San Miguel Island soon after. As a result, Bartolome Ferrelo took over the command of the expedition, continuing northward along the entire 1,000-mile coastline of Alta California. This voyage of discovery and exploration established Spain's right to legitimize its claims of the discovery and occupation of Alta California.

For several years after Cabrillo's exploratory mission in 1542, little interest was shown in further exploration or development of Upper California. However, reports of threats that the Russians planned to come from the north to occupy the territory forced the issue, and, in 1769, an exploratory expedition was ordered by the Spanish Visitador General Don José de Gálvez. Arriving in Lower California on July 1, Gálvez made plans for the exploration and occupation of the land in Alta (Upper) California through the establishment of a system of missions. Four expeditions were planned, two by sea and two by land, with San Diego as the destination. As a result, they were able to establish the mission at San Diego, the first settlement founded by whites in Alta (Upper) California, and dedicate it on July 16, 1769.

Earlier in July, a reorganized party of 62 men, headed by Gaspar de Portolá, began its trek northward through San Diego, in search of the Bay of Monterey. The intent was to establish a mission there also, as an anchor for the northern end of the chain of missions that were the dream of Father Junípero Serra. Portolá's expedition signaled the beginning of the vast changes that would soon begin to take place in the unspoiled and untamed land of California.

Entering the land that would someday be Orange County near the present site of San Onofre, Portolá and his men traveled along the bottom of the foothills. On July 24, camp was made on Aliso Creek, where the group entered a village of friendly Indians. A few days later they made camp near a spring in the foothills. Portolá and his men sighted a large Indian village on the far shore of a wide-flowing river, near the future site of the town of Olive, at the western end of a wide canyon. The soldiers had already named the mountains from which the canyon flowed in honor of Saint Ann (Santa Ana Mountains).

That Friday, July 28, the expedition experienced four strong earthquakes. Undoubtedly they were frightened because they christened the river "The river of the sweetness name of Jesus of the earthquakes." However, because the river seemed to flow from the mountains they had named in honor of Saint Ann, the soldiers gradually began calling the meandering stream the Rio Santa Ana. In those days the wide shallow river had water in it all year long. Even in the dry summer season the water averaged 12 to 16 inches in depth. The Portolá expedition moved north, traveling through the La Habra hills toward the Bay of Monterey.

If Portolá and his men had journeyed along the beach instead of inland, they would have seen the bluffs, swamps and vast tule marshes that would someday become Huntington Beach.

The California Missions

It has been estimated that there were approximately 100,000 Indians living in Alta California when the Portolá expedition arrived in 1769. The large number of natives encountered by Portolá and his party are said to have been generally friendly. Besides Portolá and Costanso, there were 27 leather-jacket troops, seven Catalonians, 15 Christian Neophytes, Father Juan Crespi, Father Francisco Gomez, an engineer, and eight or nine muleteers and servants who were members of the expedition. Portolá's journey was very significant to California's future because it

A cross crowns the east facade of the Mission San Gabriel Arcángel, called the "Queen of the Mission." Founded on September 8, 1771, by Father Junípero Serra, the mission was named for the arcángel Gabriel, the Divine Herald who announced to the Virgin Mary that she was to become the mother of Jesus. *Courtesy History Room, Santa Ana Public Library*

opened the door for the founding of the Alta California missions.

The Mission Period, which lasted 64 years, was ushered in 1769, when Father Serra and his small band of friars established the first mission at San Diego. Within a decade, there were 21 prosperous missions planted on a line approximately 700 miles long. By that time, over 30,000 neophytes were working and living at the missions.

The determined and dedicated Franciscan padres, given the job of founding the missions, accomplished a remarkable achievement by establishing 21 missions in the new territory. The best known of the founding padres was Father Junípero Serra, who provided a dynamic leadership despite his many physical problems. Among the missions he established were San Juan Capistrano (1776) and San Gabriel Arcángel (1771). A much-loved historical figure, he was determined to fulfill his dream of establishing a string of missions throughout Alta California. Sadly, he died at Carmel in 1784, 13 years after he founded the Mission San Gabriel.

The focus of the system was to bring Christianity to the natives and turn them away from their "heathen practices" and transform them into productive citizens and good Catholics. To what degree this was accomplished is open for speculation. However, scholars do agree that the mission system changed the lives of the Indians dramatically and led them on an irreversible path to a mission-centered peasant society.

MISSION SAN GABRIEL ARCÁNGEL

Founded on September 8, 1771, by Father Junípero Serra, the Mission San Gabriel Arcángel was called the "Queen of the Missions." It was named for the arcángel Gabriel, the Divine Herald who announced to the Virgin Mary that she was to become the mother of Jesus.

San Gabriel lands covered several hundred thousand acres, stretching from the sea to the mountains. It led all California missions in the agricultural production, with its output accounting for almost 25 percent of the total wealth of the Alta California missions. Over 25,000 cattle grazed on the rich grass-covered hills.

During the years of the greatest mission agricultural activity, the vast farmlands produced more than 12 million pounds of wheat.

Father José Zalvidea, known as the "Great Padre," was the driving force behind the building of San Gabriel. Known for his hard work, Father Zalvidea was constantly in the process of adding new quarters to the complex. After the earthquake of 1812 destroyed the original bell tower, Father Zalvidea redesigned the campañario to include frames for six bells.

On July 4, 1776, five years after it was founded, the mission was visited by a group of colonists led by Juan Bautista Anza. As the tired and hungry travelers straggled onto the mission grounds after making the difficult trip from Sonora, the padres rang the church bells and fired guns, welcoming them to the settlement. Father Font, the diarist and chaplain of the expedition, wrote enthusiastically about the mission and its future possibilities. He felt that the land was ideal for both agriculture and grazing. The padres had supervised the

Padre Junípero Serra founded nine of the California missions, including San Gabriel Arcángel. Heroic and intelligent, he gave his life to the establishment of the mission chain. Among his many interests were farming, irrigation, architecture, handicrafts, literature and geography. This etching was made about 1850, when he was in his middle years.
Courtesy History Room, Santa Ana Public Library

The campañario (bell tower) of the Mission San Gabriel was designed and built by Father Zalvidea after the earthquake of 1812 destroyed the original campañario. It features openings for six bells.
Courtesy History Room, Santa Ana Public Library

building of an irrigation canal which supplied ample water for the crops. Father Font was impressed by the promising herd of cattle, healthy hogs, sheep, goats, chickens and fat cows in the pasture lands. He reported that the buildings were made of adobe, reeds and logs. In those early years, the padres lived in a long shed that also served as a granary and store house. A guard house, occupied by Spanish soldiers, watched over the mission. At that point, the five-year-old mission had not yet built the main building, and was using a rectangular shed in which to hold worship services. Small tule-thatched houses, built by the Indians, formed a ring around the perimeter. The mission compound was located near a stand of large and impressive live oak trees, useful for supplying firewood and building materials.

The mission was a constant beehive of activity. Hugo Reed noted in *Life in California 1832-1852*, that the neophytes were divided into various jobs and stations. There were vaqueros, soap makers, tanners, shoemakers, carpenters, blacksmiths, bakers, cooks, general servants, pages, fishermen, agriculturists, horticulturists, brick and tile makers, musicians, singers, tallow melters, vignerons, carters, cart makers, shepherds, poultry keepers, pigeon tenders, weavers, spinners, saddlemakers, store and key keepers, deer hunters, deer and sheep-skin dressmakers, masons, plasterers and others. All were native American except for the coopers (barrel makers) who were foreign born.

In the 1810s and 1820s, at the climax of the Mission Period, there were an estimated 400,000 cattle, 62,500 horses and 320,000 sheep living on the mission lands. The cows were so wild that they were seldom used for milking. Tradition says that it took two people to hold the cow down, and a third to do the milking. The primary purpose of raising sheep was to produce wool for clothing to cover the "almost naked" Indians. The program was not a success, however, because the course and short wool was of inferior quality. Sheep were raised mainly for their hides and tallow. They were allowed to run loose on the mission lands until 1873, when a law was enacted by the State Legislature which declared that cattle and sheep would not be allowed to run loose without a herder to keep them from trespassing.

THE END OF THE MISSION PERIOD

The beginning of the end for the missions came in 1822, when Mexico assumed control of Alta California. The succession of Mexican governors who followed were said to have spent the majority of their time and energy on various rivalries, jealousies and infighting. Those were unsettling times for Southern California.

In 1826, Governor Echeancía presented a plan to organize the Indian neophyte communities into pueblos, replacing the padres with members of the secular clergy. In this drastic measure, the missions would be

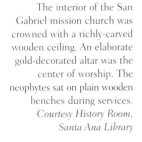

18

The interior of the San Gabriel mission church was crowned with a richly-carved wooden ceiling. An elaborate gold-decorated altar was the center of worship. The neophytes sat on plain wooden benches during services.
Courtesy History Room, Santa Ana Library

stripped of their lands. Echeancía, who was governor from 1825 to 1831 and 1832 to 1833, was able to get his plan passed by the Mexican congress in 1833, during his final year in office. The Secularization Act of 1833 effectively ended the control of hundreds of thousands of acres by the Catholic church and its missions.

The Act brought disaster and doom to the San Gabriel Mission, just as it had the other missions. The main focus of the legislation was supposed to be the turning over of the mission lands to the Indians. The churches were to be transferred from the control of the missionaries and given over to the care of resident priests. The plan did not work because graft and corruption led to the giving of the lands to friends and relatives of those in political power. Unfortunately, after the Mexicans took over California in 1822, the missions were no longer a priority. The magnificent adobe buildings, courtyards and arcades fell into decay.

In 1859, President Buchanan restored 190 acres and the vandalized and ruined buildings of the Mission San Gabriel to the Catholic Church. The restored property created the largest parcel of land given to any of the missions during the restoration period.

One of the best preserved of all of the mission churches, the Mission San Gabriel Arcángel, had been restored and refurbished by the Claretian fathers, who undertook the large project in 1908.

What happened to the Indians living at the missions? Although most of them showed no inclination to farm the land, a few did become successful farmers. Many became laborers on the Mexican ranchos. Some lived in the small towns that were beginning to appear as settlers moved to Southern California. Most intermarried with either the Mexican population or the new arrivals. They lived quiet lives, often not revealing their ancestry. Fortunately, within the last two decades many of the descendants of the Gabrielinos, Luiseños and Juanenos are rediscovering their roots and coming forward to reclaim their heritage.

THE RANCHO PERIOD

The granting of the ranchos ushered in a new period of economic and social growth. The stage was set for the establishment of the large land-grant ranchos that would control Southern California for 35 years, until the late 1860s.

A RANCH FOR JOSE MANUEL NIETO

Among the members of the expedition led by Gaspar de Portolá in 1769 was a 50-year-old soldier named José Manuel Pérez Nieto. He went on to become one of several members of that original expedition to settle on the large grants in the vast new territory.

Nieto was born in Sinola, Mexico, in 1719. He was one of the 27 soldado de cueras (leather-jacketed soldiers) who accompanied Portolá on his first expedition. Three years later, in 1772, he was stationed at the Presidio at San Diego. He and his wife, María-Teresa Morillo, a native of Baja California, lived there together with their first son, Juan José.

In 1784, the Nietos were granted permission by Governor Pedro Fages to occupy a 200,000-acre property. Accounts vary as to whether the ranch was an outright grant or merely approved for Nieto's use as grazing land. Called the Rancho La Zanja, the ranch stretched clear from the foot of the San Gabriel Mountains to the Pacific Ocean, and from the Santa Ana River to the San Gabriel River. However, in 1803, the Mission San Gabriel claimed that the ranch overlapped its property and received approximately 63,000 of those acres, cutting Nieto's ranch down to 167,000 acres.

In 1785, after many years of garrison duty in the army, the 65-year-old Nieto retired and moved with his wife and son, Juan José, to the Rancho La Zanja. Up until that time, the Nietos lived in San Diego and hired a mayordomo to run the ranch. The Nietos had four more children after they moved to the Rancho La Zanja. José Antonio Nieto was born in 1785; Antonia María Santos Pérez Nieto in 1788; María Manuela Antonio Pérez Nieto in 1791 and Antonia María Pérez Nieto in 1796. Although Antonia María Santos Pérez died as an infant, the other four Nieto children grew to adulthood.

After living a full life, José Manuel Pérez Nieto died in 1804, at the age of 85. His family continued to live on the Rancho La Zanja. Some of the children married and built their own adobe homes on the vast

Juan José Nieto built his home on Rancho Los Coyotes, granted to him as part of the original Rancho La Zanja, a 167,000-acre ranch granted to his father in 1784. The Rancho Los Coyotes was located along the El Camino Real. The Nietos, known for their hospitality, made all travelers feel welcome.
Courtesy First American Title Insurance Co.

19

property, while others moved away. For 30 years after Nieto's death, the ranch existed with few changes. There was plenty of room on the 167,000-acre ranch for each Nieto family member to settle down, build a home, and raise a family. Their cattle, sheep, and horses roamed freely about the huge ranch. According to Robert Glass Cleland, there were 3,000 mares, 1,000 fillies, 1,000 colts, 700 cows, 200 heifers and 260 bulls on José Nieto's property when he died.

THE RANCH IS DIVIDED AMONG THE NIETO HEIRS

It was not until 1834 that the José Manuel's heirs requested that the Rancho La Zanja be divided into five ranchos. Governor Figueroa partitioned the ranch into the following sections:

Ranchos Los Alamitos (Little Cottonwoods Ranch)
Rancho Los Coyotes (Ranch of the Coyotes)
Rancho Los Cerritos (Little Hills Ranch)
Rancho Las Bolsas (The Pocket Ranch)
Rancho Santa Gertrudes (Ranch of St. Gertrude)

Governor Figueroa gave Juan José Nieto, the eldest son and administrator of the estate, the largest share, The Rancho Los Alamitos. Shortly afterward, Juan José sold the rancho to Governor Figueroa for $500, or 2 cents an acre. When Figueroa died, Rancho Los Alamitos was sold to Abel Stearns. The cities of Seal Beach and Los Alamitos are now located there. Moving to Rancho Los Coyotes, Juan José Nieto built an adobe home along the El Camino Real. A haven for travelers, Ranchos Los Coyotes became a popular stopping spot

for those traveling between Los Angeles and San Diego. The Nietos sold the rancho to Juan Bautista Leandry in 1840. Leandry, an Italian by birth, bought the property on credit for a few dollars. His widow, Francisca Uribe de Leandry, inherited the ranch a few years later. Stanton, Buena Park, Cypress and La Palma now exist there.

In 1834, José Antonio Nieto was granted the Ranchos Las Bolsas on which the cities of Huntington Beach, Westminster, Garden Grove and Fountain Valley are now located. He was 20 when he married 14-year-old Catarina Ruiz, a Los Angeles native, in 1805. They built their new adobe near the mouth of the Santa Ana River, in the southern part of the ranch. When the property was divided in 1834, the Nietos christened their portion the Rancho Las Bolsas because of the pockets of dry land created when the Santa Ana River changed course in times of flooding.

The Rancho Las Bolsas contained the richest grazing lands in the region. The Nietos built up a sizable herd of cattle and owned a stable of fine riding horses. José Antonio died in 1832, two years before the land was divided into the five ranchos.

José Antonio and Catarina were the parents of two daughters and a son. José Antonio Jr. married Mariana Verdugo. María Cleofa became the wife of José Justo Morillo, who was born in Baja California and grew up in Los Angeles. Justo and María Cleofa enlarged the adobe and increased the herds of cattle and horses. The 1840s and 50s were very good years for María Cleofa and José Justo Morillo.

Three generations lived at Rancho Las Bolsas in the 1840s. Justo, his wife Cleofa, his mother-in-law Catarina Ruiz de Nieto, son José Antonio Morillo and daughter-in-law Rafaela Romero. Justo Morillo, like most of the other ranchers, was forced to defend his claim to the rancho before the United States Land Commission. To finance this action, he had to borrow money from Don Abel Stearns. On February 14, 1861, Rancho Las Bolsas was sold at public auction to satisfy a judgment of $28,043, which Stearns held against María Cleofa Nieto, José Antonio Morillo and María Rafaela Morillo. Tragically, the family had lost their homes, their land and their livelihood and Stearns had added to his growing empire.

20

In 1834, the 167,000-acre Rancho La Zanja, established by José Manuel Nieto in 1784, was divided into five ranchitos and given to the Nieto heirs. José Antonio Nieto and his wife, Catarina Ruiz de Nieto, settled on the Rancho Las Bolsas. In 1841, encouraged by his sister Catarina, Joaquín Ruiz applied for and received the grant to the Rancho Bolsa Chica.

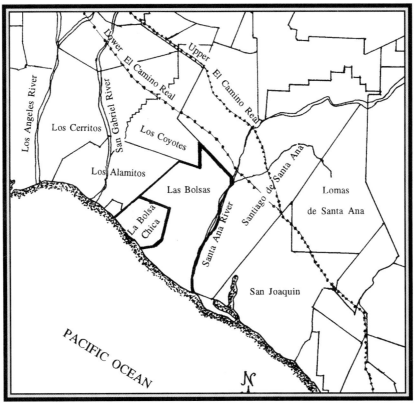

21

Another adobe ranch home in the northern part of Rancho Las Bolsas was called Las Perades. The Grijalva heirs had established the adobe on the edge of the Santa Ana River. In 1811, heavy rains and flooding changed the course of the river and the family abandoned the severely damaged house, outbuildings and corrals. According to Don Meadows in *Historic Place Names of Orange County,* "Signs of civilization were rare in early days and even ruined walls were conspicuous. These (ruins) were located .1 mile north of Sugar Avenue and .5 miles east of Brookhurst, in what is now Fountain Valley."

RANCHO BOLSA CHICA

The Rancho Bolsa Chica, an 8,107-acre rancho which ran along the ocean, was granted to Joaquín Ruiz on July 1, 1842. The present town of Sunset Beach and part of Huntington Beach are located there.

Catarina Ruiz de Nieto persuaded her brother, Joaquín Ruiz, to petition Governor Juan Bautista Alverado for a grant to the parcel of land that became the Rancho Bolsa Chica. Although Ruiz was given full title to the rancho, he was forced to defend his right of ownership before the Land Commission. He borrowed several hundred dollars from Abel Stearns to hire a lawyer to prove his case. Sadly, he died before it was approved on February 26, 1858. His family, unable to repay the loan, lost the property to Stearns.

Little is known about the modest two-room Nieto-Ruiz adobe. Surviving at least until 1889, it was located to the northeast of the site of Huntington Beach. The rancho was rather isolated because it had the ocean on one side and the Bolsa Chica swamps on the east and

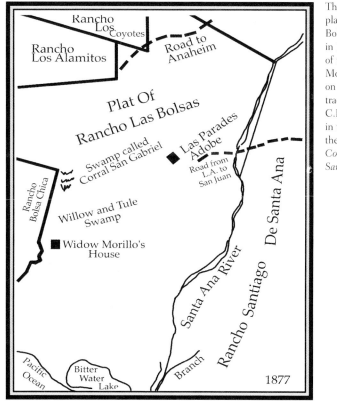

This map, which shows the plat of the Rancho Las Bolsas, was drawn by hand in 1877. It shows the location of the Las Perades and Morillo adobes, once located on the Las Bolsas property. A tracing of the original map by C.E. Roberts can be found in the volume on adobes in the 1936 W.P.A. records. *Courtesy History Room, Santa Ana Public Library*

northwest. The W.P.A. report of 1936 notes that it was used by "Bob" English as a cookhouse and bunkhouse for his farming operations on the mesa. A sheepman by the name of Sarrail lived there in the 1870s, and the adobe was occupied by members of the Stearns Ranchos Corporation at one time. John and Will English, John Graham, Henry Pankey and others remembered that the adobe was approximately 16 feet by 36 feet. It was still there in 1888-89.

LIFE ON THE GREAT RANCHOS

In *On the Old West Coast*, Major Horace Bell says of the early Californians: "...many of the families lived in comfort, some in sumptuous elegance; that is to say, they lived in fine houses, had good furniture, good kitchens, and good cooks, and wore fine clothing. These Californians were dignified people, and it is the desire of this truthful historian, so far as is able, to give them their proper standing in the history of the state they founded. They were rich, powerful, and happy in ante-gringo times. They were not lazy, neither were they shiftless, dissolute nor dishonest. On the contrary, they were a dashing and enterprising people. Their very manner of up- bring- ing... developed a vig- orous physical man- hood and womanhood."

We picture life on the early California ranchos as colorful and festive, with the typi- cal señorita wearing a tight red gown with a skirt that flares out below the calf, and a black lace mantilla

with a Spanish comb, a rose between her teeth, and, of course, the flirtatious lace fan. We tend to think that the men all wore tight black pants, bolero-style jackets and string ties. They are thought to have spent a lot of time dancing the fandango. Life was very romantic!

Of course, this vision is not accurate. The early rancho families had varied lifestyles, habits, attitudes, just as we do today. Some of the dons were hard-working, while others gambled constantly, focused on horse racing, rodeos, drinking and living the high life. Most had large families, but some did not. Celebrations such as fiestas, rodeos and family rite-of-passage cere- monies were more important to some families and less important to others. A commonality was that almost every family considered gracious hospitality as an impor- tant part of daily life.

In 1929, a member of one of California's "first families," Mrs. Florence Dodson-Schoneman, presented a paper telling about life on the ranchos. She had been born in the Diego Sepúlveda Adobe in Palos Verdes, the daughter of Rudicinda Florencia Sepúlveda Dodson, and the granddaughter of José Diego Sepúlveda, who, in the 1820s was the granted the Rancho Palos Verdes.

"Spanish women created the most hospitable homes California has ever known. Most of the 60 or so first families came from Spain and followed the traditions of that country," she said. She felt that there were many false assump- tions about life on the typical rancho that needed to be corrected, and she wanted to share her first-hand knowledge. Mrs. Dodson-Schoneman pointed out that there were two standards by which the typical family lived — the men lived one life and the women lived another. In her eyes, the women did the work and the men played. The señora who was in charge of family life, was required to be a super woman when it came to managing the household and rancho compound. Most fam- ilies had 10, 12 or more children, so she spent a lot of time being pregnant, as well as caring for babies, toddlers and young children. Along with running a home containing 30 or more rooms, the señora was also in charge of 30 or 40 Indian retainers and an extended family of widowed sons and daughters and their families. The first schools were in larger ranch homes and the schoolmaster, as well as some of the pupils, usually lived with the family.

Between the fiestas and celebrations, there were long months of serious living for the señora. The head housekeeper assisted her in managing the household, the preparation of huge meals and the care of the family's clothing. The housekeeper would go to the señora's room every morning to discuss the day's activities and menus.

Mrs. Dodson-Schoneman observed that the Spanish people loved beautiful things, and brought intricate laces, shawls, fans and satin slippers to the new world. The women treasured their heirlooms from Spain, just as we do the family silver and our mother's dishes. It was her opinion that because the families usually came by ship rather than over land, their possessions arrived intact, instead of sometimes being jettisoned along the prairie trail.

Both mothers and daughters wore long skirts. Three-flounced skirts were popular with the Spanish ladies. The señoritas of the time wore the basque blouses by day and evening finery with low shoulder lines and short, puffed sleeves. Mrs. Dodson-Schoneman pointed out that the short skirt did not come to California until the dance hall days of the 1840s. The boleros worn by bullfighter's were not worn here because bullfighting was not a part of Southern California life. Mrs. Dodson-Schoneman, who died in 1967, was very proud of her Spanish heritage. The paper she prepared on the subject has been preserved in the *1929 Orange County History Series* published by the Orange County Historical Society.

Beginning in the early 1840s, a new group of people began to move to the vast lands of Southern California. Among the immigrants was a hard-working and talented man, Abel Stearns. Arriving in 1829, Stearns would become by 1852, the owner of much of the southern half of Los Angeles County (now Orange County) as well as the richest man in Southern California.

ABEL STEARNS – PIONEER ENTREPRENEUR

Abel Stearns, a remarkable man who was one of the foremost players in one of Southern California's most dramatic and important transitional eras, truly left his mark on California's history. He made a significant impact on the region during the almost 50 years he resided there. He was a man of great daring and a great sense of adventure, combined with a profound grasp of the political and economic scene.

Born in Lunenburg, Massachusetts, on February 9, 1799, Stearns and his family were left in poverty after the death of his father. He was a young man of 12 when he went to sea.

In 1827, at the age of 29, he traveled to Mexico, lured by the tales of the fabulous treasures there. In 1828, he became a Catholic so that he might become a naturalized Mexican citizen. During the two years he spent in the country, he was able to make some important contacts that would serve him well in the future. Among these friends were Alexander Forbes and Eustace Barron, two of the most influential British merchants on the west coast.

Stearns left for California in 1829 to pursue the development of a huge tract of land promised to him by Governor Manuel Victoria. Almost immediately, however, Governor Victoria banished him from the state, reportedly because he had repeatedly nagged Victoria about the grant. Stearns, however, only went as far as San Diego, where he helped José Antonio Carillo, Juan Bandini and Pio Pico in heading up a revolt leading to the battle of Cahuenga Pass. As a result, Governor Victoria was forced out of the country.

With that event behind him, Stearns was quickly drawn to the fledgling town of Los Angeles where he established a general store dealing in dry goods, groceries and liquors. Next, he bought an adobe building in San Pedro and opened a store and warehouse.

María Francisca Paula Arcadia Bandini de Stearns married the 40-year-old Abel Stearns when she was 14. The Stearns built a beautiful adobe home on the corner of Main and Arcadia streets in Los Angeles and called it "El Palacio." Known for their hospitality, they became the center of Los Angeles society. Courtesy First American Title Insurance Co.

23

This advertisement, printed in 1869, offers for sale the vast cattle-raising empire acquired by Don Abel Stearns. By 1865, Stearns had been on the edge of ruin. In order to help him, his friend, Alfred Robinson, formed the Stearns Rancho Trust. The original ranchos were subdivided into 45-acre parcels and sold at $5 to $13 an acre. By the end of 1869, over 20,000 acres of the Stearns Rancho had been sold. *Courtesy First American Title Insurance Co.*

24

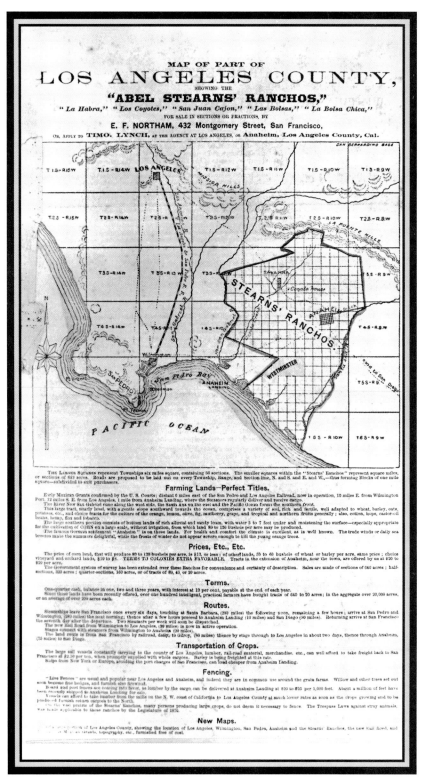

adobe home, known as the El Palacio (the palace) on the corner of Main and Arcadia streets in Los Angeles. Arcadia loved to entertain and the house rapidly became the center of Los Angeles society. As far as is known, the marriage of Arcadia and Abel Stearns was a happy one for 33 years, lasting until he died in 1871.

Stearns' first large land purchase, the Rancho Los Alamitos, came one year after his marriage, and led to his significant career as the owner of a large ranching empire. Stearns bought the rancho, consisting of 12,512 acres, in 1842, after two years of negotiations. Unknowingly, he had embarked upon the journey to become the largest landowner in Southern California.

Adding one ranch after another to his vast cattle-lands empire, he purchased the Rancho Las Bolsas piece by piece. By defending the claim of Justo Morillo to the Rancho Las Bolsas before the United States Land Commission, he was able to acquire a substantial interest in the ranch. He bought other rights to portions of the property from the Yorba and Nieto heirs. It was in 1861 that Stearns obtained, at public auction, the remainder of the Rancho Las Bolsas for a sum of $15,000.

During the early 1860s, Stearns was able to obtain the 6,800-acre Rancho La Bolsa Chica as a result of a bad debt of a few hundred dollars to Joaquín and Catarina Ruiz. Stearns owned over 200,000 acres of choice land. The Gold Rush, which began in 1849, brought to Southern California a meteoric rise in the need for cattle. During the successful 1850s, Stearns had added risky mining ventures and a flour mill to his business enterprises. He held numerous public offices and was involved in almost every charitable and civic organization in Los Angeles. In addition, he was active in business as a ranchero, merchant and property owner. Meanwhile he was lending and borrowing money at a

In 1835, Stearns, who seemed to go from one crisis to another, was charged with carrying on smuggling operations from his warehouse in San Pedro. Fortunately, he was exonerated.

At the age of 40, Stearns married 14-year-old beauty María Francisca Paula Arcadia Bandini in the little church of Our Lady of the Angels. Her father was Don Juan Bandini, one of the most influential men in Southern California. The newlyweds built a beautiful fast pace, expecting Southern California's prosperity to go on forever.

In the fall of 1862, the expected rains did not come. It was to be but the first year of what would become known as the Great Drought. Ranchers lost thousands of cattle from thirst and starvation. As the Southern California economy became a disaster, Stearns' creditors made demands on the notes he owed and pressed him for payment. By 1864, Stearns was in dire straights. In addition to his financial problems, he had failed to pay the mounting list of delinquent taxes. Consequently, the County of Los Angeles brought suit against him for payment.

Stearns borrowed money from a San Francisco capitalist, putting his ranches up for security. By 1865, he was on the edge of ruin, and in danger of losing his entire 200,000-acre estate.

In a desperate attempt to salvage his holdings, he and an old friend, Alfred Robinson, formed the Stearns Rancho Trust. In addition, they persuaded a group of northern California capitalists to found the Los Angeles and San Bernardino Land Company in which Stearns owned a one-eighth interest.

The ranches were to be subdivided into 45-acre parcels and sold at a price of from $5 to $13 an acre. A vigorous sales campaign was launched, reaching as far as Europe. Thousands of brochures were sent to eastern United States and European destinations, attracting farmers from all over. As a result, over 20,000 acres of Stearns Rancho land were sold by the end of 1869. Stearns was on his way to regaining his wealth when he died in 1871 in a San Francisco hotel. During the years between 1829 and 1871, Don Abel Stearns had changed the face of California, ushering in a new era. He was responsible for the foundation of several new towns, the rapid expansion of agriculture and the coming of the railroad.

DISASTER STRIKES SOUTHERN CALIFORNIA

A series of disasters started with the great floods of late 1861 and early 1862. The unusual winter storms began shortly before Christmas and continued for a month.

In his book, *The Cattle on a Thousand Hills*, Robert Glass Cleland reported that the tropical rain fell so continuously that the editor of the *Los Angeles Times* remarked, "On Tuesday last the sun made its appearance. The phenomenon lasted several minutes and was witnessed by a great number of persons."

The ranchers lost thousands of cattle to drowning, and a staggering amount of property and crops were destroyed as the water roared out of the mouth of the

25

By the end of the 1860s, the days when cattle and horses could roam the land freely were rapidly coming to an end. *Courtesy First American Title Insurance Co.*

Santa Ana Canyon and spilled across the flat lands, covering everything in sight. The country resembled an inland sea.

The great flood of 1861-62 was followed by two years of unparalleled drought. Between the spring of 1862 and the fall of 1865, there was so little rain that the grasses died. There was so little food that an estimated 200,000 cattle perished in Southern California. A traveler remarked about the eerie sound of dried bleached cattle bones as his wagon drove over them on the road. Even the great swamp called the Cienega de las Ranas went dry. At the same time, a serious smallpox epidemic arrived in Southern California.

The heirs of the great ranchos were forced to endure ceaseless litigation regarding clouded land titles. Large tracts of land had passed to speculators instead of being systematically subdivided and sold in sections. The long and expensive litigations not only brought bitterness but also destruction of property and bloodshed. Many of the rancho heirs had to borrow money at high interest rates to pay the costs of litigation. The situation contributed strongly to the demise of the great Mexican ranchos. It was into this dramatic and depressing situation that the Americanos began to arrive. After purchasing property, often from the heirs of the ranchos, they set about building houses and corrals, clearing the land and planting crops.

The lifestyle of the newly arrived settlers differed sharply from that of the Spanish ranchero. Owning great tracts of land, the Californios did not think about developing the thousands of acres they owned, but were content to allow cattle and wild horses roam freely on the vast open ranch lands. Newly arrived farmers were upset because the marauding animals were destroying their crops. The settlers sometimes had to guard their crops at night in order to prevent new seedlings from being trampled and ruined. Tempers flared as two distinctly different lifestyles and philosophies clashed.

Soon the Americans would arrive in greater and greater numbers, looking for rich farmland on which to settle and a new era would begin.

BOOM OF THE EIGHTIES

Although Huntington Beach was not founded until 1901, the land boom of the 1880s affected the farming areas between Santa Ana and the beach as well as the previously established towns.

The "Boom of the 1880s" is considered to have started in March of 1886 when the competition between the Southern Pacific and Santa Fe railroads escalated into a full-fledged rate war. The Southern Pacific Railroad, which had been extended to Santa Ana in 1878, had already provided improved access to

Southern California. Many of the county's founding pioneer families arrived in the late 1870s and the early 1880s. When the tracks for the Santa Fe Railroad were laid in 1885, the rate war brought the price of going west down to as low as $1 a person for those traveling from the towns along the Missouri River to Los Angeles. Extensive advertising campaigns from both railroads began to appear, attracting hundreds to the rich farmlands surrounding the established towns.

According to Glenn S. Dumke in *The Boom of the Eighties*, the publicity consciousness born during this historically significant period has characterized the Southland ever since. It was, to a large degree, responsible for Southern California's phenomenal growth. Dumke surmises that perhaps the greatest effect of the boom, as far as the Santa Ana Valley is concerned, was to inspire the formation of Orange County, which was carved out of the south half of Los Angeles County in 1889.

In 1886-1887, with thousands of new arrivals coming daily to settle the new lands, local real estate entrepreneurs seized the opportunity to plat 12 new towns in two years. Among them were Olive Heights, St. James, Yorba, Richfield, Carlton, Aliso City, Fairview, Buena Park and San-Juan-By-The-Sea. Of these, El Toro (Aliso City), Olive (Olive Heights), Capistrano Beach (San-Juan-By-The-Sea), Atwood (Richfield) and Buena Park were the only ones to survive.

FAIRVIEW: THE BOOM TOWN THAT WENT BUST

The only tangible reminders of the once-promising town of Fairview are the street name and the name of Fairview State Hospital. Founded in 1887 on 1,762 acres purchased by a local syndicate, Fairview, with its artesian wells, seemed to hold great promise as a resort. Purchased for $297,500, the prime land was platted and lots advertised for sale in late 1887. An elaborate three-story Victorian hotel, several frame business buildings, a school, a bath house, a few cottages and a church were built the next year. The centerpiece of the town was the artesian well, flowing abundantly with warm mineral water. The resort claimed to have "the only genuine Celery-Peat Mud Baths," guaranteed to cure rheumatism, gout and blood disorders. Tennis, swimming, hunting and croquet were available for the entertainment of the guests.

At night Fairview glowed with that special light emitted when natural gas is used for illumination. A huge tub was inverted over the mineral well water tank and held flat to the ground with chains. Pipes led from the tank to the bath house and other buildings in town, providing the gas for the light fixtures.

The downfall of Fairview resulted because too much of the development of the relatively expensive project was financed on credit. Through 1888 and 1889 the syndicate borrowed more and more money, in an effort to bale themselves out. By 1889, families began leaving, and by 1905, the town's sad fate was sealed.

Blanche Collings, in the *Orange County History Series*, recalls her family's stay in Fairview:

"My father came in January, 1889. Ignorant of the booms, he was advised by an old acquaintance to see Fairview, found the people pleasant and the climate delightful and bought the E.L. Buck home. My mother and sister came next month and went from Santa Ana to Fairview on the last trip of the Fairview and Pacific car. A heavy rain just afterward put part of the railroad under water, and to repair the damage would have been folly. Later my father bought the Fairview store from the Henderson Brothers and my parents made their home in Fairview until 1904 when they sold the store and moved to Santa Ana.

"When I went to Fairview in June 1890, we had a resident pastor with regular services in the little church, and a school house with a full nine months term, the pupils from Newport Beach and Pollerino attending there. The three-story hotel was occupied as a residence by the A.L. Clarke family. After our removal to Santa Ana in 1904, the church was wrecked. It is no longer there...where Fairview stood are one or two dairy farms and a few Japanese raising strawberries."

THE END OF AN ERA

The boom burst in the last 1880s, but not before it had brought many new settlers to the Santa Ana Valley. Linn Shaw tells us, in the *History of Orange County, California*, that the whole economic structure collapsed, "leaving the fair face of Southern California strewn with pitiful wrecks of erstwhile handsome fortunes."

By this time, the Gabrielino Indians had blended into the local populace; the once-great missions were abandoned and in a state of disrepair, and the large ranchos were divided into smaller parcels. The stage was set for the arrival and settlement of the Americano pioneers.

For those with rheumatism, gout and blood disorders, a stay at Fairview Hot Springs undoubtedly provided a sure cure. In addition to swimming in the warm Plunge, guests could go duck, quail and dove shooting. The elegant three-story building was a fine example of the rare Second Empire Victorian style.
Courtesy History Room, Santa Ana Library

Chapter Two

THE ARRIVAL OF THE PIONEERS

Who were the pioneers that settled Huntington Beach and its surrounding farmlands? Where did they come from? Why did they come to this particular territory? Where did they get the money to buy their land?

Perhaps one of the most surprising things about the early pioneers is how often they moved, always pushing the frontier west — from Ohio and Indiana to Illinois or Iowa, to Colorado or Utah and on to California. At first they crossed the great prairie and mountains in wagons pulled by oxen, sailed around stormy Cape Horn, or trekked through the jungles of Panama to reach their new home on the west coast. In the 1880s, the railroads brought many new settlers to Southern California, to an unseen and unknown territory. Leaving friends and family behind, the pioneers often arrived with few possessions and a lot of hope and faith in their future.

The pioneers settled the land, started the schools, platted the towns, opened the stores, founded the banks and brought civilization to the miles of desert, foothills and marshy land that was to become Orange County.

WILLIAM AND MARY JUANITA NEWLAND

When the pioneer Newland family built their new home on the edge of the mesa, in the year 1898, there were no other houses around. Their Queen Anne Victorian house sat on a picturesque knoll high above the marshy lowlands. On a clear day the Newlands could see both the sandy beach and the Santa Ana Mountains.

The Newlands were pioneers in the true sense. They had the courage to purchase and to undertake the cultivation of property that had been, in the beginning, marshy peat lands, considered by everyone else to be of no value.

The Newlands, like so many of the new settlers, had come west to find a new life. William was a native of Adams County, Illinois. His parents, John and Mary, grew up in Laurel Hill, Allegheny, PA. William could trace his ancestors living in America back to the Revolutionary War. His paternal great-great-grandmother, Nancy Irving Newland, was a young girl at the time of the war and devoted most of her teenage years to making haversacks for her seven brothers, all of whom were in the Army.

William was very proud of his father, John Newland. Born in Pennsylvania, John lived most of his life in Adams County, Illinois. When the Civil War reared its ugly head, John joined the Third Missouri Cavalry. On two occasions he was captured by the Confederates, but each time he escaped before the rebels could take him to their camp. Known for his bravery, John was killed on March 3, 1862, leaving his wife and six young children to care for themselves.

William, being the oldest, was only 11 when his father went to war. Two years later, when his father died, he was expected to become the man of the house. When he was 19, his mother died and William became the head of the family, caring for the five younger children until they were grown.

William went to work as a farmhand for John DeLapp in Morgan County, Illinois. Six years later, William married John's daughter, Mary Juanita. In

FROM VAST RANCHO TO AGRICULTURAL RICHNESS

Courtesy First American Title Insurance Company

This large group of children attended the Ocean View Elementary School, built in 1886 for the children who lived in the vast farmlands around Wintersburg. It was located on what is now called Beach Boulevard, near Warner.
Courtesy Arline Huff Howard

November of 1882 the family made the big move to California and lived in San Mateo County for one year.

According to Bernice Newland Frost, her parents "came on what was called 'the first immigrant train to California.' They landed at Half Moon Bay up near San Francisco, and Mother couldn't stand that damp climate up there. She got rheumatism so bad, so they moved down to what is now Compton. Some of the family was born there. Then they moved out to Irvine and he just got it into his bonnet that he was going

The Newland House, constructed in 1898 on a picturesque bluff overlooking the peat lands, was the home of William and Mary Newland and their 10 children.
Courtesy Huntington Beach Historical Society

to finally make the break and do something for himself and that's when he bought the acreage at Huntington Beach."

Moving to Southern California in 1883, the Newlands purchased 80 acres in Compton. After eight years in the Compton area, the family moved to Orange County so that William could take charge of 1,300 acres on the San Joaquin Ranch. He raised the first crop of barley ever grown in that area, which led him to be called "The Barley King." Around 1897, the family purchased the 520 acres of farmland that would become the Newland Ranch. In May of 1898, they moved into their charming Victorian house on the bluff. Dawes and Kuechel, a firm based in Santa Ana, were the contractors for the redwood frame house. The Newland household must have undoubtedly been a very busy one as there were eventually 10 children to feed, clothe and care for. The last two, Helen and Bernice Margaret, were born in the house.

Newland's keen eye and instinct for farming told him that the peat lands would be an especially productive place to grow vegetable crops, if only the water could be drained off the top. Not one to be stopped by such a big problem, he made plans for draining the swamp. Ditches were dug that successfully drained the water from the rich soil. William invented a special tool to yank willow trees out of the swamp, so that he could clear it and then plant crops. For the first 10 years or so, celery was the main crop raised by the Newlands, with sugar beets, lima beans and chili peppers as secondary crops. In later years he focused on the raising of

The Newland barn, which sat on the bluff, was unusually large and spacious. *Courtesy Huntington Beach Historical Society*

sandy beachfront. Mr. Newland scraped gravel out of the ocean at low tide. He let the rains wash the salt out. The gravel was then used in the cement foundation of the house."

The Newland Ranch had all of the accouterments of the typical American farm. A large garden provided a big variety of fresh vegetables. There was an orchard bearing many kinds of fruit in front of the house, and a vineyard that provided grapes. Eggs and meat were obtained from the chickens. Turkeys, cows and horses were among the farm animals kept in the barns and corrals. The Newlands obviously lived a very healthy lifestyle. Their daughter, Helen Newland Tarbox, remembers: "You see, youngsters in those days had so much more to do than children do now. When we came home from school, we had our little dresses changed and we had our little aprons put on and we had the eggs to gather; we had the chicks to feed and if the hens were away from the other chickens, we had them to take care of. We had things to do when we got home! The brothers would have to milk the

sugar beets. The fertile valley became nationally known for the variety and excellence of its vegetables.

Delbert "Bud" Higgins, a local historian, observed that: "Newland faced a difficult task in building his home on the mesa overlooking the fertile farm lands of Fountain Valley. The site is about a mile from the ocean. There were no roads connecting this area to Newport Beach in those days. So Mr. Newland hitched a team of horses to a wagon and hauled lumber from McFadden's Wharf in Newport to his site along the

The Newland family attended a DeLapp family reunion in Pomona, CA, about 1902. Helen Newland is the child sitting on her mother's lap in the second row. Her father, William, is standing behind them. *Courtesy Huntington Beach Historical Society*

Delphia Newland, William and Mary's fourth child, lived in the Newland house until she married C.D. McConahy in 1907. *Courtesy Huntington Beach Historical Society*

cows and see that all the milk was brought to the house. The milk had to be strained through strainers and put into those big pans. I can see those big pans yet that the milk was put in... So you see, we didn't have time to think about running around and doing this or that or the other thing."

Helen goes on to remember how hard her mother worked. She fixed three meals a day for about 50 farmhands, many of whom lived in the bunkhouse on the property. In addition, she canned everything from chili sauce to peaches. When the Newlands first lived in the house, there was no electricity. They used acetylene lamps, which burned a type of gas. When the electric power was at last brought to

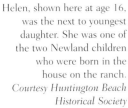

32

Helen, shown here at age 16, was the next to youngest daughter. She was one of the two Newland children who were born in the house on the ranch. *Courtesy Huntington Beach Historical Society*

the house, they had to bring the wires a long distance, because the Newland Ranch was still far out in the country.

The Newlands had frequent guests because in the early years there was no hotel in which to stay. A great many of them were relatives from Illinois. Henry Huntington stayed in the guest room when he came to talk to the Newlands about the founding of Pacific City (Huntington Beach). Helen Newland Tarbox remembers when the circus came to Santa Ana — P.T. Barnum came to stay at their house.

THE FOUNDING OF PACIFIC CITY

William Newland not only pioneered in his occupation as a farmer, but also was one of the leading forces behind the founding of Pacific City. The Newlands bought stock in the West Coast Land and Water Company, which, in 1901, platted and sold the first lots at Pacific City.

Bud Higgins claims that "Newland was the real leader in organizing the town. He insisted that it include four services — a blacksmith shop, a school, a church and a country store. In almost every segment of the development of Pacific City (Huntington Beach), the Newland name is mentioned."

Tradition says that it was William who convinced Henry Huntington to bring the Pacific Electric "Red Car" Railway to the newly-platted town. Newland was active on the Board of Trade that was so instrumental in developing the new community. He helped found the First National Bank, the local newspaper and several businesses. He was active in the celery grower's association and he established the Huntington Beach Canning Company.

Both of the Newlands were strong supporters of the local school system. They served on the boards of the elementary and high school boards for a number of years. Because the Ocean View Elementary School District (located near Wintersburg) was too far away, the Newlands were, in 1902, instrumental in founding the elementary school system in what would become Huntington Beach. Mary served on the school board for 16 years and founded the first P.T.A. in Huntington Beach. In addition, the Newlands helped found the Methodist Church.

THE INDIAN BASKETS

In addition to the back-breaking work of raising a family and helping run the ranch, Mary had the added responsibility of car-

Costumed nymphs, crowned with garlands, appear to be looking out at the audience in this long-forgotten play. Helen Newland is fifth from left. *Courtesy Huntington Beach Historical Society*

Mary Juanita Newland spades the first shovelful of dirt for the groundbreaking of the new Huntington Beach Elementary School in 1916. The Newlands, who believed strongly in a good educational system, were active on various Huntington Beach school boards. *Courtesy Huntington Beach Historical Society*

Chapter Two

Helen Newland, shown here in the second row from the top, fourth from the left, attended the first Huntington Beach Elementary School in the 1910s. Her parents were influential in establishing the school. *Courtesy Huntington Beach Historical Society*

34

ing for two children with severe illnesses. Mary Frances, who had tuberculosis, had to go to Palm Springs to a sanitarium for awhile. The Newlands built a sunroom for her on the south side of the house in 1915-1916.

While Mary was visiting her daughter in Palm Springs, she would stop off at the Indian reservation for rest and refreshment. She became interested in Indian baskets and began to collect them, adding to her already impressive collection of artifacts found on the Newland Ranch. She even visited Indian tribes in Arizona to collect rare baskets. Eventually, they were all over the house, and were used for wastebaskets, sewing baskets and decoration. At one point an Indian chief came to visit and help catalog the baskets. The valuable

collection was given to Bowers Museum and several of the baskets were sent back to the Smithsonian Institution for display in 1976.

Archaeologists say that the Gabrielino Indians lived on the mesa where the house is now located as long as 1,000 years ago. They would gather clams from the tidal basin and mud flats below the mesa and cook them. In the summers they lived on the mesa above the tidelands, retreating back to the canyons in the winter. Layers of clamshells and Indian artifacts were plowed up during the years that the Newlands farmed the large ranch. In addition, cog stones, arrow points, fish weights, metates and pestles were being discovered. Mrs. Newland would go out to the fields after a hard rain to pick up artifacts, and almost always found some. Several large mortars were found by Mr. Newland as he plowed the fields. The family said that there was an Indian graveyard on the next hill.

THE FAMILY GROWS UP

After William died in 1933, Mary, who was in her 70s, continued to run the ranch on her own. To make matters worse, the entire country was in the midst of the Great Depression and the Newlands were suffering financially, along with almost everybody else. The family managed, however, to keep their heads above water.

In 1939, Mary Newland was named Huntington Beach Woman of the Year for her many contributions to the welfare and progress of the community. Mary continued to live in the house on the mesa until she died in 1952, at the age of 93.

Bernice Margaret, the youngest child, had fond memories of the many family holiday festivities held in the house. Family members almost always came home for Christmas; as a result, she remembers 50 beautiful Christmases there.

The 10 children who grew up in the house all turned out

Mary Newland and her vacuum cleaner pose in the sunroom of the Newland House. To the right and in the case behind her is part of her impressive Indian basket collection. She collected all kinds of Indian artifacts, including arrowheads, cog stones, fishing weights and mortars. The majority of the collection was later given to Bowers Museum. *Courtesy Huntington Beach Historical Society*

The Adams Ranch featured a small square single-walled house made of board-and-batten construction.
Courtesy First American Title Insurance Company

to be fine, responsible people. Clara, the oldest child, married Peter Isenor, a prominent farmer in the Talbert district. Wilmuth married Irving Thompson in 1903. Mary Frances, the third child, remained at home with her parents. Delpha married C.D. McConahy in 1907. John went into the Army and served in Siberia during World War I. Jessie and her husband, John Corbin, ran the Newland Ranch in Asteanchia, New Mexico. William and Clinton were ranchers on the home place. Helen married into the Tarbox family, and Bernice married and moved to Seattle. At that point, the Victorian house on the mesa faced an uncertain future.

THE PEOPLE WHO SETTLED THE PEAT LANDS

Although most came from the Midwest and East, the pioneer families also came from other parts of the world. Sometimes they were of different religions and cultures. Many had large families at a time when all family members, from toddler age on up, were expected to do their share. Others had no children. However, they all had one goal — to become successful farmers.

The Buck Family, as an example, came to the Westminster territory from Illinois about 1870. Otho J. Buck and his two sons, Sherman and Charles, were successful farmers who raised celery, alfalfa, corn, beets and potatoes. Sherman left California for awhile to pursue an adventuresome life in mining and prospecting in Arizona, returning in 1902 to farm his father's ranch.

Harry Woodington's father, George, a native of Jo Daviess County, Illinois, came to California in 1870 to take a look, turned around and went back home. Ten years later, he came back again, bringing his family to settle in Westminster. After Harry grew up, he worked for Mr. Smeltzer and, in 1903, became the foreman at the Golden West Celery and Product Company. In 1908, he saved the celery crop almost single-handedly by experimenting with a successful chemical mix that destroyed the blight that was killing the celery. Harry loved Percheron horses and raised them at his ranch.

Daniel Boyde, a native of the Isle of Man, was born in 1843 on the tiny island off the coast of England. He had little opportunity to get an education because he had to support himself. Consequently, he joined the fishing industry when he was very young.

Otho J. Buck
Courtesy History Room, Santa Ana Public Library

At the age of 25, Daniel crossed the Atlantic Ocean, traveled through the Isthmus of Panama and headed up the coast. He arrived in San Francisco in May of 1868, and went to live in Salinas for two years. In 1889, he settled near Old Newport in Orange County and went into farming.

In his biography, David tells us that when he first came to the area, he found that one of his greatest troubles was the crop damage by wild horses that roamed the range at will, often destroying in one night the labors of many months of weary work. Frequently he found it necessary to kill the animals in order to save his crops. It was not until the country became more settled and fences more numerous that the annoyance ceased.

Born in 1864, Peter Eisenor was a native of Halifax County, Nova Scotia. After deciding, at the age of 17, that he did not want to become a farmer in his homeland, he went to Winnipeg, Manitoba, to work for the Canadian Pacific Railroad Company. After traveling

around for a number of years, he settled in the Bolsa area in 1890. In 1894, he married Clara, the oldest of the Newland daughters, and they settled down to raise a family of four children. Peter farmed hay, barley and sugar beets near Wintersburg.

Michael Babylon was born in Aschofenburg, Bavaria, in the year 1864. He crossed the seas to America at the age of 17. He traveled first to Sterling, Illinois, where he learned both farming and the English language. In 1885, he came to California and went to work for "Lucky" Baldwin. Michael's wife, Mary, whom he wed in 1895, was a native of Holland.

Samuel Talbert

Born in Piatt County, Illinois, on February 4, 1874, Sam Talbert worked on his father's farm until he was 18 years old. After he crossed the plains, he settled in Long Beach where he farmed for four years. He fell in love with and married 15-year-old Hattie Brady of Long Beach and they married in 1894.

Seeing opportunities in the Fountain Valley area, he moved his family there in 1897. Paying $40 an acre for 320 acres of tule-covered peat lands, he became a leader in converting a useless wasteland into one of the most productive sections of the county.

After the Talberts established a small commercial center in Fountain Valley, the town was renamed "Talbert" in his honor.

William Tedford

In 1864, William and Nancy Tedford and their five children crossed the plains in a prairie schooner pulled by an oxen team. Born in Tennessee on August 18, 1826, William moved to Missouri with his family in 1831. The Tedfords eventually settled in Solano County. Unhappy with the situation for farmers there, they moved to Orange County in 1868, settling on 60 acres of raw land near Old Newport. Mrs. Tedford was one of the first American women in the territory. She

came to a land full of wild animals, rattlesnakes, flocks of birds, Indians, wild cattle and horses. Luckily, she was met with kindness on the part of the Spanish women who lived on the ranchos that dotted the countryside. The Tedfords had five more babies while living on their ranch. All 10 of the children survived into adulthood. Active in political circles, William was elected supervisor of Orange County for four years.

William Babb

Born in Appanoose County, Iowa, on January 6, 1865, William Babb and his family moved to Sumner County, Kansas, in 1877, when William was a boy of 12. In 1880, they moved to Coffeyville, Kansas, to farm. Two years later, they moved their farming operations to the Cherokee and Osage reservations in a wild and sparsely populated country known for its considerable lawlessness.

William later went on the range as a cowboy, driving cattle to market. He saved enough money to buy a herd of his own. In 1894, he and his wife, Minerva, bought a dairy farm in Fairview. They had only one child. Sadly, he died when he was quite young.

George Stanton

One of those men who answered the call, "go west young man," several times was George Stanton. Born in Litchfield County, Connecticut, in 1832, he was nine when his family moved to Ashtabula County, Ohio. In 1859, he moved to Wisconsin to try his hand at farming. He married his first wife, Elsie, who passed away eight years later, leaving a daughter.

At the beginning of the Civil War, he joined the Union Army and served until 1864. Unfortunately, he suffered a severe sunstroke and never really recovered from the ordeal.

George and his second wife, Sarah, had one son, Charles. They moved to Orange County in 1887, purchasing 16 acres on which they raised apples, peaches, plums, apricots and walnuts. On June 19, 1908, Sarah attended a wedding in Los Angeles. A terrible railroad accident left her a cripple for life. In poor health, the Stantons retired to their ranch to live out their years.

George Gothard

A native of Jo Daviess County, Illinois, George Gothard was born on February 24, 1852. In 1874, he came to California, settled in Anaheim, and went into the grape growing business. After five years he moved to the wild tule lands near Wintersburg and began raising celery.

George's first wife, Elizabeth, died, leaving him with a young son, B.T. His second wife, Ellen, and he had four children. George acted as a road overseer for his area for 12 years. Besides raising celery, he also discovered and activated a gravel pit near Huntington Beach. Fittingly, Gothard Street is named for him.

The Borchard Family

Several pioneer families came to the Bolsa area from Oxnard in Ventura County, California. The head of the Borchard family was Casper, who came from Germany and settled in Oxnard in the 1870s. He and his sons, Leo, Frank and Charles, farmed 1,500 acres together. Sugar beet raising was the chief industry of the home place. They also owned 4,000 acres in Newbury Park, and several thousand acres in Madera County.

In 1898, 19-year-old Leo Borchard was the first of the brothers to come to Orange County. Ten years later,

The Babb family, from Appanoose County, Iowa, came to California in 1894, and started a successful dairy business. *Courtesy First American Title Insurance Company*

This Road District map was produced in 1913 and lists each property owner having property outside the city limits. The numbers represent the number of acres. Included on the map are the names of farmers, gun clubs, rivers and small towns. *Courtesy History Room, Santa Ana Public Library*

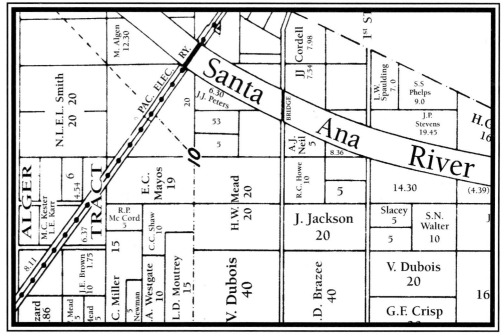

Frank and Charles followed Leo, establishing themselves on nearby ranches. They liked the Bolsa area so much that they bought 560 acres on which to raise beets and beans.

John B. Bushard

John B. Bushard's grandfather, John Bushard, was born in France in the late 1700s, and immigrated to Rosser Point in Canada. John's father, James Bushard, moved to Clinton, New York, and took up farming on a large scale. Life was hard for the farmers of the northeast. In his autobiography he notes that he was "compelled to walk through dense timber to Plattsburg or Saranac with a sack of corn on his back in order to have it ground at the mill." John, the oldest of nine children, was born in Clinton, New York, on March 20, 1843. After he reached maturity, he moved to St. Paul, Minnesota, and became a farmer.

In 1861, John enlisted in the

Union Army and became a member of Company A, the Minnesota Cavalry. He participated in several battles such as Mail Springs, Somerset, Kentucky — one of the war's first major battles, on January 19, 1862. Later, he fought in the Battle of Gettysburg.

After the war ended, John moved to California and went into the teaming business, hauling freight between Los Angeles and Prescott, Arizona. The job was dangerous because the wagons were often the target of Indians and the criminal element among the miners.

While living in Los Angeles, he married Mary Virginia Page, a native of Michigan. They had four daughters and a son.

After returning to the east for a year, John opened a real estate office in Los Angeles. In the early 1870s, he settled on the 1,800-acre Bolsa Ranch, which he had purchased earlier. Unfortunately, the property was in litigation and John lost it in the court case. Not a man to become discouraged, he purchased a half section of land and sold all but 190 acres to the new settlers. The Bushards built a house on the ranch, which was located near Huntington Beach.

F.P. Bowland

It was 1854 when F.P. Bowland came across the plains with a party of immigrants in a prairie schooner pulled by oxen. He was headed for the gold fields of California to make his fortune.

After four years of limited success, the Clay County, Missouri, native came to Southern California and settled in San Bernardino. He went into the drug store business with Dr. J.C. Peacock. He promptly fell in love with and married the demure and dainty Martha Elizabeth Peacock. Sadly, she died six years later, at the age of 24.

Mary Anna Bates, a native of Leeds, England, was F.P.'s second wife. She died in San Bernardino at the age of 33. The Bowlands had two daughters, Anna and Lillian May.

In 1880, F.P. came to the Bolsa area with his new wife, Martha McDonald. A widow, she had three small children when they were married. While living on their 203-acre ranch in Bolsa, the Bowlands had three children of their own.

F.P. was interested in politics and held office a few times. However, he claimed that it had always been against his wishes and that "his tastes inclined him toward a private life and domestic affairs rather than the excitement and turmoil of partisan life." The Bowlands were staunch Presbyterians.

Samuel Gisler

A native of Switzerland, Samuel Gisler was born in Canton Uri, on February 6, 1860. He dreamed of coming to the United States, the land of opportunity. In 1883, at the age of 23, he sailed from Havre, France to New York.

Settling for awhile in Oxnard in Ventura County, Samuel farmed 228 acres of beans and beets. His enthusiasm for the United States overflowed to the extent that he brought his seven brothers to California. Six of them settled in Oxnard, while one went to farm in Sawtelle.

Samuel and his wife, Annie, also of Swiss descent, were married in Ventura County. Tragically, she died in 1891, leaving three small children. Samuel and his second wife, Rosa, also a native of Switzerland, had 12 children, including a pair of twins. During the summer of 1909, the Gislers went to a baby show in Long Beach. The couple, who at the time had 11 children, won a prize of $1,500 for having the largest family.

In 1903, Samuel came to Huntington Beach and established a ranch. Again, his chief crop was sugar beets, with barley as the second crop. He operated a dairy, providing milk to most of the people in the fledgling town of Huntington Beach.

Perry T. Neeley

Born at the end of the Civil War in Lancaster, Missouri, Perry Neeley was one of 11 children. His mother, Sarah, was his father's second wife. She raised the widower's three young children and bore eight of her own. The three youngest died in infancy.

Perry was 14 when his family decided to take up and move to Alamosa, Colorado. He went into wheat farming and well drilling in that state. In 1889, he married Mary Josephine Carter of Alamosa, who was one of 8 children.

In 1891, the Neeleys set out for California and the Mojave Desert. They built a roadhouse about 25 miles northeast of Mojave, at a junction in Inyo County. Next, they moved to Panamint country, bordering on Death Valley. During the five years they spent there, Perry tried his hand at mining. In 1897, he returned to the Colorado ranch and went into the cattle business.

In 1904, the family sold the ranch and moved to Pomona, California, where they spent a year as proprietors of the Pomona Hotel. He and his family settled down on a ranch at Old Newport in October of 1905. Perry became actively involved in the drainage problems of the tule-covered peat lands.

Isaac M. Clippinger

Born in Fairfield County, Ohio, on February 22, 1843, Isaac M. Clippinger was a member of a typical family from the Midwest. After living for several years in Ohio, the family moved on to Kansas, where his father operated a general store for about three years. The west beckoned, however, and his father, Solomon, sold his store and took 17-year-old Isaac on a pleasure and prospecting trip to Pikes Peak, Colorado. The trip, which took six months, was made in wagons pulled by teams of oxen.

39

Harvest time called for all hands to work long hours. *Courtesy First American Title Insurance Company*

40

On January 13, 1905, Southern Pacific engine No. 2215 sank when the tracks gave way because of the softness of the peat. It took five days and nights of constant work to get the engine out of the peat. The town in the background is Smeltzer. *Courtesy First American Title Insurance Company*

In 1861, the family moved back to Ohio and Isaac married Jennie Ashton, a member of a prominent pioneer Ohio family. But Isaac, having tasted the greater freedom of the west, was not content to remain permanently in Ohio. At that time, Iowa was a new frontier, and in 1877, the family moved there to try their hand at farming. Isaac's next job was as an oil-driller in the oil fields of Pennsylvania. He moved on to take a job on a railroad in Pennsylvania.

In 1886, the Clippingers, with their two daughters, Rosa Frances and Anna Ashton, decided it was time to move to the west coast. They settled in Tropico, Los Angeles County, where Isaac became one of the town's leading citizens. A prominent member of the Republican Party, he represented his district at the Republican state convention. He went into real estate, catering especially to the permanent settler rather than to the speculator. The Clippingers lived in Tropico for 14 years.

In 1905, Isaac saw the possibilities of the fledgling community of Huntington Beach, and opened a real estate office in town. In July of 1906, he became postmaster of the town, a position he held for many years.

THE EGYPT OF AMERICA

Thompson and West in *The History of Los Angeles County*, called the vast peat lands in the Gospel Swamp-Bolsa Chica area "The Egypt of America" because of the richness of the soil in the swampy peat lands.

Before the Bolsa Ditch was constructed in 1890, the land in the Bolsa area was worth approximately $15 per acre. After the ditch was built, the price of land went up to approximately $500 an acre.

Not everyone was in favor of the ditch. The work was contested before the Orange County Board of Supervisors and even landed in the courts for about three years. The Drainage Act of 1881, which authorized the cost and care of the ditch, decreed that the farmers should be assessed according to the benefits each received from the construction of the ditch.

Finally, the ditch was completed and put into operation, along with other smaller drainage systems. Thousands of acres of comparatively worthless land to the north and east of Huntington Beach were turned into some of the most productive soil in Southern California. The ditch opened the way to the establishment of high-quality celery crops in Orange County. The celery industry went on to become famous throughout the nation.

By 1910, the sugar beet was rapidly replacing celery as the most important crop. However, barley, corn, alfalfa, potatoes, pumpkins, beans and other vegetables continued to be grown commercially.

THE PEAT LANDS

The remarkable fertility of the soil in the region was attributed to the presence of the richest peat lands in the world. Plans were made for the peat, which was said to have been from 20 to 90 feet in thickness, to be used as a fuel, replacing the more expensive coal.

The Anthracite Peat Fuel Company, with headquarters in downtown Los Angeles, was formed for the purpose of manufacturing and selling the peat throughout California. The company acquired the rights to use the Carpenter patent, a process by which the peat was turned into a high-grade commercial fuel.

By combining certain inexpensive chemicals with the peat soil, the company planned to make briquettes of a convenient size and shape for easy handling and use. The process was the result of many years of trying to find a substitute for coal, which would produce no smoke, soot, gas or clinkers. The briquettes could be used for domestic heating, cooking and the generation of power.

The officers of the Anthracite Peat Fuel Company were all from Los Angeles. Henry Schaefer was president, Joseph Meszler was vice president and W.B.

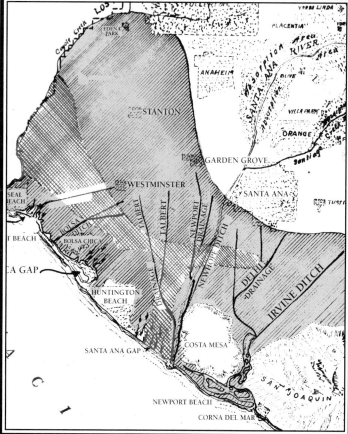

The Artesian Water Belt, where a man could drive a pipe in the ground and get an instant well, is shown as the shaded area of the map above. Note the drainage ditches, with names such as Talbert and Newhope, which empty the collected water into the ocean. *Courtesy First American Title Insurance Company*

Chapter Two

42

bituminous coal, very little of which will give out 14,000 heat units to the pound, which would place it considerably above run-of-the-mill coal of high grade. For domestic use peat briquettes seem to be in every way as good as anthracite, and in some respects better than any kind of bituminous coal. They are free burning, give a clear smokeless flame; they are clinkerless and hardly need any draft when started. The cost of digging and drying peat is much cheaper and safer than coal mining, being all surface work..."

For those farming in the peat lands, however, the peat brought a unique and bothersome problem. The horses' feet kept sinking in the peat when they were pulling agricultural machinery. To help solve the problem, large flat plates made of wood were strapped to the bottom of the horses' feet. The horses looked like they were wearing modern-day thongs as they plodded through the fields.

Unfortunately, the dreams of many regarding the popularity and commercialization of peat fuels were never realized.

Simmons was the secretary/treasurer. C.H. Carpenter became the superintendent. He was very enthusiastic about the prospect of the peat lands, stating that the Bolsa Chica area contained the richest peat deposits in the world. Considered the foremost expert in the manufacturing of peat, Carpenter had spent his adult life analyzing the quality of peat soils.

The site chosen for the company's first manufacturing plant was on the mesa 2.5 miles north of Huntington Beach and a mile south of Wintersburg. An office building, residences for the officers and employees, a machinery building and manufacturing facilities were planned for the site. A single-storied boarding house, complete with large dining room and model kitchen, was built for the employees.

As soon as it was practical, the company planned to build another plant that would obtain gas from the peat. With the gas, the company could manufacture its own light and power.

C.L. Norton of the Massachusetts Institute of Technology, says of the peat: "This cheap fuel is swamp and marsh mud. Its caloric value when dried is from 6,600 to 14,500 B.T. units per pound. This compares with very good grades of both anthracite and

THE BIRTH OF THE CELERY INDUSTRY

A great marshy wasteland, alive with birds, fish and wild animals, covered many square miles of the area between Westminster and the ocean. Raccoons, possums, bobcats, wild hogs and coyotes roamed the area in great numbers. Millions of ducks, wild geese, herons, brown pelicans and other birds made the swamplands their home. For hundreds of years the winter rains had brought rich topsoil into the swamp. Few knew that underneath the tule grasses, willows, wild celery and a variety of water plants, was some of the richest soil in California.

D.E. Smeltzer, owner of the D.E. Smeltzer Company of Michigan, came west to find land on which celery could be grown year round. His company had experienced great success in growing celery in Michigan, but, due to the cold climate, could not raise a crop in the winter.

Beginning his search, Smeltzer went to Los Angeles, where he found some Chinese truck gardeners who were having some success with celery. Like so many midwesterners, he was impressed with the opportunities to raise a crop year round in the sunny Southern California climate. He set out to look for a location with the type of soil needed for celery. After seeing the wild celery growing in the swamp called Las Cienagas, he knew that he had at last found his Garden of Eden.

The big problem was the large amount of water that needed to be drained from the swamp in order to make it into producible land. Smeltzer was convinced, however, that it could be done. Local settlers, who had

Celery was introduced to the area by D.E. Smeltzer and E.A. Curtis in the early 1890s. By 1904, over 1,800 carloads of celery were being shipped each year from Smeltzer and Wintersburg. Courtesy First American Title Insurance Company

been draining small portions of the swamp for at least 10 years, were apprehensive about the large scope of the plans. They were sure that the project would be too expensive. However, E.A. Curtis, an employee of the Earl Fruit Company, thought the plan had possibilities. On land that had been previously drained, Curtis and Smeltzer planted a small experimental crop but it failed.

Deciding to try again the next year (1894), the men planted 80 acres of rented land with celery. The Earl Fruit Company supplied the seed, farm implements and water for $5,000. Chinese truck gardeners were hired to supply the labor. That first year, 50 carloads of prime quality celery were shipped to the Midwest and East. Because the crop was of such superior quality, it brought premium prices at the marketplace.

Armed with new plans to drain large areas of the swamp, Smeltzer drained the entire area. Wide canals were dug to carry the water from the swampland into Alamitos Bay. Leading into the canals were smaller

43

The planting and raising of celery, sugar beets and vegetable crops required a lot of hand labor in order to produce a successful yield. Courtesy History Room, Santa Ana Public Library

44

open ditches, which brought the water from the fields. As the land was improved, tile drains were installed under the ground at 40-foot intervals. Whole sections of swampland were drained by this network of tile drains.

THE TOWN OF SMELTZER

The fledgling town of Smeltzer, owned by the D.E. Smeltzer Company, featured a small hotel, a warehouse, crate-making facility, blacksmith shop, store, bunk house, post office, telephone office and several houses, all dedicated to the process of raising celery. A huge barn housed the 50 teams of fine draft horses. In 1900, Smeltzer had a post office for the six months from March 23 to September 15. The settlement was located a half of a mile west of what is now Beach Boulevard, where the railroad tracks crossed Edinger Street.

A pamphlet entitled, *Orange County, California: Its Progress, Resources, and Prosperity*, described the celery lands in 1897: "The land is rich and fertile beyond the expectancy of the most extravagant dreamer. Within a one-and-a-half miles south of Westminster the world famous celery fields are located. This land is positively so fat the owner can squeeze the coin right out of it. The average yield of celery is 1,000 dozen bunches to the acre and the minimum price 18 cents per dozen bunches, or $180 per acre. The estimated cost of producing it is $50 per acre leaving a snug profit of $130 per acre. One man can take care of ten acres after the plants are set out. Most celery is grown on what is commonly called 'peat land', which lies adjacent to Westminster. The product has the world for its market. Owing to its very superior quality, it finds ready sale wherever it is placed. Six or seven hundred carloads finds its way east while large orders are distributed over this coast."

As the fields were drained, the water situation changed. At first, artesian wells and springs were used to irrigate the celery fields in the summer. As the ground dried up, a unique irrigation system came into use. During the dry season, plugs were placed at the ends of the tile drains that led to the canals. The water would back up in the drains and become absorbed into the extremely porous soil. Eventually, wells were dug and pumps installed because the water table had fallen so low.

Growing thousands of stalks of celery was tedious backbreaking work. The tiny celery seeds were first planted in seedbeds in the spring. During the summer the seedlings were transplanted to the fields, where they were weeded and irrigated for several months. The stalks were cut and prepared for shipping by trimming the tops. After being tied in bunches of 12, the celery was packed in layers in refrigerated railroad cars. The fields were then planted with barley, a crop which was harvested in June, just before the little celery plants were transplanted into the long rows.

Getting the harvested crop to market was a significant and almost insurmountable problem. Because the swampy boggy land had been a kind of no-man's land, there were few roads leading into or out of the area. The celery was shipped in the months between November and March. The months of January through March almost always produced some rain. Most years the peat lands became an impassible quagmire. After the celery was cut and placed in baskets, the workers had to carry it by hand as much as a quarter of a mile. The loaded wagons had to make their way through the sloshy slush of the peat lands. The wagons were then sent to the railroad station in Anaheim.

THE SANTA ANA-NEWPORT RAILROAD

In 1902, the Santa Ana-Newport Railroad, a branch of the Southern Pacific, was extended from Newport to Smeltzer. The railroad installed shipping points at La Bolsa, Smeltzer and Celery.

With this significant improvement in the marketing process, the celery industry became a major economic force in Orange County. The area being used to grow celery increased, and by 1902, there was over 1,200 acres of celery fields. In 1904, the amount doubled to 2,400 acres.

A MULTI-CULTURAL SCENE

The celery fields provided a lively multi-cultural scene, with Chinese, Japanese, Italian and American workers performing the various chores. The Italians, brought in by D.E. Smeltzer, kept to their own customs and foods. The Japanese, numbering over 70, lived in a bunkhouse at the small settlement at Smeltzer. Following their national custom, they bathed in a special bathhouse every evening and changed into their kimonos for an Oriental-style dinner. A dozen or so American teamsters also lived in houses in Smeltzer.

The Chinese laborers, who did most of the work, lived in small wooden houses scattered about the countryside. There was, at the time, a strong anti-Chinese sentiment in Orange County. Accordingly, several of the homes where the Chinese workers lived were burned and their tools stolen. The Chinese acquired large savage dogs to guard their homes. The Company hired a guard to protect their property and ordered him to shoot anyone who bothered the Chinese. In spite of this, the Earl Fruit Company buildings were burned to the ground by an arsonist anyway.

THE CELERY CROP BECOMES A MEMORY

Because the peat lands were extremely fertile, the first several years of celery production yielded high-quality crops. After approximately 14 years, the fertility of the soil began to decline and the plants became less hardy. It was then that celery blight reared its ugly head and the only solution was to spray the crop with a mixture of bluestone and lime. At first the solution worked and the celery regained its profitability. Eventually, the land became so worn out and the blight so bad that celery growing gradually diminished.

The town of Smeltzer became a ghost town and most of the buildings were torn down or moved to a new location.

THE SUGAR BEET

In the 1890s, S.W. Smith was instructed by the Santa Ana Chamber of Commerce to go to Watsonville, California, and find out what the raising of sugar beets was all about. He returned with a good deal of valuable information and a large quantity of seeds.

At first there was no sugar beet processing plants in the county and farmers had to send their beets all the way to a plant in Chino. In order to remedy the problem, a sugar beet factory was built at Los Alamitos by Montana Senator W.A. Clark in 1896-97. The Southern California Sugar Company, located in Santa Ana, was the second. The Anaheim Sugar Company, the Santa Ana Co-operative and the Huntington Beach Holly Sugar Factory were built in 1911. These five factories made Orange County the most prolific sugar beet region in the United States. Their combined investment numbered about $4 million.

By 1911, over 30,000 acres of sugar beets were grown in the county. The crop was the most labor intensive of any crop under cultivation at the time. The fertility of the land was crucial. After the land was cleared, the farmer would plow the fields nine to 12 inches deep, usually in November or December. Next, the soil was harrowed until it was fine and rolled with a large roller. In February and March the seed was planted with a beet drill. After the plants came up and had four to six leaves, they were rolled lightly. Next came the thinning of the rows; one acre contains 5.5 miles of rows. In addition, the crop had to be weeded by hand at least four times during the growing season. When the beets were ready for harvest at last, from August to October, a special implement, pulled by horses, was used to harvest the beets. Tagging along behind the pullers were the toppers, men who were required to crawl down the rows in order to cut the tops off of the beets. The beets were then ready to go into wagons and taken to an elevated beet dump.

The beet dump, invented by Tim Carroll of Anaheim, revolutionized the beet industry. A "sample snatcher" stood by the railroad cars, gathering a bushel basket load of beets from each batch. The samples would be sent to a laboratory to test the amount of saccharin contained in the beets.

Sugar beets were dumped into a railroad car that was parked on the track. The wagons are driven up the ramp on the left, and after the load was dumped, taken down the ramp on the right. The mules that were often used to pull the wagons can barely be seen at the right of the dump.
Courtesy First American Title Insurance Company

46

Arriving at the factory in cars, the beets were unloaded into special bins with sloping bottoms. The beets were then forked into a flume filled with water.

The flume delivered them to machines which washed them and placed them in position for the slicer. The slices, called cossets, passed through a chute to the diffusion battery, which consisted of 14 tanks connected by pipes and valves.

The sugar in the beets was extracted by a series of leachings with hot water. The juice, heated to a temperature near the boiling point, was then treated with milk of lime. Passing through filter presses, the purified juice was conducted into immense evaporators. When the juice left the last evaporator, it had been reduced to about one-fourth. Lastly, the sugar was boiled in a vacuum strike pan and became crystallized. It is obvious that sugar beet growing and processing were very labor intensive.

VEGETABLE CROPS

When vegetable gardens are mentioned, we picture small plots with a row or two of each kind of vegetable. However, to the farmers in the peat lands, the miles of rows of vegetables provided their livelihood. Most of the towns existed because of the economic support generated by the farmers who lived throughout the endless miles of rich agricultural lands.

County farmers won many prizes with their large high-quality vegetables. At the St. Louis World's Fair in 1910, for instance, they brought home 12 gold medals and four silver medals for their vegetable displays. A good example of the richness of the Bolsa lands was a 50-pound sweet potato raised by the Rev. Dr. Fackler, a minister and horticulturist. It was sent to the New Orleans World's Fair as part of an exhibit.

A wide variety of vegetables was grown throughout the region. Lima beans once grew in only two places on the globe — Southern California and the island of Madagascar. Lima bean growing in Orange County can be traced back to 1886, when James Irvine, the owner of the San Joaquin Rancho, planted 120 acres as an experiment. However, the other farmers were slow to follow Mr. Irvine's example. By 1908, Irvine had 17,000 acres of beans. It was considered to be the largest bean field in the world belonging to one man. In 1910, the county's lima bean crop amounted to 1,175,000 bags, and was valued at about $5 million. There were approximately 28,000 acres of lima beans in the county. The mesas around Huntington Beach and Smeltzer, La Habra Valley and the San Joaquin Ranch were the prime producers. Chili peppers, grown in rows, were also a popular crop.

The peppers were usually dried in warehouses. Two crops of potatoes a year could be harvested from each parcel of land. Sweet potatoes were introduced into the county by Thomas Nicholson of El Modena. Endless rows of onions grew near Anaheim. Peas were grown on the mesa in areas that had comparatively little frost. Large fields of cabbage were grown near Anaheim, Garden Grove and Fullerton, and shipped east during the winter. Celery and cauliflower were major crops in the Wintersburg area. Several kinds of melons, as well as pumpkins, produced gigantic fruit when grown in the peat lands.

Pumpkins, raised primarily as food for stock, often grew so large that it took two men to load one into a wagon. In the early 1900s, Orange County was credited with producing 38,000 pounds of asparagus a year. Beautiful large tomatoes grew in profusion throughout the peat lands. Some of them were canned, but most were sold fresh.

Peanuts, which did well in the county, were often grown in the rows between fruit trees. However, because of the competition from Japan, the crop was not very profitable.

The rich farmlands around Huntington Beach continued to be very profitable, producing a wide variety of crops. However, by the 1960s and 70s, something new would be grown on the land — block after block of new tract houses.

THE GUN CLUBS

The Bolsa Chica section of the coast, between Long Beach and Newport Beach, has been called one of the greatest natural habitats in the world. Wild ducks, plover, doves, egrets, herons, gulls, geese, jacksnipe, pelicans, coots, land birds and waterfowl of almost any kind can be found in the swamps, ponds, grain fields and tules of the Bolsa Chica. Tom Talbert recalls: "…Birds by the thousands so thick in flight as to almost eclipse the sun. The hours-long flight of ducks patterned against the blazing sunset sky was most amazingly spectacular and beautiful. When startled, great flocks of birds arose to circle around and return to their beloved haven."

One of the big industries in the county began before the turn of the century, as numerous duck clubs began to be established in the lowlands from the entrance of Newport Bay to the sloughs west of Huntington Beach. The area was home to such clubs as the Creedmore, Green Wing, Los Patos, Lomita, Westminster, Golden West, Blue Wing, Chico, Samae, McAleer and Bolsa Chica clubs.

Each club purchased a large area of marshland, prepared the ponds and built a clubhouse. According to Richard Vining, in the February 1996 issue of the *Orange*

County Historical Society Courier, the clubs were a year-round activity. Large areas were enclosed with dirt dikes and water grass was grown within the boundaries. Late in the summer, after cattle had grazed the grasses, the fields were set afire to burn off the remaining stubble, leaving just the grass seed. Later, wastewater from the sugar beet mill was used to flood the dike area, creating acre after acre of shallow ponds.

Hunters came from all over the state to hunt in the huge haven for wildlife. It was said that a man had to be downright clumsy with a gun not to bag his limit every time he went hunting. Jackson A. Graves, president of the Farmers and Merchants Bank, in his book, *My Sixty Years in California*, tells the following story: "The Bolsa Chica, a very aristocratic gun club, which brought a large body of land in the Bolsa Chica Rancho, near the present town of Huntington Beach, always had the most excellent shooting until quite recently. I was one of the organizers. I remember hearing a shot from the nearby Blue Wing Club, followed by a yell from various members. He looked up and saw the sky raining with ducks. It seems that a man needed one duck to complete his limit, so he picked out a big sprig and fired. A flock of sprig were circling, ready to light. They came in range, he fired, and with one shot killed 14 sprig. We presume he shared his catch with a less fortunate club member."

The hunters, who often came from the Los Angeles area, usually traveled to their clubs on the Pacific Electric trains. They were met at the station by a wagon and team that took them to their destination. Sometimes the hunters drove down through Westminster, taking unpaved country roads to the marshlands.

The Bolsa Chica Gun Club, pictured here, was a popular retreat for sportsmen from Los Angeles. The Blue Wing Gun Club, another of the dozen or so gun clubs in the Bolsa Chica and San Joaquin (Irvine) area, owned 160 acres near Westminster. *Courtesy History Room, Santa Ana Public Library*

Count Jasco Von Schmidt, a wealthy sportsman from Los Angeles, was one of the founders of the Bolsa Chica and San Joaquin Gun clubs. *Courtesy History Room, Santa Ana Public Library*

A DAY AT THE BEACH

Arline Huff Howard, who grew up in Huntington Beach, remembers her childhood days at the beach: "In the summertime we would go to the beach early on Wednesday for the entire day. We left home at 7:00 a.m. and stayed with Mother and my sisters until Dad picked us up at 4:00 p.m. at the beach. Mom stayed under the umbrella to avoid sunburn. Playing in the ocean, I'd try to get on a sandbar, pick up a lot of shells."

All Photos Courtesy Huntington Beach Historical Society

48

Chapter Three

THE STAGE IS SET

The potential of the beautiful shoreline of the place called Shell Beach was bound to become noticed by enterprising entrepreneurs when the nearby farmlands were settled. Much of the Pacific coastline in Southern California is bordered by cliffs and the steep rocky terrain while the flat beaches and rolling waves of Shell Beach had an obvious potential, if access were improved, as a future tourist attraction.

Before the turn of the century there were no railroads or roads leading to the beach. Therefore, it was difficult for people to get to the isolated shoreline. As the land was drained, the beaches became more accessible and a road was built. By the turn of the century, the mesa was surrounded on three sides by a crazy quilt of farms, primarily known for their success in growing vegetable crops.

In the 1880s and 90s, Colonel Robert J. Northam, manager of the Stearns Rancho Company, raised barley where Huntington Beach now stands, and ran cattle and horses on the swampy land surrounding the mesa.

During the last quarter of the 19th century, a handful of small towns had sprung up in the 6,000-plus-acre farmlands to the north and east of the future site of Huntington Beach. These small towns were the lifeblood of the many farmers and their families who lived in the rich peat lands northwest of the Santa Ana River. They are important to mention because they, with the exception Westminster, eventually became part of Huntington Beach.

Bolsa

A school was established as early as 1870 in Bolsa, located at the crossroads of Bolsa and Brookhurst Street. The company store, owned at that time by W.L.Gaines, was important to the farm families who lived in the surrounding area. According to Don Meadows, a post office was established at the store on February 26, 1886, with Mr. Gaines serving as postmaster. Although the mail stop was discontinued on October 28, 1891, the tiny settlement of Bolsa served as a daily focus for farm families. The school, with its celebrations, plays and holiday events, was the social center for the surrounding farms. Most of the nearby farmers took their milk products to the Bolls Creamery, located across the street from the school. The owner was P.A. Raab.

Smeltzer

The small town of Smeltzer (discussed in detail in Chapter 2) was founded in 1894 when D.E. Smeltzer built a celery packing house along the Huntington Beach branch of the Southern Pacific Railroad, approximately half a mile west of Beach Boulevard and Edinger Street. Several buildings were constructed to house the celery workers and to prepare the stalks for packing. Briefly from March 23 to September 15, 1900, Smeltzer had its own post office.

The Smeltzer Telegraph and Telephone Company organized by Tom Talbert, J. B. Lossing, the Heils, Ed Larter, Bruce Wardlow, Sterling Price and others had a modest beginning. The lines were strung along fence posts and tree trunks. Two to six parties shared each line. Using the old-fashioned ring system, each telephone had its own set of rings, using long and short signals created by turning a crank. Subscribers paid $1 a month per phone. Eventually the S.T. and T. Company was bought out by the Huntington Beach Telephone Company.

PACIFIC CITY BECOMES HUNTINGTON BEACH

October of 1887 with great expectations, the small town enjoyed a brief and interesting life. A syndicate spent $297,500 to purchase 1,762 acres of land with a warm flowing artesian well as its centerpiece. A road was built between Santa Ana and Newport Bay. The portion that led through Fairview was a 100-foot-wide grand boulevard. A business district was established and residential lots laid out. A picturesque three-story Second Empire-style hotel along with several stores were built with the objective of attracting the public. A plunge and dressing rooms were constructed and a school and church opened. As the town failed, the post office was closed. The hotel was demolished around 1910. The details of the failure of this anticipated boomtown is described by Blanche Collings in Chapter 1.

Within 10 years much of the celery crop, as a result of blight and overtaxed soil, was replaced by sugar beets, and consequently Smeltzer, the center of the celery crop, disappeared.

Fairview

In contrast to the other settlements surrounding the future site of Huntington Beach, Fairview was developed specifically as a resort town. Founded in

Fountain Valley

In his book *Historic Place Names in Orange County*, Don Meadows quotes A.F. Hawley who wrote

52

The graduating class from Fountain Valley School in about 1904.
Courtesy First American Title Insurance Co.

in 1875, "lying to the south of Westminster between it and the ocean, is a tract of 30,000 acres or more known to the residents thereon as Squatters Country or Fountain Valley." The name, Fountain Valley, was first the name of a school built in the 1890s, and was derived from the abundance of artesian water. The water was so close to the surface that all one needed to do to get a stream of water was drive a pipe into the ground.

Hawley goes on to say that there were 145 farms of 160 acres each and five 80-acre farms in the tract. The name was revived when the City of Fountain Valley was incorporated in 1957. The city offices were first located on the site of the village of Talbert.

The first country doctor in Huntington Beach, Dr. Samuel D. Huff (pictured left) , purchased the land and house known as the Morse Ranch in 1901. *Courtesy Arline Huff Howard*

Gospel Swamp

Historically, the Santa Ana River formed the boundary between two great ranchos, granted by the Mexican government to the Californios. The Rancho Las Bolsas, 29,000 acres granted to Manuel Nieto in 1784, stretched to the north and west of the river, while the 62,516-acre Rancho Santiago de Santa Ana, given to Jose Antonio Yorba and Juan Pablo Peralta in July of 1810, was located to the east and south.

Don Meadows explains that the flood of 1828 changed the course of the river, leaving about 30,000 acres of marshy ground between the old and new channels. Those who moved in and claimed the land, which they believed belonged to the government, were called squatters. It should be pointed out that the word "squatter" can be misinterpreted. Those who settled the fertile land and established farms were hardworking people who felt they had a right to settle there. Being very religious, they held frequent camp meetings. For this reason, the region was given the unofficial name of Gospel Swamp.

After the United States Land Court awarded the Gospel Swamp area to the Rancho Las Bolsas, some of the squatters bought the land upon which their farms were located. Others moved away.

Tom Talbert pointed out that the swampy land was not only a perfect haven for all kinds of animals and waterfowl, but for criminals as well. They sometimes set up secret island camps, building huts out of tule thatch. The swamp was not only good place to hide, but the sloshing sound produced by the sheriff's party

as it advanced through the swamp gave the fugitives plenty of time to escape.

Talbert

In 1896, the Talbert family of Long Beach purchased 320 acres near Bolsa. Samuel, Thomas and Henry, the sons of James Talbert, went into farming together. The family later developed a small town at the intersection of present-day Bushard Street and Talbert Avenue. Tom, who wrote the book *My Sixty Years in Orange County*, tells how the family established the town on one of the few high spots of the ranch.

John Corbett, a successful blacksmith, opened the first business in Talbert and soon after opened the first grocery store in a 20-by-30-foot wooden building. After a few months, Corbett left Talbert forever and returned to New York to manage his share of his inheritance from his brother's estate. He sold the store to Tom Talbert for $200 in cash, $600 in debt to the wholesalers and a $700 note.

Tom took advantage of the barter system, trading farm animals for groceries, poultry, horses, eggs, butter and other necessities. Gradually, Tom added chicken feed, shoes, work clothing and hats, hardware, soda pop, rolled barley, cigars and patent medicines to his line of products. A trip to the general store was an exciting treat for farm children at the turn of the century. In 1903, Tom Talbert sold his store to B.F. Taylor of Glendora for $10,000 cash, and moved a few miles to the new village of Huntington Beach.

The residents of the lively little town wanted its own post office. Talbert remembers how his father, James, rode throughout the district with his petition which asked for permission to establish a new post office named Fountain Valley. The petition was returned with the statement that a two-word name for a post office could no longer be used except in the case of unusual historical significance. So it was decided to name the post office "Talbert" instead. The petition was granted in 1899, and a young Tom, at age 21, was appointed postmaster by President William McKinley. This was the first official office for Tom. He went on to hold many important government positions, including that of Orange County Supervisor.

Wintersburg

The town of Wintersburg, established by Henry Winter in 1890, was located on the Huntington Beach branch of the Southern Pacific Railroad, one-half mile west of Beach Boulevard. It did not develop beyond its role as a shipping center for celery. The school, which served about 200 students, was moved, Victorian building and all, from Ocean View to Wintersburg.

Springdale

Springdale was the name given to the school district organized in 1904, and located on the northwest corner of Warner Avenue and Springdale Street.

Westminster

The farm country surrounding Westminster and Huntington Beach join at some unknown point between the two. Westminster, which went on to become a substantial town, was first a temperance colony that was founded in 1872 by Rev. L.F. Webber, a Presbyterian minister from nearby Anaheim. He purchased 7,000 acres of Gospel Swamp with the idea of setting up his own religious colony. His new town was centered around a school house, a Presbyterian church and a few stores. The original town center of Westminster was located on Westminster Avenue where it crossed the Southern Pacific tracks. *Westminster Colony, California: 1869-1879* by Ivana Freeman Bollman is a scholarly work that delves into the first 10 years of the community.

The Newbert River Protection District

At the turn of the century there was a fine quality of water everywhere in the region surrounding the future site of Huntington Beach. When a farmer dug holes to set fence posts, water often spouted up from the ground. During the flood of 1893, it was possible to go by boat from Costa Mesa to Long Beach.

The Newbert River Protection District, formed in 1900, was created to determine and purchase a right of way for the permanent location of the meandering Santa Ana River. The district covered 18,000 acres of prime farm land. The name "Newbert" is a combination of Newport and Talbert. $185,000 in bond money was used to purchase a 300-foot strip of land that would become a permanent bed for the river. After the ditch was dredged, taxes were levied to provide for the repair and upkeep of the new riverbed.

The Freeman River, which no longer exists, was named for J.G.Freeman, a prominent landowner in the area. A beautiful and important river, it flowed south by southwest, passing just west of Wintersburg, past the edge of Huntington Beach and entered the ocean at Bolsa Bay. As the number of artesian wells that drew the water out of the water table increased, the river disappeared.

PACIFIC CITY IS FOUNDED ON THE MESA ABOVE THE BEACH

In 1901 something happened that would change the face of the beach town forever, bringing a flurry of real estate activity that was unprecedented along the picturesque Orange County coastline.

That spring, Philip Stanton headed a partnership which purchased 150,000 acres of the Rancho Las Bolsas for $100,000 from Col. Robert J. Northam. The California promoters hoped to create a resort that would rival the popular east coast resort at Atlantic City, New Jersey. For this reason the group called their new development Pacific City. The mesa, a beautiful piece of land, was dotted with chains of fresh water lakes.

Sometime between 1902 and 1904 (accounts differ) the first Huntington Beach Pier was constructed of wood. It was an important feature in the plan to attract tourists to the new town. Courtesy First American Title Insurance Co.

Incorporating as the West Coast Land and Water Company, the new company had among its members William T. Newland, Sen. John N. Anderson, S. H. Finley, Simeon Kalisher, Mr. Weatherbee and Judson House. They made a $10,000 down payment and agreed to pay $10,000 a year until the loan was paid. The company proceeded to lay out streets and lots in a 40-acre tract on the mesa, overlooking Shell Beach. The required water system was installed, the streets paved and general improvements made. A pavilion formed the centerpiece of the beach front.

In August of 1901, the first lots were offered for sale. Tom Talbert remembers that a church and residence were moved on wheels from the declining town of Fairview to make Pacific City look a little more settled. The first lots sold for $100 or $200 each. Parcels were given away to any person willing to build a structure on the property immediately. A perplexing problem surfaced, however. When the company drilled a well to obtain domestic water, the gas fumes emitted by the hole were annoying and unpleasant.

In keeping with the resort theme of the proposed new town, the construction of a rough wooden pier began in 1902.

PACIFIC CITY BECOMES HUNTINGTON BEACH

In 1902, Philip Stanton sold his interest in the West Coast Land and Water Company to the Vail and Gate Group of Los Angeles. At this point, Henry E. Huntington, the wealthy owner of the Pacific Electric Railway Company and a heavy stockholder in the Southern Pacific Railroad, became interested in Pacific City. (The Pacific Electric Railway had already been established between Los Angeles and Long Beach.)

Huntington soon made plans to extend the electric railroad system to Newport Beach.

In 1903, the impressive Huntington Inn, a large Craftsman-style two-story hotel, was built across Ocean Avenue from the beach.

In a gesture of appreciation to Henry Huntington, the name Pacific City was changed to Huntington Beach. On June 22, 1903, a first post office was established in a wooden piano case. Huntington Beach was on the verge of a real estate boom. Lots that had sold only a couple of years before for $100 to $200 suddenly commanded prices of around $3,000 each.

In 1901, Philip A. Stanton headed a partnership which formed the West Coast Land and Water Company, founders of Pacific City. He and others dreamed that the new resort would be as popular and successful as Atlantic City. *Courtesy First American Title Insurance Co.*

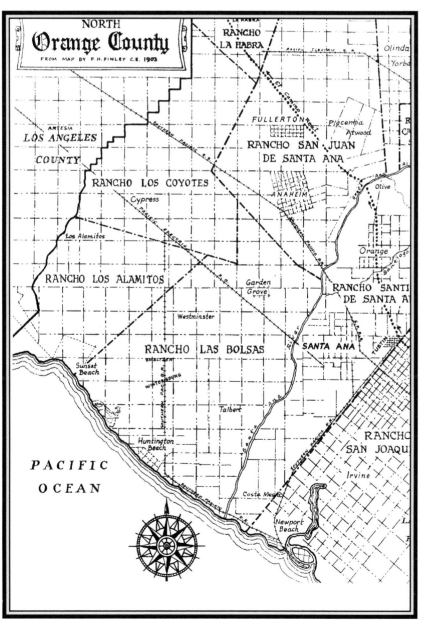

Huntington Beach, Smeltzer, Wintersburg and Talbert are shown on this 1903 map, prepared by S. H. Finley, county surveyor. The vast area between Huntington Beach and Westminster contained approximately 30,000 acres of rich farmland. *Courtesy First American Title Insurance Co*

55

These early photos of Huntington Beach, taken about 1903, show the mesa that would, within a year, be developed into the new community. *Courtesy First American Title Insurance Co.*

PHILIP A. STANTON, ENTREPRENEUR

One of Orange County's most prominent early 20th century developers and politicians was Philip A. Stanton. He was a man who had big dreams and was willing to take chances to fulfill them. In addition to becoming the prime mover in establishing the town of Pacific City, he founded in 1904, the Bayside Land Company, which developed Bay City, located between Anaheim Landing and the Los Angeles County line. The town of Stanton was named for Mr. Stanton, who had served as speaker of the State Assembly. In 1911, he led the fight to keep the tiny town of Benedict and its surrounding farms from being developed into a sewer farm by the city of Anaheim. The farmers were able to stop the plan by incorporating the village. In gratitude, they named the new town after Stanton.

HUNTINGTON BEACH GRAND OPENING

One of the most important days in the history of the new town of Huntington Beach was July 4, 1904. On that day the village was resplendent with banners and decorations. A large crowd stood to greet the first official Pacific Electric Red Car as it came rolling in from Long Beach. The event marked the inauguration of the daily electric car service between Huntington Beach and Los Angeles, via Long Beach.

It has been estimated that more than 50,000 people came to the town to help celebrate the event. Tom Talbert recalls that there were Red Cars coming all day long, with some of the passengers even riding on the tops of the cars. Buggies, spring wagons, saddle horses and bicycles brought thousands more into town. Many walked long distances to attend the festivities. Eleven sides of beef were barbecued in a huge pit at Fifth and Walnut streets, with a hearty dinner served from noon to 4 p.m.

On May 31, 1904, it was reported that there was only a two-mile gap remaining to finish the line between Long Beach and Huntington Beach. Some 300 teams worked feverishly on the road bed, preparing it for the installation of the rails.

On that day, the crowds cheered the inspiring talk given by Mr. Vickers, the president of the Huntington Beach Company. Speaking from the back of a farm wagon, he described the plans the company had for the beautification and development of the community. The day was heralded as "Founders Day." Through the

The Huntington Inn, a dramatic Craftsman-style building built in 1903, faced Ocean Avenue, at Eighth Street. It was the destination of many beach-going tourists and prospective property owners. During the oil boom of 1920, the hotel was occupied by many of the men who came to town to work in the oil fields. *Courtesy First American Title Insurance Co*

56

years, Huntington Beach has become known for its special Fourth of July celebrations.

HUNTINGTON BEACH BECOMES A REALITY

In the spring of 1904, the new town was becoming one of the most prominent seaside resorts in Orange County. According to the *Daily Evening Blade* "lots were being sold rapidly and houses were going up in all directions."

The streets were being oiled under the personal supervision of Theo F. White, the inventor of the new White patent paving process. People from other localities came to take a look at the smoothly finished road surface. Fortunately for Mr. White, the drainage and soil were ideal to create the perfect job.

An 80-foot-wide boulevard called Ocean Avenue, was built parallel to the ocean front. The road became part of the Pacific Coast Highway in 1926.

The previous year, Dave Stewart and Frank Gibbs built Pacific City's first frame business building at the corner of Walnut and Main Street. W. T. Collins bought the southeast corner of Ocean and Main Street for $16,000. Meanwhile, the Huntington Beach Company had purchased a large tract of land on the Bolsa mesa, to the north of the townsite. A grand boulevard that would circle the company's property was planned. Enthusiastic property owners granted a right of way to build a major road that would connect Huntington Beach to Santa Ana.

In 1904, the original road had to be rebuilt. Special pilings that were wrapped in canvas and dipped in asphalt were obtained to resist the ravages of bad weather.

The new commercial center, located on Main Street and extending east from Ocean Avenue, was rapidly taking shape. H. E. Pack of Denver, Colorado, bought the 50-by-110-foot corner of Main and Ocean. Pack, a realtor, had made a careful study of beach towns and was enthusiastic about the future of Huntington Beach. The word quickly spread that he purchased a significant commercial location, and more property was sold during the next three weeks (May of 1904) than during the preceding 12 months. The purchases amounted to more that $20,000.

Pack's new building was immediately occupied by the Townsend-Robinson Investment Company. J.B. Corbett was the manager and C.E. Robinson was the secretary of the company, which offered lots for sale with immediate possession.

Such a growing town obviously needed a Board of Trade. According to historian Jerry Person, J.B. Corbett was the first president of the group formed in 1904. The Board of Trade became synonymous with the Chamber of Commerce.

The opportunities to build four-, five- and six-room cottages to be used as rentals and rooming houses held much promise. In June of 1904, lots in the brand new townsite were being sold even more rapidly than the previous month. The price of lots was rising at a phenom-

The street plan of Huntington Beach, shown here in 1913, featured streets numbered from First to Twenty-third perpendicular to the ocean, with Main Street taking the place of Fourth Street. Cross streets were named after trees and Ocean Avenue bordered the beach. The original plat extended only to Orange Street.
Courtesy History Room, Santa Ana Public Library

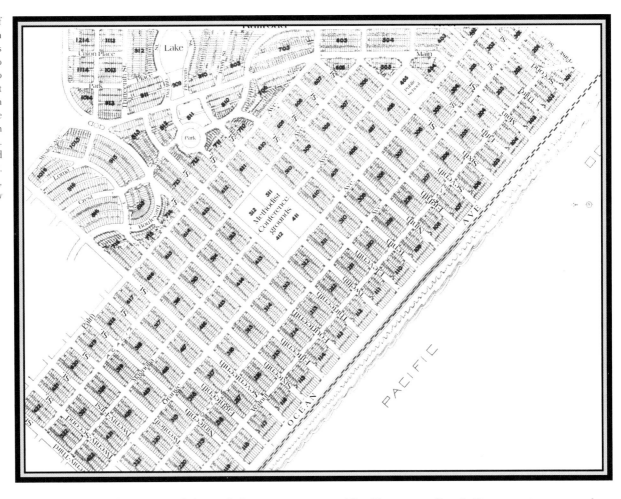

enal rate. The *Daily Evening Blade* cited the instance where a lot was sold for $1,500 on a Saturday in June. Smaller lots were going for the sums from $700 to $1,000 each.

The Huntington Beach Company, incorporated on May 4, 1903, devoted itself to improving the land and selling real estate. Vickers, who was president, was assisted by two Los Angeles businessmen, Walter Vail and Carroll W. Gates. The men saw to it that a great variety of trees was planted along the streets and ordered a huge horse-drawn water wagon to irrigate the plantings on a regular schedule.

Water, a necessity for any successful community, was supplied by the first well at Olive and Main Street. The second was drilled on Atlanta east of the Southern Pacific tracks and the third in Lake Park.

Henry Huntington, for whom the city is named, was the nephew of railroad magnate Collis P. Huntington. Henry recognized the possibilities of electric railways in 1902 while he was living in San Francisco. After moving to Los Angeles, he began developing the Pacific Electric Railway system, known as the "Red Cars" in 1903. He extended the line from Long Beach to Huntington Beach in 1904.
Courtesy First American Title Insurance Co.

THE RED CARS AND HENRY E. HUNTINGTON

Henry Huntington, the nephew of railroad magnate Collis Huntington, became interested in the possibilities of the electric railway while living in San Francisco in 1902. After moving to Los Angeles, he purchased and immediately began connecting, consolidating and extending the existing lines of the Pacific Electric Railway. In doing so, he created an efficient urban railway system. His effort to bring the Pacific Electric Red Car to Huntington Beach from Long Beach was the major contribution to the survival of the new town.

In order to persuade Huntington to bring his railroad to the new community, Vickers, Vail and Gates made him a deal he could not refuse. He was offered a block of stock at the ridiculously low price of 17 cents a share, a free right-of-way along the beach, one-twelfth of all the subdivided lots and a one-fifth interest in all of the ocean front property. Huntington was reluctant, but was finally swayed by the inducement that the community would be renamed for him.

Huntington, who served on as many as 60 executive boards at one time, loved fine art and beautiful things. In 1910, he retired from business and devoted himself completely to the collecting of antique furniture, fine art, rare books and other treasures. His home, located on the 50-acre San Marino Ranch, became the Henry E. Huntington Library and Art Gallery.

THE TROUBLE OVER TOWN LOTS

A battle ensued in 1904 between the original owners of the townsite of Huntington Beach and outside speculators who had acquired property with the idea of making it part of the new town. A group of real estate operators from Long Beach purchased a tract of land to the east of the Huntington Beach Company's property, intending to divide it into town lots and advertise them for sale. However, the Huntington Beach Company still had many town lots to sell and did not like the idea of the competition.

As a result, a five-foot barbed wire fence was erected along the company's eastern boundary. The fence stretched north from the ocean front to a point far enough to make it out of the question for the owners of the proposed addition to connect with the new town in anything but the most circuitous way.

The Long Beach outlanders, having been shut out, were not willing to surrender. They tried to convince the Huntington Beach Company that it was unfair to keep them out. The district attorney was consulted to help end the dispute expeditiously. To straighten out the problem, a petition was presented to the supervisors requesting that a road be opened between Huntington Beach and the new addition. A suit to condemn the land for the highways was instituted and the road built. However, the barbed wire fence stayed put for several months, marking the eastern boundaries of the company's property.

THE CHURCHES—A MARK OF STABILITY

By 1908, the Baptists, Methodists and Christian church had all built houses of worship on Orange Avenue.

The Methodist Episcopal Church, organized in 1904, held its first services in the bank building. The congregation grew quickly, and on January 9, 1906, its

Mr. Selby, the conductor of the first Red Car to reach Huntington Beach. *Courtesy Huntington Beach Historical Society*

The first Pacific Electric Railway "Red Car" arrived in Huntington Beach on July 4, 1904, in the midst of a grand celebration. It was estimated that 50,000 people attended the festivities that day. *Courtesy Arline Huff Howard*

59

The First Christian Church, which first met at Ocean View School in December of 1895, built this traditional Gothic-inspired building at the corner of 8th and Orange streets in 1908. *Courtesy Arline Huff Howard*

In 1906, the Huntington Beach Tent City Company incorporated and immediately began setting up tents next to the tabernacle in anticipation of the annual July 4 celebration. The tents were popular with vacationers as well as those who came to attend the Methodist revivals.

In 1906, the G.A.R. (Grand Army of the Republic) began holding its annual encampment in Huntington Beach. The Board of Trade was successful in persuading the G.A.R. Executive Board in Los Angeles to plan its annual meeting in the new town as a result. The month of September brought a week of patriotic programs, parades and memories.

SALOONS

From its beginning, saloons were not allowed in Huntington Beach. A clause in each deed given or sold by the Huntington Beach Company prohibited the sale of intoxicating liquors.

According to long-time resident Virginia Payne, city ordinances prohibited (1) the sale of, gift or delivery of any alcoholic beverage; (2) gambling of any kind; (3) the game of pool or other related games found in pool halls.

However, the law did not stop bootleggers. Constable Winslow was forced to wage an active campaign against the transporting of alcoholic beverages.

EARLY SCHOOLS

According to Tom Talbert, the first school in the area was the Ocean View School. It was so named because it had a beautiful panoramic view of the Pacific Ocean, including Catalina Island. Talbert notes that the buildings were later moved to the corner of Smeltzer and Hampshire Avenue (Hwy. 39), with about 200 students attending. Originally, the Springsdale School District was not part of Ocean View, but later joined it.

60

first chapel was dedicated. The Reverend Pitner of Los Angeles was the special guest preacher for the morning service. Reverend Thompson, presiding Elder of the Pasadena District of the Methodist Church, filled the pulpit at the evening service.

The formal opening of the First Baptist Church occurred on June 17, 1906 with the Rev. Herndon Ganett of the Church in Santa Ana as the guest speaker. Scott's orchestra provided special music during the service.

The 14 founding members of the Christian Church first met on December 29, 1895, at the Ocean View School. The group worshiped together without benefit of a minister until January of 1905, when L. C. Haulman became their pastor. After meeting in a bicycle shop at 6th and Walnut for awhile, the congregation purchased a lot at the corner of 8th and Orange street, and built their first church building.

THE METHODIST TABERNACLE AND TENT CITY

In 1906, the Southern California Methodist Association decided to move its annual conference headquarters from Long Beach to Huntington Beach. The Huntington Beach Company donated four square blocks between Acacia and Orange avenues and 11th and 13th streets to the organization. The Board of Trade guaranteed a subsidy of $5,000, in return, the conference was to make $20,000 in improvements. One block was reserved for the tabernacle, one for the playground and park, one for retired ministers' home and one for a tent city. The cornerstone for the tabernacle (assembly hall) was laid in on April 18, 1906. At the end of 10 years, the Methodists received the deed to the land, as was agreed upon in 1906. Eventually, however, they traded the property to Frank Bundy for a piece of land in Santa Monica Canyon and moved the Methodist conference there.

The Methodist Tabernacle in the center of a four-square-block campground, was also used for many civic events, and served as a temporary high school while the permanent building was being constructed. *Courtesy First American Title Insurance Co*

Members and families of the Malvern Hill Post of the Grand Army of the Republic pose in front of their tent about 1904. The G. A. R. used the tent city campground for many years. *Courtesy First American Title Insurance Co.*

The Tent City campground was located next to the Methodist Tabernacle. It was a popular summertime destination for vacationers and camp meeting attendees from Orange and Los Angeles counties. *Courtesy First American Title Insurance Co.*

Chapter Three

the turn of the century. He used a huge old cylinder-type phonograph to provide the music for the skaters. In 1905, he sold the building to C. W. Sawyer, who opened an implement and tool store there. The first bowling alley was located in the pavilion on the beach side of Ocean Avenue at Main. It was operated by Boxie Huston.

Tom Talbert was a member of the swimming club that gathered at the beach for a 6 a.m. swim every day, whether it was summer or winter. Every New Year's Day a large group gathered to pose for publicity pictures of their "Polar Bear" surf activities. The photos were sent back east to show that folks in Southern California could play in the ocean year-round.

The Huntington Beach Company donated the land for the first elementary school within the city limits. The grammar school, a fine two-story building topped with a bell tower, was located in the 500 block of Orange Avenue. In 1908, the first Huntington Beach Union High School building, a grand two-story Mission-style edifice, was built at Main and Mansion street.

TIME FOR SOME FUN

On a more recreational note, Tom Talbert owned and operated a large rollerskating rink. Rollerskating was one of the most popular pastimes in the years after

THE TOWN GAINS SEVERAL PROMINENT EARLY CITIZENS

By 1904, several of Huntington Beach's most important pioneers moved into the new village. Recognizing the new town's potential, several adventuresome souls built residences and commercial buildings, investing their time and effort in its establishment.

The prospects of the new resort city were noticed by many in Orange County. For example, John Shirley, a prominent restaurateur from Santa Ana, purchased

62

WELCOME TO HUNTINGTON BEACH

several town lots and built a charming cottage. According to the *Daily Evening Blade*, Mr. Shirley served "spreads that would put to shame most of the hotel tables in the country. The full menu was too long to remember off hand, but among the good things to eat were strawberries as big as ordinary potatoes and grown right at the beach, potatoes as big and nice and dry as any ever placed on a table, and also a home product, green peas as big as cherries and as tender as the very best green peas can be, and a beefsteak that came from the choicest cut of a very choice beef. Then there were a lot of other fixings too numerous to mention and to cap all there was the cordial welcome given the visitor that made him feel at home."

Vegetable crops were an all-important part of the economic life of the community, providing the basis for the survival of the stores in town. As an example of the continuing importance, Mr. Woodward and Mr. Frank Drarrow moved down from Portland, Oregon, where they had been in the vegetable business for years. After leasing 80 acres from Will Shamrock, they planted horseradish, onions and cucumbers. Mr. Woodward, while speaking of the farm's impressive success, noted that he had harvested as high as $600 worth of onions from one acre of land, and that $1,000 was not an uncommon yield for one acre of horseradish.

Dr. Samuel G. Huff the First Country Doctor

Dr. Samuel Huff who was born in Salem, Illinois, on October 4, 1845, arrived in Wintersburg in 1901 and served as a beloved country doctor for 17 years. Dr. Huff first came to California in the 1860s, but returned to Illinois to get his medical degree. He graduated from the Washington Medical Department in St. Louis in 1870. After living in San Bernardino for 20 years, he and his family purchased a 40-acre ranch and Victorian farm house from Mr. Lanfair. Located on the highest hill on the mesa, the ranch featured 30 graceful English Walnut trees. Before the surrounding land was drained, a swamp of tules, willows and blackberry patches encircled the hill.

In addition to being a physician, Dr. Huff, who was known for his interest in education, served as president of the Board of Trustees of Huntington Beach.

The Matthew Helme family poses on the front porch of the house they moved from Fifth and Verano streets to the corner of Sixth and Walnut streets in 1903. The house is still in the Helme-Worthy family. *Courtesy First American Title Insurance Co.*

After Dr. Huff died in 1922, his son Ralph, and his wife, the former Alice Gallienne, inherited the ranch and raised their four daughters there. Ralph grew tomatoes, corn, lima beans, sugar beets and other crops on the 40 acres.

Matthew and Mary Josephine Helme

In 1903, Matthew and Mary Josephine Helme moved their two-story house from the farm country near 5th and Verano (now Euclid Street) to the corner of Sixth and Walnut streets in Huntington Beach. The wooden house, previously owned by the Leatherman family, was moved 11 miles by a mule team into the heart of town.

The next year the Helmes built a two-story wooden commercial building and opened the M. E. Helme House Furnishing Company. Located next to their residence, the business was the first furniture company in the new village and was quite successful, offering all kinds of household goods ranging from

In 1904, Matthew Helme built Huntington Beach's first furniture store on Walnut Street, just south of his home. The second floor of the wooden building contained seven furnished rental rooms and two one-bedroom apartments. *Courtesy First American Title Insurance Co.*

63

furniture to bird cages, baby buggies and mirrors. In addition, there were seven furnished rental rooms and two one-bedroom units on the second floor.

Mary Josephine Helme, born on October 4, 1862, in Indiana, was a woman of courage and fortitude. She was orphaned at an early age when her father was killed in the Civil War and her mother passed away. She moved in with her grandparents who already had 12 children of their own. In 1883, she married Charles E. Helme. Sadly, he lived only two years after their marriage. Heading west in the spring of 1886, she homesteaded 160 acres on Rattlesnake Flat in Washington State. Three years later she and Matthew, her deceased husband's brother, were married. They moved to Santa Ana so that their three children might get a better education than what was then available in Washington.

Matthew Helme went on to become one of Huntington Beach's most influential citizens. After fighting for incorporation in 1909, he was elected to the new city's first Board of Trustees(City Council). He worked hard to bring water, that all-important commodity, flowing in the new town. He helped set up the modern fire department, and in 1916, worked to get the city manager system in place. His next important tasks were to introduce an ordinance to set up the city's first gas bonds, and to begin a substantial street paving and lighting program. He served as president of the Huntington Beach Tent City Company in 1914.

Helme was the town's fourth mayor in 1916 and 1917. Among his accomplishments were the gas lighting system, with gas lights installed along Main Street; paving Ocean Avenue from Main to 17th streets and providing a new brick boulevard along Fifth Street. He introduced the action resulting in the purchase of the water system from the Huntington Beach Company by the city.

In 1917, Helme resigned from the Board of Trustees and he and Mary Josephine moved back to their wheat farm in Washington. The house and the store remained in the family, however, when their daughter, Amy, and her husband, Lawrence Worthy, opened a plumbing business in the store building and continued the Helme-Worthy family legacy of active involvement in the community.

The M. E. Helme House Furnishing Company handled all kinds of furnishings and household goods including bird cages, lamps, mirrors, baby buggies and a full line of furniture. Courtesy First American Title Insurance Co.

64

THE FIRST BANK BUILDING: A SIGN OF PROSPERITY IN 1905

The two-story stone building which was to house the Huntington Beach Bank and the Savings Bank of Huntington Beach was constructed in 1905 at the corner of Walnut and Main streets.

In 1904, the founding of two lumber companies, Starr Lumber and San Pedro Lumber that made construction much easier because it provided the availability of materials. San Pedro Lumber that eventually bought out Starr, provided employment and a tax revenue for the new townsite.

The Anthracite Peat Fuel Company, founded in 1905, was a commercial outlet for the vast peat lands. The peat ranged from 20 to 50 feet deep over a wide area. In 1906, the company built a large bunk house and cook house to be used by the employees. The La Bolsa Tile Factory and Raine Tile Company made clay tiles to drain the field to the north and east of the townsite.

The Huntington Beach Canning, Pickling and Produce Company was founded in 1905 by W. T. Newland, J. F. Corbett and others. They planned to provide $100,000 in capital by selling 1,000 shares at $100 each. Using this method they were able to raise $20,000 quickly. The funds were used to buy the land and construct the cannery and box units of the factory. The company bought and sold fruits, vegetables and produce. Some of the varieties were canned, while others were pickled. The company also manufactured cans, crates and boxes for the purpose of storing and shipping its products.

Mr. M. R. Frie was hired as the first manager. He had been associated with the Heintz Company, producers of a well-known brand of pickles, for 18 of the 36 years he had been in the canning business. In the March 12, 1906, edition of the *Daily Evening Blade*, he is quoted as saying "From what I saw yesterday in your wonderful section I am fully convinced that you folks have something better than a gold mine, as the soil there is inexhaustible. That section, when devoted to raising vegetables should be called the pride of California vegetable gardens, for there is no other section in the United States that can show varieties like you have in that low section. If properly developed, that land will bring safely, from $800 to $1,000 per acre in vegetables."

Unfortunately, Mr. Frie and the Huntington Beach Canning, Pickling and Produce Company could not come to an agreement and Mr. Frie never went to work there. Mr. W. Boulder of Ontario, Canada, and his two sons were the first to take charge of the company's operations.

THE FIRST ARCHAEOLOGIST

The region's first recorded archaeologist arrived in 1906. Dr. F. M. Palmer, the curator of the Southwest Society of the Archaeologist Institute of America, explored the Bolsa Chica wetlands, hoping to find relics that would date back to the days of prehistoric inhabitants. The *Daily Evening Blade* reported that residents had been finding mortars, pestles, arrowheads, crude tools and many relics for many years.

TOM TALBERT

One of Huntington Beach's most prominent citizens was Tom Talbert. He became a well-known civic leader and county supervisor. Moving to the new settlement of Huntington Beach in 1903 he went into the real estate business. Fortunately his friends, W. D. Maateer and William Newland, convinced the 26-year-old man to move to Huntington Beach instead of the much larger town of Santa Ana.

As Tom joined the 52 realtors already working in town, it was easy to see that the new town was booming. When the boom went bust in 1905 and most of the other realtors went out of business, Tom stayed on, using his time, talents and enthusiasm to improve Huntington Beach in many ways. He was a director of the First National Bank of Huntington Beach, an agent for the Huntington Beach Company, and active in almost every civic organization.

The "Goddess of Liberty" float appeared in the Fourth of July parade of 1908. Each girl represented one of the 13 original states. *Courtesy Huntington Beach Historical Society*

nized the economic value of the gun club and their visitors, they did not always agree on the privatization of the land.

On November 26, 1906, Will Burdick and his hunting buddies entered the property of the Bolsa Chica Gun Club by propelling their boat down the Freeman River to its junction with Bolsa Chica Bay, destroying fences as they progressed down the river. Carrying shotguns, the interlopers had been shooting game. In their opinion, they had a right to enter the property because they thought the Freeman River was a navigable stream of water.

The Bolsa Land Company and the gun club denied that the local hunters had access to their property and filed suit against them.

On May 15, 1907, the California Supreme Court sided with the Bolsa Land Company and the Bolsa Chica Gun Club, making the determination that the Freeman River was an irrigation ditch, not a river.

The Bolsa Land Company replaced all of the fences across the waterways, preventing hunters from bringing their boats through the area.

In 1909, Tom was appointed to the office of county supervisor, representing the Second District. After winning the election for the seat in 1910, Talbert was elected chairman of the Board of Supervisors. He served in that capacity eight times in 16 years during his 17 years in office. This was a period of great constructive activity in Orange County and Talbert was right there, participating in many important decisions.

THE BOLSA CHICA GUN CLUB VS. THE HUNTERS

The gun clubs were still thriving in the Bolsa Chica area during the 1910s, controlling large areas of swamp land. While the local residents usually recog-

The basketball team from Huntington Beach High pose in front of the Methodist Auditorium in 1908-09, after winning the Orange County championship tournament. *Courtesy First American Title Insurance Co.*

A GRAND SIGHT:
THE GREAT WHITE FLEET SAILS PAST
ORANGE COUNTY

In April of 1908, a majestic and patriotic parade of battleships, The Great White Fleet, streamed slowly past the beach towns along Orange County's coast. Teddy Roosevelt had planned the worldwide tour of the fleet to demonstrate the extent of our nation's naval power. Crowds gathered along the shore from San Juan Capistrano to Bay City. A large and enthusiastic crowd gathered in Huntington Beach to see the 16 battleships and two auxiliary boats sail by approximately two and half miles off shore. Over 5,000 people made their way to the town that day. Huntington Beach was in gala dress, with flags and bunting everywhere. The crowds were excited and enthusiastic about seeing the splendid naval pageant.

Almost everyone brought a big lunch basket. Families could be seen everywhere putting out their food on tablecloths spread on the sandy beach, on boat bottoms on the wharf and almost any available spot. It was reported that practically every city in the county was deserted and most of the inland stores closed so that everyone could go to the shore to see the splendid array of ships. In all, an estimated 12,000 to 14,000 people watched the ship pass Orange County shores. While the ships could be seen easily with the naked eye, only those using field glasses could see the men on the decks.

The Evangeline Hotel, constructed in 1908 in the Craftsman Bungalow style, provided lodging for visitors and prospective residents. *Courtesy First American Title Insurance Co.*

W. T. Newland and S. W. Price headed the committee to welcome the crowd. Almost every resident of Huntington Beach served on one of the committees that helped to make the day run with remarkable smoothness.

THE EXCITING ADVENTURE OF THE GALLIENNE FAMILY

In 1910, the H .A. Gallienne and the George Lake families came from the Island of Guernsey in the English Channel, directly to Huntington Beach to begin their new life in America. The move itself must have been quite a challenge because of the changes in atmosphere and culture.

Before coming to America, the Galliennes briefly considered moving to Australia or Canada, but changed their minds and headed for California. They boarded the ocean liner, the *Mauretania* from Southampton,

The H. A. Gallienne family, shown here in 1910, was one of pioneer families from diverse backgrounds who settled in the Huntington Beach area. They came directly to the new town from the Island of Guernsey in the English Channel. H. A. Gallienne went on to become an important landscaper for the Holly Sugar Company and the Huntington Beach Union High School. *Courtesy Arline Huff Howard*

Ed Manning (left), the first mayor of Huntington Beach, appeared in the 1909 parade celebrating the incorporation of the city. Councilman C. H. Howard sits beside him. *Courtesy First American Title Insurance Co.*

England, on December 2, 1910, setting sail for New York. The Galliennes and the Lakes were very excited and proud when they passed the Statue of Liberty. Shortly thereafter, on a cold and dark day, they landed at Ellis Island. After being scrutinized by the Ellis Island official, they were allowed to enter the United States.

After transferring to a freighter, the families sailed to New Orleans. The next leg of the journey was aboard a train headed for Los Angeles. When crossing the great Texas plains and the arid stretches of New Mexico and Arizona, the travelers were awestruck by the sights of the new country and lifestyle. The Mexican atmosphere was exciting, especially for the young people. On December 18, they arrived in Los Angeles, where they transferred to the Red Car. When they disembarked in Huntington Beach, they were taken by surrey to a relative's home at 17th and Yorktown. What an adventure!

The Gallienne family found rooms on the second floor of the National Bank Building. At first the women were very unhappy because Huntington Beach had no paved streets, street lights or gas, and only one cafe. Its saving grace was the beautiful beach only a block away.

H. A. Gallienne who was a well-known nurseryman in his home country, had to start his career over again, taking any job available. He found employment at the La Bolsa Tile Company. A short time later, he was hired at the newly established Holly Sugar factory. It was there that he was able to use his talent and experience as a nurseryman when he was put in charge of the landscaping of the grounds. Within a few years he became the custodian of building and grounds at Huntington Beach High School.

HUNTINGTON BEACH INCORPORATES

In February of 1909, Huntington Beach took a major step in its civic history when it incorporated as a city of the sixth class. 94 residents voted for incorporation and 2 against the measure. A Board of Trustees was selected and Ed Manning became the first mayor. The city boundaries consisted of 3.7 square miles, and the population was 915.

The first city hall that was located in the rear of the First National Bank Building, rented for $12 a month. The first jail was constructed sometime during that first year. It consisted of an open metal cage placed on the platform constructed for the fire bell.

THE FIRE DEPARTMENT

A history of the Fire Department notes that "Mayor Manning asked John Philip, a hardware merchant to organize a volunteer fire company. On March 1, 1909,

20 men held the first meeting and organized the Huntington Beach Volunteer Fire Department. John Philip was elected Fire Chief." Most of the businessmen in town became members of the new department.

The group immediately petitioned the city council for recognition and approval, which was granted on April 26, 1909. The organization's first official act was to ask for the money to buy the necessary equipment to fight fires.

They requested funds for a large fire bell, a hose cart with 600 feet of tubed fire hose, a nozzle, a hydrant wrench and the installation of fire hydrants along the alleys. The equipment was received and the system was in place by late fall.

The fire department history tells us that two members of the city council went to Los Angeles to listen to the sounds of several types of fire bells. The bell they chose was mounted on a platform 20 feet above the ground at the corner of Main and Walnut streets.

The next task was to find a place for a fire station. A location was found at the horse and carriage stable on the northwest corner of Third and Orange streets. The rent.was $8 a month.

THE CITY GAINS
A NEW CARNEGIE LIBRARY

The Woman's Club was one of the first to identify the need for a public library. Pressing forward to make the idea a reality, a mass meeting was called by the Woman's Club on February 15, 1909, for the purpose of founding a library association. Mrs. R. H. Lindgren and R. W. Blodget had contacted the Board of Trade, who also got behind idea. The first library committee consisted of Mrs. Lindgren, Mrs. Mary Manske, Mrs. C.D. Heartwell, Mrs. Minnie Nutt and Mrs. Blodget. A $1 membership drive was immediately instituted. The Huntington Beach Woman's Club donated $50.

The community enthusiastically supported the project. One of the first needs was a building. Mr. Reed donated $50 for the purchase of an old roofless building that was moved to the southwest corner of Walnut and Main Street. The owner of the lot, S.E.Hearn, agreed to the use of

the lot for a nominal fee. Local carpenters and painters donated services to repair the building. Second-hand furniture was painted or stained and varnished. Mr. H. Gibbs furnished fuel for the first winter and the Huntington Beach Company furnished electricity and water.

In June of 1909, soon after the city's incorporation, the Board of Trustees agreed to take over the responsibility for the library and to appoint a Library Board. Members of that first group were A. W. Everett, Mrs. Lindgren, Mrs.S. L. Blodget, Mrs. Manske and Mrs. Ida Vincent. In July of 1909, Miss Edith Brown of Long Beach was named as the first librarian. There were 338 volumes on the shelves.

In 1910, Mrs. Maude Andrews became the new librarian and the library was moved to the southwest corner of Third and Walnut and enlarged. The completion of the Holly Sugar Company a year later, brought many new people to town.

Mrs. Bertha Proctor became the first permanent librarian in May of 1911, receiving a salary of $35 a month. She was one of the best known of the many persons who devoted their time and energy to the improvement of the library throughout the years. In

The first Huntington Beach Union High School, an imposing building designed in the Mission Revival style, was built in 1910. *Courtesy First American Title Insurance Co.*

The classical red brick Huntington Beach Public Library was built in 1913 thanks to a gift of $10,000 from the Carnegie Foundation. The land was donated by the city. The original library association was formed in 1909. *Courtesy First American Title Insurance Co.*

In 1914, Huntington Beach celebrated the completion of its 1,350-foot concrete pier, considered to be one of the finest in the nation.
Courtesy Huntington Beach Historical Society

Municipal Concrete Pier, Huntington Beach, Cal.
(Length 1350 feet.)

1912, the city bought four lots on the corner of Walnut and Eighth Street as a future site for a new library.

On February 13, 1913, Huntington Beach was notified that the Carnegie Foundation had granted $10,000 for the erection of a library building. In November, the cornerstone was laid for the new edifice. The Carnegie library building was indeed grand. Constructed of red tapestry brick with light gray brick trim, the building was crowned with a roof clad in mission tiles. At a size of 35 feet by 61 feet, the building also included a large basement with a lecture room, reference room, work room and furnace space. The main floor contained the bookshelves, general reading room, children's room and librarian's room.

On May 7, 1914, the library moved into its new home. The Huntington Beach High School class of 1914 gifted the library with a fine grandfather's clock.

THE NEW CONCRETE PIER

In 1910, the chamber of commerce, recognizing that the pier constructed in 1902 was ready to fall down, appointed a special committee to study the problem. The Huntington Beach Company wanted a new wooden pier built at 23rd Street instead of Main Street, so that the properties they were developing at the west end of town could be promoted. However, after committee members studied the situation, they decided that a new reinforced concrete pier at Main and Ocean would be of greater benefit to the city.

Tom Talbert remembers that this was the beginning of what he considered the bitterest fight in the early history of Huntington Beach. In 1911, a bond issue of $70,000 to pay for the pier, was proposed. Several families, including the Talberts, Chapins, O'Connors, Herrons and many others campaigned for the concrete pier and bond issue; the Huntington Beach Company, Whitneys, Warners and others opposed the bonds, claiming the expense would bankrupt the city. The bond issue carried by more than two-thirds majority.

Although the $70,000 was approved in 1911, it would be 1914 before the pier was finished. In 1912, a powerful storm damaged the pier even further. Mr. James, the engineer for the new concrete piers in Santa Monica and Venice, helped supervise the new pier's construction. The Mercereau Construction Company received the contract for the building of the pier.

The total cost of the pier was $100,000 — $30,000 more than originally expected. One reason for the long construction period was the method of construction used. Each piling was cut and left to season for months along the bluff. A narrow gauge railroad car brought the wood onto the new pier and the pilings were individually fitted and driven into the ocean floor. By the time it was finished in June of 1914, most residents were enthusiastic about the impressive reinforced concrete pleasure pier.

THE GRAND OPENING OF A NEW PIER

A festive two-day celebration marked the opening of the new pier, considered to be one of the finest concrete piers on both coasts. A committee made up of Board of Trade members planned the festivities.

The formal dedication was led by the Santa Ana Lodge No.794 B.P.O. Elks. Included in the ceremonies on June 20 were music by the Long Beach Municipal Band, the laying of the cornerstone, and the inspection of the pier by the public. In the afternoon a variety of foot races, a baseball game and a diving and swimming exposition provided entertainment for everyone.

The Pacific Electric Depot, located next to the ocean, was the lifeblood of the community. Not only did it bring passengers from Los Angeles via Long Beach, but it was also used to transport goods and freight for local merchants.
Courtesy First American Title Insurance Co.

The 75-yard race for boys under 14 offered a $1 for the first prize and 50 cents for the second place. The girl's race featured the same amount of prize money, but was only 50 yards in length. There was also a three-legged race, sack race and a ladies 75-yard competition.

An admission fee of 25 cents was charged for those attending the baseball game that starred teams from Garden Grove and the Pacific Electric Company.

The Los Angeles Athletic Club provided

the swimming and divers for the exposition. Champion Juvenile Divers Ray Kegeris (11), Tommie Witt (9) and Paul Lisle (9) were among those athletes featured. Later in the program a Japanese fencing and sword dance exhibition added drama to the festivities.

At 8:00 p.m. an event listed as the "Ocean Illumination" was presented. The evening was concluded with a Carnival Dance on the new Pier.

Sunday began with a Casting Tournament by members of the Southern California Rod and Reel Club. Donatelli's Italian Band then provided some lively music. A union church service at the end of the pier was led by the Rev. R. A. Torrey listed as "the world's most famous evangelist." Miss Annie McClaurin, well-known gospel singer and soloist, appeared with the Big Chorus Choir. More music by Donatelli's Italian Band and the Great Festival Chorus of Southern California, along with more diving and swimming demonstrations by the champions from the Los Angeles Athletic Club occupied the afternoon.

Participating Board of Trade committee members included H.T. Sundbye, president of the Board of Trade and chairman of the event; R. M. Dickinson, local manager for the Sharer Investment Company and H. B. Little, assistant cashier of the First National Bank. Leonard Obarr, of Obarr's Drug Store, confectionery dealer H.E. Talbert and City Marshal John Tinsley rounded out committee.

THE PACIFIC OIL CLOTH AND LINOLEUM COMPANY BUILDS A NEW PLANT

The new oil cloth and linoleum factory, completed in 1914, helped bring new economic stability to the 10-year-old city.

The community watched in anticipation as the brick factory building took shape. An 83-foot-high smokestack that was five feet in diameter, reached into the sky. A transformer house provided the electricity (equivalent to 100 horses pulling on the traces).

In that same year the merchants who owned businesses downtown decided to form a permanent organization. Among those helping to organize the group were jeweler T. R. Canady, Henry Gibbs from the Pioneer Feed and Fuel Company, M. A. Turner, Mr. McElfresh and Mr. Eader.

The opening of the Princess Theater was heralded by the *Huntington Beach News* during June of 1914.

Pacific Oil Cloth and Linoleum Factory, Huntington Beach, Cal.

W.P. Harrison, the manager of the Princess, felt that the city was a good place to open a first-class picture show.

By 1915, the town's slow but steady growth had produced a pleasant place in which to live as well as a budding resort town. An electric lighting system, oiled and paved streets and substantial business blocks gave the city an air of stability. The splendid new $25,000 high school was the pride of the community. Streets lined with neat homes, five churches and a new library were among the attributes of the city. The new 1,315-foot-long municipal pleasure and fishing pier, lit by electric lamps, was a big attraction for tourists.

In addition to the surrounding rich productive farms land, a handful of factories added to the economic security of the community. The Holly Sugar Company built a factory, its third in the county, which cost $1,250,000. The Pacific Oil Cloth and Linoleum Factory, the Pacific Broom Company facility and La Bolsa Drain Tile Company were among those operating in Huntington Beach. Their presence brought hundreds of jobs to the city, proving a strong economic base for the economy.

THE END OF AN ERA

Huntington Beach, after many years of peaceful and stable existence, was, along with the rest of Southern California, headed for many changes. On the horizon were disastrous floods, the excitement caused by Pancho Villa, and, most significantly, World War I.

In January of 1916, two flash floods did a great deal of damage in Orange County. In June of that year the border activities caused by the actions of Pancho Villa had much of Southern California in a state of excitement. Life had barely settled down again when World War I began in April of 1917. The nation had thought of little else but the dangerous situation in Europe in the years between 1916 and 1919, and the American sense of patriotism was very strong. For more than two years before the United States officially entered the war, the dark threatening cloud of our nation's involvement had created an unsettled mood across the United States.

THE FLOODS OF 1916

The year 1916 is known for not one, but two raging floods. Each did considerable damage to Orange County, Riverside, San Diego and Los Angeles counties. Adding to the problem were the many changes in the face of Southern California that had taken place since the well-remembered flood of 1884.

Since that time, many of the small villages had grown into large towns, new communities developed and miles of brush-covered land were cleared for farming. New arrivals, seeing the arid country and dry rivers and creeks, often settled down smack in the middle of a dry flood plain, not realizing the potential for danger until the waters began to rise.

Several days of heavy rain on January 15, 16, 17 and 18, thoroughly soaked the ground throughout Orange, Los Angeles, San Diego and Riverside counties. The second storm, a few days later, hit even harder. The Santa Ana River raged out of its banks in several places. Rushing out of the Santa Ana Canyon from the Corona area, the river flooded most of Yorba, located on the north side at the mouth of the canyon, and both sides of the river west of Olive. The Anaheim Sugar Factory property and the barrios in Anaheim, Atwood and Richfield, were covered by fast-moving floodwaters, forcing rescuers to bring the Mexican families out by horseback. The approach to the new Olive-Anaheim bridge was washed out.

The floodwaters poured onto the grounds of old Orange County Hospital and the Poor Farm west of Orange. Significant amounts of debris lodged against the Southern Pacific railroad tracks, sending water across the flat land. In the downtown section of Garden Grove, water stood two or three feet deep in some stores. In order to relieve the pressure there, dynamite was used to blow holes in the embankment on which the Pacific Electric tracks were located. Three persons drowned as a result of the first flood.

The town of Huntington Beach, sitting on its mesa, was relatively unscathed; however, the surrounding farmland, from the ocean to Santa Ana Canyon, was inundated with flooding.

Damages to agricultural lands in Orange County totaled $350,000 in 1916 dollars. The loss along the entire length of the river, estimated at over $1 million, included the loss of bridges, railroads and roads. The floods of 1916 taught Orange County a lesson, alerting residents and officials to the need for better and more extensive flood control measures.

HUNTINGTON BEACH ON THE BRINK OF NEW DISCOVERIES

After the Armistice was signed on November 11, 1918, the tired soldiers came home to settle down. They were anxious to take up where they left off by getting married, starting a family, buying a cozy house and getting back to civilian work.

Connie Brockway, in *Huntington Beach Notes*, reports that the city council, on March 10, 1919, established a Placement Bureau at City Hall where returning soldiers and sailors could register for jobs and for employers to list their needs.

In 1919 and 1920, the face of the peaceful and picturesque beach town of Huntington Beach would be dramatically changed forever as the presence of black gold was discovered under its peatland soils.

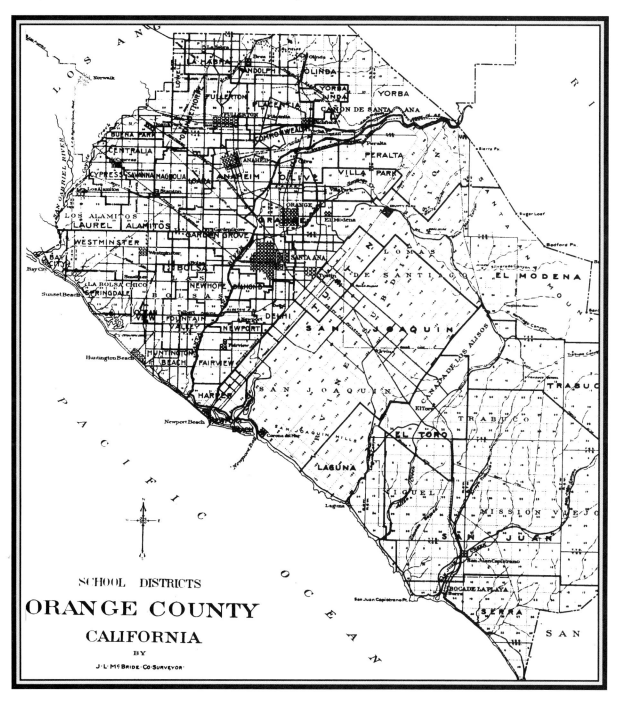

The 1913 School District Map of Orange County, mapped by surveyor J. L. McBride, shows Bolsa, Newhope, Fountain Valley, Diamond, Ocean View, Springdale, Old Newport, Fairview, Harper and Delhi in the country surrounding the Huntington Beach School District. *Courtesy History Room, Santa Ana Public Library*

73

Chapter Four

THE ENCYCLOPEDIA LOTS

Almost everyone enjoys a true rags to riches tale, and the story of Huntington Beach's encyclopedia lots is one of the best. The encyclopedia lots were part of an advertising promotion to encourage families to buy sets of the Students Reference Encyclopedia, a special edition of the Encyclopedia Britannica. The encyclopedia company purchased and subdivided seven five-acre tracts into lots, creating 420 lots in all. The company gave the lots away as an inducement, at no extra cost, to purchasers of the sets of books. Most of the people who bought the books lived in other parts of the country and had never been to sunny Southern California, the land of milk and honey.

In the 1910s, Valery O. Appel, an attorney for the company, came west looking for the cheapest possible land to give away with the special sets of books. He purchased the seven worthless tracts of land from the Huntington Beach Company. The property was cheap because it was two-and-a-half miles from the beach and consisted mostly of unbuildable hillsides and canyons. The Huntington Beach Company was glad to get $200 an acre for such worthless land.

K. Philip Frederick wrote an article entitled, "Oil Fortunes That Were Gained From Books," about the case of Ezra Hapfield and his family. Ezra bought an encyclopedia for his daughter, Hattie, who was attending a girl's finishing school. He paid little attention to the deed for his new lot when it arrived and threw it into a desk. Later, it was transferred to a horsehair trunk and promptly forgotten. Hattie got married, had a son and became a widow within a short time. After she and her son moved back to her father's farm, the family received an inquiry from an attorney concerning the long-forgotten lot.

Living in New England they had not heard of the oil boom and were only mildly curious about the letter. Soon, they received an offer of over $300 for the property. This amazed Mr. Hapfield because the amount was more than he had paid for the entire set of encyclopedias. He decided it was time to investigate.

The family paid the back taxes on the lot, sold their livestock and bought tickets for California. Ezra, Hattie and her son quickly discovered that their parcel was located over the heart of a huge subterranean oil reservoir. They decided to keep the lot, and with their first oil royalties bought a handsome bungalow, complete with orange trees, on a slope overlooking the Pacific Ocean. The oil royalties kept coming in.

City Historian Alicia Wentworth has an original contract for one of the Encyclopedia Lots on the wall of her office. It reads, in part:

> *The Americana*, published by the Scientific American Compiling Department with 18 volumes bound in Three-Quarter Morocco Binding, which I agree to accept and pay $126. Title of said books shall remain with you until payment of the full amount.
>
> Fred C. Hathaway
> Salt Lake City, Utah

(Lot) 25 x 112 feet in the Fairview Addition to Huntington Beach, Orange County, California. The lot is free from marsh or swampland. All taxes of every kind from date hereof will be paid by the under-

HUNTINGTON BEACH — ON THE BRINK OF A NEW DISCOVERY

Courtesy Huntington Beach Historical Society

A stone monument and brass plaque mark the location of the Discovery Well, properly named the "Huntington A" No. 1. Oil was struck on May 24, 1920, at a depth of 2,199 feet. The plaque was dedicated on September 30, 1960, by the Standard Oil Company of California and the Petroleum Pioneers, Inc.
Courtesy Huntington Beach Historical Society

signed. (Lot) could be exchanged for any unassigned lot in the entire tract for purchase of four books only.

Fairview Addition is located within five furlongs of the Northern City Limits of the original town site, twelve furlongs from the ocean-front, and six furlongs from the Pacific Electric Interurban Station. Fairview Addition is about 60 feet above the sea level. Its contour is that of a high level plain, slightly rolling. The soil is a rich topsoil with a clay sub-soil. Huntington Beach is 30 miles from Los Angeles, an hour's ride by the Pacific Electric Railway hourly service.

Tom Talbert recalls that after the oil boom hit in 1920, he and his friends, William Schumacher, James

Macklin, J.K. McDonald and an unnamed man from Buena Park formed a syndicate with the idea of buying as many of the lots as possible. They sent out a letter to every lot owner offering to buy his or her property. They were able to buy 33 lots at a price from $5 to $15 each. One owner asked $50 for his lot, but in 1920 the syndicate thought that was outrageous and refused to buy the property. The encyclopedia company, after learning of the oil strike, would not sell its remaining five lots. When the plot plans of the property had been originally finalized by the Orange County Board of Supervisors, the Encyclopedia Britannica Company agreed to dedicate the streets. However, after oil was discovered, the company tried to rescind that promise so that they might keep that portion of the tracts designed for streets and receive the royalties from the oil company. The streets represented approximately one-third of the land tracts and could mean a fortune in black gold profits.

The Board of Supervisors reacted by passing a resolution that would declare the potential streets as county roads. As a result, the encyclopedia company filed suit against the County, attempting to quiet the title of the property contained in the unbuilt streets. Meanwhile, Tom Talbert's syndicate filed its own suit, as intervenors, protesting the withdrawal of the dedication of the streets. The syndicate won its case.

The syndicate then approached the oil company and requested that they not pay any royalties pertaining to the streets to the encyclopedia company. Its case

76

The discovery of oil changed the face of Huntington Beach at an eye-popping rate in the early 1920s. People who lived in the city when oil reigned supreme will tell you that the smell of oil and the noises made by the pumps severely impacted the quiet beach town.
Courtesy Huntington Beach Historical Society

was based on the claim that the streets belonged to the lot owners and that each lot owner should receive a share of the royalties. Of course, the encyclopedia company objected to this and filed another suit. By this time, there were six sets of lawyers involved in the case. Any action was delayed and postponed for about two years. This created a hostile and angry atmosphere among all involved.

Tom Talbert, seeing the hopelessness of a settlement, tells in *My Sixty Years in Orange County*, that he called a conference of all participants. Within two hours the group reached a compromise and settled their differences. From the $51,000 deposited in a holding account in the bank, the encyclopedia company received $2,500 and the lot owners received the balance.

HUNTINGTON BEACH – THE GEM OF THE SOUTH COAST

You can picture the Huntington Beach of 1920 — a stable and respectable community possessing all of the components needed to make it a good place in which to live. In addition, the beach and the tourist trade helped to make it unique, adding a certain excitement and gaiety during the summer season.

In 1920, the assessed valuation of all city properties was $1,023,635 with a tax rate of $1.50. The population was 1,687. The community had its own light and power plant, waterworks system and gas plant. The village was especially proud of its new ornamental and useful streetlights. Three-light cluster lampposts had been placed at alternate street corners and fitted with the latest electric lamps. A modern sewer system had been installed in the mid-teens. The telephone exchange was connected to both the Home and Sunset systems. Mail delivery to each home and business had been inaugurated in 1917.

In addition to the exciting activities held in the area surrounding the new concrete pier, there were four parks to serve the residents. The city hired a pro-

fessional forester to take charge of the planting and maintenance of the parks and the trees, flowers and shrubbery planted on the parking strips on each side of the residential streets.

The Huntington Beach Municipal Band, under the direction of C.H. "Pop" Endicott, enlivened many events.

The Methodists, Baptists, Church of Christ, Christian, Catholic and Christian Science churches were well established and had built substantial buildings. The Southern California Methodist Association had continued to maintain its large auditorium and tent city. Other organizations such as the Southern California Veteran's Association, Epworth League of the Methodist Church, Church of Latter Day Saints and Grand Army of the Republic held their annual conventions in the auditorium.

Considered by some to be the most important manufacturing plant in the city, the Holly Sugar Company claimed to be the most modern sugar beet factory in the world. Located about a quarter of a mile from the city limits, it had its own electric power and was equipped with a refrigerated plant. Using the Steffens method of sugar extraction, the facility employed approximately 400 skilled and unskilled laborers during the four-month-long sugar beet season.

The smartly-dressed Huntington Beach Municipal Band, in the 1920s. *Courtesy Huntington Beach Historical Society*

The saltwater plunge, located on the ocean side of the Pacific Electric tracks, is shown here in 1918. Constructed in 1911, it attracted residents from all over Orange County. *Courtesy Huntington Beach Historical Society*

Bathers frolic in the surf against a backdrop of the oil derricks. The building with the long wall in the background is the salt water municipal plunge.
Courtesy Huntington Beach Historical Society

During that time, more than 1,000 tons of beets were crushed daily. The yearly output of marketable sugar was valued at $2,225,000.

La Bolsa Tile Company had grown to become the largest clay tile factory west of Chicago. Luckily, an inexhaustible quantity of the right kind of clay needed to make tile for irrigation purposes existed at the plant location, about half a mile from the Huntington Beach city limits. It provided almost year-round employment for many Huntington Beach residents.

A successful fish and frog farm was established at the fresh-water lakes that once were prevalent on the Huntington Beach mesa. Nearby artesian wells provided a plentiful supply of additional water. Trout, terrapin, crawfish and bullfrogs were raised to be sold to the finest

restaurants in Los Angeles and nearby cities. In addition, the Beach Broom Company factory produced an annual output of $40,000 worth of products and the Pacific Linoleum and Oil Cloth Company had an output of $250,000 annually.

The Board of Trustees (City Council) included Ed Manning (president), Albert Onson (clerk), Richard Drew, C.J. Andrews and R.L. Obarr. Charles Nutt was the city treasurer and E.E. Lovering served as city attorney. L.W. Blodget was city recorder, C.W. Warner was the city engineer, C.R. Sumner was the superintendent of gas and sewers, F.L. Snyder was the marshal and George M. Taylor was superintendent of streets.

The 1920s was considered the "golden age of volunteer organizations." Almost

78

The Huntington Beach High School football team poses with its coach in 1924. Bud Higgins is the fourth from the left on the bottom row.
Courtesy Huntington Beach Historical Society

everyone was involved in one or more civic or fraternal groups, in addition to his or her church. The Free and Accepted Masons, Independent Order of Odd Fellows, Order of Eastern Star, Rebekah Lodge and Huntington Beach Woman's Club were among those organizations that were active in Huntington Beach. In addition, there were two fraternal insurance lodges, the Modern Woodmen and the Woodmen of the World. The American Federation of Musicians, an affiliate of the American Federation of Labor, was also active in the city. A very busy Chamber of Commerce claimed over 70 members, and worked actively to promote the commercial center.

Huntington Beach might have gone on for many years as a substantial and stable community, supplemented by the lively summer tourist season and its proximity to the wide sandy beach. Few realized in 1919, that within a year the daily life, appearance, focus and level of activity of the city would change dramatically. Huntington Beach was on the brink of its most important and explosive era. Oil was about to be discovered!

OIL FEVER

The evidence was there, speaking loud and clear. The Huntington Beach area was resting on a vast domed pool of oil. The real potential was not realized, however, until May 24, 1920, when the Standard Oil Company of California completed "Huntington A" No. 1 well at a depth of 2,199 feet, producing 45 barrels a day.

Sam Talbert recalled that when the shepherds of the early days grazed their sheep in pastures to the north of town, the gas constantly escaping into the air through natural vents in the earth was very noticeable. The shepherds, after blocking off the surrounding vents, would light a match to the gas flowing from one vent, and cook their dinner over the resulting fire.

Throughout the development of the Huntington Beach area there were complaints about the problems of attempting to drill a water well and getting so much gas that the well was not usable. In some places the heavy oil and asphalt oozed from the earth. Free for the taking, the asphalt was

The Huntington Beach Light and Power Plant, made of manufactured blocks, has a distinctive Mission-style parapet and quatrefoil window. *Courtesy Huntington Beach Historical Society*

used by residents to repair roofs and other purposes. Some farmers had their own small gas wells which they utilized for the light and fuel supply for their homes and barns.

BLACK GOLD ENRICHES ORANGE COUNTY

The search for oil on the Huntington Beach mesa was not by any means the first interest shown regarding the discovery of oil in Orange County. As early as 1894 oil was discovered by the Union Oil Company in the Brea-Olinda area. Most of the early development of oil in California was based on the presence of oil seepages or by oil-colored sand or shale on the ground. As petroleum developments progressed, oil formations were sought at greater and greater depths. The Huntington Beach fields, along with the oil developments at Coyote Hill, Richfield, Santa Fe Springs, Signal Hill, Dominguez and Torrance, were the result

Rows of oil derricks crowd the land behind the sea wall along the Pacific Ocean. *Courtesy Huntington Beach Historical Society*

Pacific Coast Highway
(U.S. 101 Alternate) is
flanked by oil derricks
in this dramatic scene.
*Courtesy Huntington Beach
Historical Society*

of a dome formation. In his book, *Orange County Through Four Centuries*, Leo Friis credits the Chapman Well No. 1 northeast of Placentia with the beginning of the second oil boom in the county. On March 11, 1919, the well came in with a mighty torrent of gas and oil.

By 1919 there were oil wells in many areas of north Orange County. The Standard Oil Company, already successful locally, paid $458,721.20 in taxes on the production of its wells in 1919-1920. By the end of March of that year, wells in Orange County were producing over 1,475,000 barrels a month, with a value of $22,125,000 a year. Prices ranged from $1.43 per barrel for the lowest gravity oil to $1.93 for the highest in quality. Samuel Armor said in his *History of Orange County* that "the oil industry is clearly the largest asset of Orange County, and makes this county safe from light, heat and power troubles."

THE FIRST EXCITEMENT AND DISCOVERY

On October 20, 1919, the Standard Oil Company and others leased a large section of land on the Huntington Beach mesa. Some of the leases carried a cash bonus and a monthly rental as well. There was guarded excitement over the potential for oil development. Friis, in his book, called the Huntington Beach of that time "a quiet little village." He noted that "There are no saloons or drinking in Huntington Beach and the moral atmosphere is of the highest order." Perhaps that is what made the village so quiet.

As you can imagine, there was a lot of excitement over the potential of the oil industry because the discovery of oil meant almost instant untold riches to the owner of lands that were previously used for pasture, crops and groves.

THE SCRAMBLE FOR BLACK GOLD

When Huntington Beach A No. 1 came in on May 24, 1920, it established the character of the Huntington Beach mesa as proven oil territory. Soon the well was producing nearly 150 barrels of good quality oil per day. On November 13, Bolsa Chica No. 1 came in and produced over 2,000 barrels a day. However, few people even in their wildest dreams, could predict the success of the oil business in Huntington Beach or the lengths to which it would influence the entire life of the city.

According to C.W. Patrick, in the W.P.A. papers, "...each summer season brings many hundred people to the Methodist Camp Ground where religious meetings were held. With the leasing of a large portion of the area for oil drilling by Standard Oil Company,

impetus was given to the sale of lots. The Huntington Beach Company put on an auction sale that brought eager buyers from far and near. The camp meeting ground became an auto camp for oil workers and their families."

C.F. Roberts, in the September 1921 issue of *The Orange County Review*, reported, "Seventeen months ago Huntington Beach was a sleepy little town of 2,400 souls. Today there are about 8,500 permanent residents and a floating population of perhaps 4,000."

Quiet, lush and picturesque country landscapes were replaced by tall wooden oil derricks that emitted a sometimes ear-splitting noise and the overpowering smell of oil. Houses and barns were torn down or, in the case of some of the city's fine Craftsman Bungalows, were moved from the new oil fields into the downtown neighborhoods.

The 2,500-acre Huntington Beach oil field was destined to become the third largest field in Southern California.

THE OIL BOOM BRINGS DRAMATIC CHANGES

Oscar L. Stricklin, who worked as an oil rig builder after his arrival from the Midwest in 1920, recalled that people came pouring into Huntington Beach "like there was a gold rush." He worked seven days a week during those exciting days, and did not even think about a day off or a vacation. According to C.E. Roberts, in the W.P.A. papers: "The next big excitement in the field broke when the people voted to open 36 blocks in the west end of the city. The oil operators found a rich field there and several hundred wells were drilled in what became the closest drilled oil field in the world. The oil drilling was intense during the holiday period of the Christmas season, and the brilliantly lighted derricks attracted thousands of night visitors. Hundreds of homes were moved out of the new town lot oil field and many families with no other

The First Baptist Church, shown here, sits among the beach cottages. It was built in 1909, in the Gothic style, and sports a three-story high bell tower.
Courtesy Huntington Beach Historical Society

shelter stayed with their houses while they were being moved over the streets. Oil derricks sprang up as the houses were moved off little town lots 26 feet wide and 117 feet deep. Row after row of oil derricks lined the paved streets from 23rd to 17th Street.

The major oil companies established gasoline refineries nearby. The Holly Sugar Company plant was turned into an oil refinery operated by its subsidiary, the Holly Development Company. The Pacific Linoleum and Oil Cloth Factory, which relied on crude oil at the location, was turned into an oil refinery.

Many smaller companies, having caught oil fever, opened new factories based on oil or gas production. As an example, the O.C. Field Company was founded by a brilliant young chemist who used his newly invented process of making gasoline from wet gas to build a large factory.

The Standard Oil Company, having been responsible for the original discovery of the field, first leased its land from the Huntington Beach Company. Later Standard Oil acquired control of the land company and, by the 1930s, owned much of the land within the city limits and paid almost half of the taxes. Also involved in oil and gas refinement, the Standard Oil Company had a plant where canned gas was manufactured and shipped over the western half of the United States.

OIL RIGGING: A DANGEROUS OCCUPATION

Throughout the years that oil dominated the community, there were frequent stories in the newspapers describing the injuries, and sometimes deaths, of the workers who kept that industry going. In 1926, for instance, Homer Person of the Wiltshire Oil Company received a broken arm and crushed hip when the tongs at the well on which he was working fell and struck him. C.S. Clayer and Fred Loney narrowly escaped death when a dry gas line on which the men were working exploded and caught fire. The fire department, who were called immediately, "could do nothing with the huge gusher of flame." Working in the oil fields was not only dangerous, it was also smelly and noisy.

Bud Higgins recalled in his oral history by Cal State Fullerton: "Most of the wells that came in, they just put them on production. But when a well got away from them or something happened, why, everybody would go there. The Bolsa Chica well, when it got away, came in under such high pressure and such great production that they could not control it, so it blew for a couple of days. Everybody around the country was there to see it during the time that it was blowing. I can remember during this period of time I was going to high school, and when a gasser would come in, the noise was so terrific that they would let school out. We would go over and watch the gasser; sometimes they would

82

The Holly Sugar Factory, built in 1910, went from crushing and processing sugar beets to working as an oil refinery in the late 1920s. *Courtesy Huntington Beach Historical Society*

blow all day and all night, and maybe the next day or two before they could get it shut in, or before it would sand itself up and they could get it and control it."

No matter what dangers, noises, dirt and smells came with the oil business, the industry would dominate Huntington Beach for many years to come.

THE VOLUNTEER FIRE DEPARTMENT

When Huntington Beach's first mayor, Ed Manning, took office in February of 1909, he recognized the immediate need to organize a fire department. John Philip, a local hardware merchant, brought 20 prospective volunteers together in March of that year. Philip was elected the first fire chief of the new city. Most of the businessmen in town were members and between 15 and 18 hardy souls would show up for drills. A Fireman's Ball was held to raise the first funds. The City Council voted to purchase a hose cart with 600 feet of tubed hose, a nozzle, hydrant wrench and a large fire bell.

In 1918 the Fire Department and the city recognized the need for the latest mechanized equipment and a

1922.

The Pacific Electric tracks, along with the poles that carry the electric lines, form a diagonal line across the photograph. The classic standards flank the stairs to the beach. *Courtesy Huntington Beach Historical Society*

place to house it. A metal shed to park the new Model T Ford fire truck was built at the new City Hall on Fifth Street. The truck was equipped with two 40 gallon chemical extinguishers and 100-foot-long hoses.

On March 10, 1919, Fire Chief French reported that the Volunteer Fire Department had been reorganized. He requested that the fire truck be fixed so that it could carry ladders.

The oil situation, which increased Huntington Beach's population from 1,400 to 6,000, drastically changed the face of the city and pointed out the need

Bathing beauty contests added spice to the annual Fourth of July celebrations. *Courtesy Huntington Beach Historical Society*

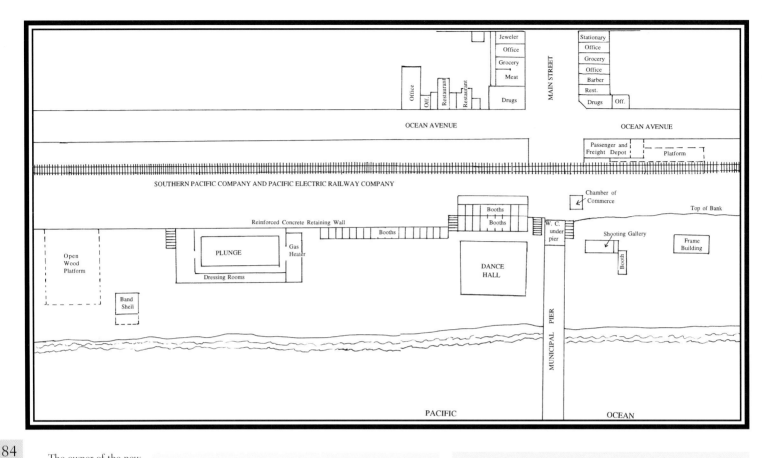

Jeweler
Office
Grocery
Meat

Office
Off.
Restaurant
Restaurant

Drugs

MAIN STREET

Stationary
Office
Grocery
Office
Barber
Rest.
Drugs
Off.

OCEAN AVENUE   OCEAN AVENUE

Passenger and
Freight Depot   Platform

SOUTHERN PACIFIC COMPANY AND PACIFIC ELECTRIC RAILWAY COMPANY

Chamber of
Commerce

Top of Bank

Reinforced Concrete Retaining Wall

Booths
Booths

Booths

W. C.
under
pier

Shooting Gallery

Frame
Building

Open
Wood
Platform

PLUNGE

Gas
Heater

Dressing Rooms

DANCE
HALL

Booth

Band
Shell

MUNICIPAL PIER

PACIFIC   OCEAN

84

The owner of the new
M.A. Johnson
Building, constructed in
1915 at 112 Main Street,
stands to the right of the
center door. Built of pressed
brick, with luxor glass
transoms, the two-story
commercial building had
the latest in modern
storefront facades.
*Courtesy Huntington Beach
Historical Society*

The intersection of Main Street and Ocean
Avenue was, from the beginning, the "center" of the
community. Taking the Red Car from Los Angeles
to points north, passengers would disembark at the
depot on the corner of Main and Ocean. They
could spend the day in a variety of fun activities,
from swimming in the Salt Water Plunge to attending
a band concert. In addition, businesses such as
restaurants and grocery stores were close by.

The Smiley and Smith store
sold gasoline, wood, coal,
hay, grain, flour and all
kinds of staples in their
store on Main Street in
early Huntington Beach.
*Courtesy Huntington Beach
Historical Society*

(Far right) John and Minnie
Eader, the owners of the
Eader's Bakery at 113
Main Street, prepare food
over an open fire in the alley
behind their bakery. John is
the first man on the left.
*Courtesy Arline Huff
Howard Collection*

Huntington Beach: The Gem of the South Coast

Mr. and Mrs. A. A. Cole, their daughter and Grace Reed pose in front of the Cole's confectionery and tobacco store on Main Street. *Courtesy Huntington Beach Historical Society*

Minnie O. Higgins was the proprietor of Huntington Beach's first Alpha Beta Store. She is shown here in the vegetable department in September of 1921. *Courtesy Huntington Beach Historical Society*

In 1927, disaster struck when the Alfred Gasoline Company plant at 18th and Olive streets exploded and set fire to a whole field of oil derricks. An entire block was wiped out, at a loss of several million dollars. The incident forced the City Council to rethink the fire danger situation. It was decided to create separate fire and police departments. In 1928, James K. Sergeant was appointed the first full-time fire chief.

for better fire equipment. A Seagrave motorized pumper, costing $10,000, was purchased in 1920. It featured an apparatus that pumped 750 gallons per minute and carried 1,500 feet of fire hose, as well as the firemen's equipment. Jack Kenneth, hired as the first full-time driver, also served as first aid fireman and fire engineer. He lived at the fire station and was on call 24 hours a day. A new five-horsepower double-end siren, mounted at City Hall, called the volunteer firemen to duty.

In 1924, the fire department moved to a new station at Fifth and Orange streets. There were two stalls to hold the two fire pumpers, the second of which was purchased in 1927. A spacious dormitory provided a home-away-from-home with six beds.

THE KIT CARSON TROOP IS FORMED

The first Boy Scouts Troop, an organization that has contributed much to the youth of Huntington Beach, was formed in the city in March of 1917. Organized by the Rev. M.W. Coates of the First Baptist Church, it was called the Kit Carson Troop.

Within the first year the troop was headed by three different Scoutmasters. After Reverend Coates was transferred to a church in another town, the Reverend J. Alvah replaced him as leader. Before the year was out, however, Mr. Boyden Hall was elected as Scoutmaster. A month later, Cecil McCoy was elected to the post, serving until he went off to fight in World War I in November of 1918. By 1921 the troop had dwindled.

In 1922 C.E. Morris, who was elected Scoutmaster from 1922 to 1926, is credited with the rebirth of the Scout troop. Russ Paxson, in a tribute to the Boy Scouts in a booklet prepared for the Troop's 75th Anniversary, tells this interesting story: "In the early months of 1922, a young man from Ohio came to Huntington Beach by the name of C.E. Morris. He was not here long when he saw a need for a boys' organization. The incident that prompted this action happened on the beach. Mr. Morris was employed by the Huntington Beach Land Company. On this particular day, he was working for the company on the beach when he observed a small group of boys who had dug a hole in the sand and then covered it with newspapers. They lay back patiently waiting for some unfortunate soul to fall into their booby trap.

"Mr. Morris went over and began talking with the boys and excited them with the notion to join a good boy's organization. With this need he met with Mr. R.J. Prescott, then an active member of the Lion's Club, requesting to reorganize the Boy Scout troop under the sponsorship of the Lion's Club. A committee was formed and on June 9, 1922, Troop I was officially organized and Morris was elected scout master."

THE BOY SCOUT CABIN IS BUILT

Troop No. 1 met at various places, including the library, the rear of a store and the back of Boxie Huston's Bowling Alley, but it clearly needed a place of its own. The troop was growing and had proved itself worthy of a larger meeting place.

The Huntington Beach Land Company gave the Scouts a piece of land on which to have their campouts. Located behind the ice house, next to the railroad tracks on the southwest side of Atlanta Street, they had their very first campout on May 25, 1923.

The Lion's Club, the troop's new sponsors, requested that a more centrally located site be established, with the idea of erecting a building for the troop's use. The City of Huntington Beach granted the troop permission to relocate in Lake Park. The park, which had been deeded in 1912 to the City by the Huntington Beach Land Company for $10 in gold and the promise that it would be used and maintained as a park, was at that time used as a water sump. Nothing had been done to improve the park, which was at a low point on the mesa. During the early 1920s oil boom, it was often occupied by a pool of oily smelly water.

Scoutmaster Morris was credited by Russ Paxson with the vision of creating the troop's home. Aided by the community, Troop I members embarked upon the building of the Scout Cabin in 1923. The telephone company donated the logs for the walls, while the local Carpenter's Union and members of the Lion's Club donated the labor. Paxson remembers that the log shell of the cabin was six tiers high on the first day and the logs had all been used. The Edison Company donated the additional logs needed to finish the building, and on May 2, 1924, the cabin was completed.

By the 1920s, the Pacific Electric Railway system was well developed and stopped at many small stations along its complicated system of routes. Red Cars headed in four different directions from Huntington Beach. If the person's destination was Balboa Island, Newport Beach, the Pacific Gun Club or the Surf Club, he caught the car going south. Another line went to Bolsa and the Holly Sugar Plant, while still another went to Santa Ana. By heading north travelers could make connections to almost anyplace in the Los Angeles and Orange County, as well as some cities in the Inland Empire.

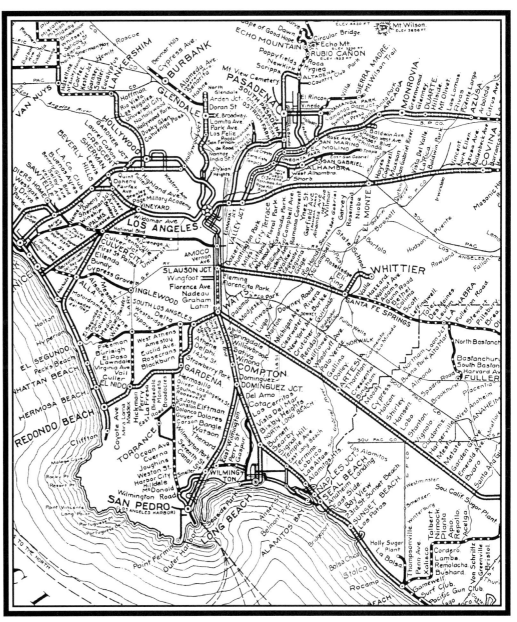

The Huntington Beach City Hall, constructed in 1923 at the corner of 5th and Orange streets, illustrated the new wealth brought into the community by the oil industry. It was demolished in 1981. *Courtesy First American Title Insurance Company*

88

During World war II, the United States took over the cabin and the park, using them for war-time needs. Fortunately, Scoutmaster Leroy Paxson, son of former leader Russ Paxson, was able to hold the troop meetings in his garage. He is credited with keeping the troop alive during the war years.

On March 9, 1917, the *Huntington Beach News* praised the Boy Scouts of America as "an institution which readily commends itself in any community, as it has a tendency to bring out all the finer and nobler traits in a boy's character, and to suppress the less laudable ones."

Boy Scout Troop No. 1 holds the record of being the oldest organized Boy Scout troop west of the Mississippi. It can be credited with having an important and positive influence on the young men of Huntington Beach and providing many unforgettable experiences for its members.

WATER BECOMES AN ISSUE

For many years after the founding of Huntington Beach, the community and the vast farming region surrounding the small town reveled in the abundance of water. The resources of the Santa Ana River and its tributaries, its watershed, the artesian wells, the lakes on the mesa and the remaining swamplands led most to believe that the ample water would be available forever.

From the late 1880s through the 1910s, the dramatic draining of the swamplands opened new tracts for successful farming. The underground water supply gradually became depleted as more farms were established. Where once a farmer had to dig down only a few feet to bring in a new well, the water level in the wells had dropped dramatically until even some wells that were 95-feet deep quit flowing. In addition, there was a danger of salt water from the ocean infiltrating the fresh water because the water level in the lakes had dropped significantly.

The S.H. Bowen Company, located at 1980 Lake Avenue, was one of several oil-related businesses that came to town as a result of the discovery of oil. The firm manufactured oil well tools. *Courtesy Huntington Beach Historical Society*

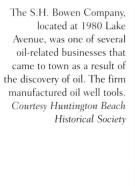

It was time to consider the installation of pumping plants to facilitate the irrigation of the crops. Many farmers thought that method of water would be too expensive. In spite of these reservations, the unincorporated town of Garden Grove proceeded to build the first pumping plant in about 1912. Soon, almost every farm between Garden Grove and Huntington Beach was taking part in the pumping system.

By 1918, the lowering of the water table had become a serious matter. The Orange County Board of Supervisors recognized the problem and hired the J.P. Lippincott Company, civil engineers, to survey the resources and write a report on the water situation in Orange County. It was the Lippincott Company that discovered the dangers of the underground salt water invasion. The surveyors discovered a great underground wall which ran along the coast and kept out the salt water. In addition, the pressure from the underground fresh water level inland had created a natural dam to keep the salt water out. As the water level dropped, the existence of a gap in the wall between Huntington Beach and Newport caused much concern. It was clear to all of those involved that something needed to be done to correct the county's serious water problems.

PACIFIC COAST HIGHWAY – THE DREAM BEGINS

Proposed as early as 1909, a dramatic scenic road running along the Pacific Coast from San Juan Capistrano to Oxnard was the dream of several far-sighted citizens. Tom Talbert notes that in those early years "many coastal towns were not even connected by a cow trail and could be reached only from inland points." He credits Huntington Beach pioneer William T. Newland with starting the ball rolling on the visionary project.

In 1913 the South Coast Improvement Association was organized to promote the coastal towns and the coast highway. Some citizens, including the group's first president, P. A. Stanton, were concerned that the Board of Supervisors wanted all tax monies to be spent on the interior towns and were not interested in the development of the small coastal towns. Tom Talbert echoed the feelings of the association when he said that the goal was to overcome "the antagonistic opposition of jealous, disinterested or unthoughtful people of the interior and northern part of the county."

W. T. Newland, Harry Welch, Lew Wallace, Tom Talbert, Jess Armitage and P. A. Stanton were the prime movers behind the project. They traveled many miles making speeches and attending meetings to promote the building of a scenic highway along the sea.

In 1915, the Board of Supervisors appointed the first county Highway Commission. Supervisor Tom Talbert of Huntington Beach was chairman, with William Schumacher, Jasper Leck, H.E. Smith and

Popular performers and bands appearing in the band shell attracted visitors to the pier and beach. The impressive concrete pier, built in 1914, was considered the finest in Southern California when it was constructed. *Courtesy First American Title Insurance Company*

By 1927, downtown Huntington Beach had developed into a thriving commercial center with rows of two-story brick buildings on each side. On the right is the "Let's Eat" café, a paint store, dentist and a shoe store selling Florsheim Shoes. On the left are the Rexall Drug Store, a bakery and a marvelous street clock. *Courtesy Huntington Beach Historical Society*

89

Fred Struck as members. The commission's first task was to plan an extensive highway building program.

A year later, Huntington Beach pioneer William Newland was on the second Highway Commission. By this time, the commission had proposed a bond issue for $1,270,000 to build 117 miles of highways. The Board of Supervisors passed a resolution calling for the issue to be placed on the ballot. The measure would require a two-thirds majority for passage. The Associated Chambers of Commerce, organized by Dr. Dodson, took on the huge task of educating the public on the need for the important funding source. As a result, their efforts were successful and the bond issue was passed.

The first road built under this program, according to Tom Talbert, was the highway from Santa Ana to the tiny town of Bolsa, a few miles north of Huntington Beach. Talbert, in *My Sixty Years in Orange County*, tells about the supervisor's visit to inspect the new highway. They had several small holes bored in the 18-foot-wide slabs, and were surprised to find out that the concrete was only 2 1/2 to 2 3/4 inches thick instead of the required four inches. Because the Supervisors refused to accept the job, the contractor had to tear out the entire road, haul the concrete pieces away and build a new road. As a result, the contractor went bankrupt, the bonding company lost money, and the county

Famous movie star Mary Pickford was the guest of honor at the ribbon cutting celebrating the opening of the Pacific Coast Highway in 1926. Those who assisted her are from left: County Supervisor George Jeffries, Board of Supervisors Chairman Tom Talbert, Supervisor Leon Whitsell and State Highway Commissioner Nelson Edwards. Tom Talbert's young son can be seen peeking over Miss Pickford's shoulder.
Courtesy First American Title Insurance Company

90

The Dr. Shank House, one of several large Craftsman Bungalows that were relocated from the site of new oil strikes in the late 1920s, was moved into the developing downtown section of the city and used by the doctor as a combination home and office. An excellent example of Craftsman architecture, it features a combination of Swiss and Japanese influences.
Courtesy Huntington Beach Historical Society

inspector was fired. Talbert notes that Orange County used the same plans and specifications as Los Angeles County during concurrent road-building programs. Mysteriously, L.A. County purchased 10 carloads of cement and gravel for each one bought by Orange County. As a result, the L.A. County roads cost $12,000 miles per mile while those in Orange County's ran $9,500 per mile. It appears that such an obvious mystery was never officially solved.

PACIFIC COAST HIGHWAY BECOMES A REALITY

The idea of a coast highway had been around for more than 10 years when it finally became a reality in 1926.

Los Angeles County, the first to build its section of Coast Highway 101 Alternate, set the standards and specifications for the project. Sensibly, Orange County used the same plans.

There was no road from Huntington Beach to Seal Beach when the highway was begun. At that time, Ocean Avenue, which fronted the beach in Huntington Beach, stopped at 23rd Street on the north end and was scheduled to become a part of the new highway. In 1915, $50,000 was budgeted by the Board of Supervisors to build a bridge at Anaheim Landing. The first step in the road-building process involved hauling dirt from the mesa of the Bolsa Chica Gun Club and dumping it across the sandy beach. This created a rough and difficult roadbed that was almost impossible to navigate. At that point, the lack of available funding caused the project to reach a standstill.

The next task of the proponents was to try to interest the State Highway Commission in providing the funds to turn the rough road into a modern highway.

There were several good reasons for the construction of the route. A strong contributing factor was the military importance of the road, which would connect fortifications along the coast. The Automobile Club of Southern California, a forward-looking body, worked hard to convince the state to include this highway in their system. The public, many of whom envisioned being able to travel a scenic highway along the coast, supported the need for the first-class coast route.

As can usually be expected on any government project, there was also an opposition stance. The farmers from Springdale and Wintersburg objected strongly to the building of the road. The gun clubs, owners of much of the swampland to the north of Huntington Beach, also did not want a highway along the ocean front. Both groups did everything they could to prevent the obtaining of the needed easement through the Bolsa Chica.

The situation between the two sides continued in a stalemate until the proponents decided that there was no other way to gain the right-of-way but by condemnation proceedings. District Attorney L.A. West was authorized to start legal action. At that point, according to Tom Talbert, the opposition asked the proponents to come to Los Angeles to settle the matter. All present agreed that building a good fence on both sides of the road would provide the solution, satisfying the farmers and gun club owners. Talbert, who represented Huntington Beach on the Orange County Board of Supervisors from 1909 to 1927, worked tirelessly to make the Highway 101 Alternate a reality.

Philip A. Stanton, one of the founders of Pacific City (now Huntington Beach) played a large role in the complicated scenario that finally granted an easement along a large portion of the ocean. According to Talbert, Stanton discovered a discrepancy in the title of the Rancho Los Alamitos. The original Spanish grant, made in 1834, specified that the boundary line of the

ranch extended to the tidewaters of the Pacific Ocean. By 1920, the tidewaters reached the northern border of Anaheim Bay, making it possible that the Surfside Peninsula was not included in the ranch property. Stanton filed a claim on this parcel of land under the name of Ord Land and Water Company. After a long drawn-out court case, the court granted the land to the Ord Company. However, before the patent was issued, the Board of Supervisors made an application to the U.S. Government for an easement strip 40 feet wide for the purposes of building a highway.

The Ord Land and Water Company protested the easement and the matter landed in court again. The court decided that because Orange County had only improved a 20-foot-wide strip of road, it would have to pay the Ord Land and Water Company $10,000 for the other 20-foot strip. The settlement of this suit paved

92

the way toward the construction of Highway 101 Alternate (Pacific Coast Highway). It was a day for much celebration in 1926, when the Coast Highway was at last open to the public, creating a scenic highway that reached from San Diego to Oxnard.

DONKEYS, BOWLING, DANCING AND CROQUET

Huntington Beach, in the 1920s, was an active and lively place with lots of entertainment. Connie Brockway, in *Huntington Beach History Notes*, describes the actions taken by the City Council through the years.

In June of 1922, the Council granted permission to allow boxing matches in the Airdrome located at Atlanta Avenue and Alabama streets, on the Fourth of July.

On August 2, 1926, the Council approved a motion to allow donkeys on the beach front in connection with the amusement concessions near the municipal pier. On December 6 of that year, Charles E. Merryfield was granted a request to install and operate a six-alley bowling parlor at 216 Fifth Street.

In May of 1927, the City Council appointed a committee to investigate the problem of noise caused by dances at the Woman's Club. It was noted that some of the dances lasted until 2 a.m. Presumably it was the parties to whom the building was rented, not the women themselves, who were causing the noise.

In October of 1927, the Council directed the city engineer to lay out and install a tennis court and croquet grounds at the center of 6th and Main streets.

HUNTINGTON BEACH UNION HIGH SCHOOL

In 1926, Huntington Beach built an impressive, spacious and beautiful high school in the classic Lombard Romanesque Revival style. Designed by prominent Santa Ana architects Allison and Allison, the building complex was judged by the *Los Angeles Times* as one of the six most beautiful school buildings in Southern California.

In the 1926 high school year book, *The Cauldron*, students recalled the rather unusual groundbreaking held on Monday, February 8. After singing the National Anthem and saying a prayer, the students grasped two long ropes attached to a plow. William Newland, senior member of the Board of Education, held the plow in its course as the students pulled it about 100 feet, creating a deep furrow. The program was concluded with the singing of "America."

The four-story tower and the auditorium, the first buildings to be built, were considered the focal point of the new complex. Three pairs of double entry doors, set in richly decorated arched recesses, lead into the interior of the auditorium. The square tower features

arched openings, pinnacles at each corner and a conical roof. The building is embellished with decorative trim, an arcaded corbel table at the eaves line, classical columns and arched multi-paned windows. The interior is richly decorated in the Mediterranean style.

During the 1920s and 30s, Huntington Beach was known for its strong athletic teams. In *Oiler History and Tradition*, Coach Harry Sheue recalls the championships in football, basketball, baseball, track, swimming, tennis, volleyball, water polo and wrestling won by the school's teams. He was proud to have discovered Eddie Morris, called the World's Fastest Boy, in the 1930s. Eddie won every 100-and 220-yard dash race in which he participated and was selected to be on the C. I. F., State and All-American Track Teams in the late 1930s.

Both the Boys and Girls Glee Clubs entered countywide music contests. In 1926, the Girls Glee Club not only won the county contest, but also brought home first place in the California Girls Glee Club championship. In addition, the girl's group, in 1926, won first place in the County Music Memory Contest. The event required each person to memorize 40 musical numbers, the composer's name and his nationality.

Other important school activities included the Girls' League, Scholarship Society, Debating Team, Dramatic Club, Yearbook Staff and Orchestra.

When the rest of the high school buildings were torn down in 1976, the community insisted that the tower and auditorium be saved. On September 30, 1987, Mayor Jack Kelly and Supervisor Harriet Weider officiated at a ceremony which dedicated the tower and auditorium as an Orange County Historical Landmarks.

The new Huntington Beach High School, constructed in 1926, was built by prominent Orange County contractors Alison and Alison.

DUKE KAHANAMOKU BRINGS SURFING TO HUNTINGTON BEACH

Bud Higgins remembered the days in 1925 when Duke Kahanamoku and his friends brought the sport of surfing to Southern California shores. The Duke, who had graduated from Stanford University, was a friend of Captain Sheffield who ran a bath house at Newport Beach. When the Duke came over from Hawaii to make some pictures, he and his fellow surfers introduced the sport to the west coast.

Bud Higgins remembers his introduction to the sport: "...nobody gives anybody pointers on surfboards, you just watch what they do and go out and try to kill yourself. It's something you have to learn and a lot of times you become so exhausted that you would just as soon fall off of your board and drown yourself, because in those days with the boards we had, it was a very exhausting sport. The boards weighed 135 pounds, so it required a lot of energy to paddle the board out."

Junior class members are shown here in one of the many plays held in the Auditorium. Set in four acts, the play was titled, "My Country Sweetheart." *Courtesy Arline Huff Howard*

Rows of trailers line the road along the beach. The Pacific Electric Railway (Red Car) tracks, a row of telephone poles and the Pacific Coast highway cut a diagonal line across the photo. *Courtesy Huntington Beach Historical Society*

THE GREAT DEPRESSION

Orange County had some particularly prosperous years during the 1920s because of the success and growth of the citrus and dairy industry, vegetable farms and burgeoning commercial centers.

This prosperity came to a screeching halt with the stock market crash that began in October of 1929. That same year, 659 banks closed nationwide. Two years later, the number of bank closures jumped to 2,293. In 1932, another 1,453 ceased to do business. Throughout the early 1930s, tax delinquencies and property repossessions increased dramatically, and retail and manufacturing businesses were adversely affected. Local and federal agencies were unable to cope with the thousands of applications for welfare from people thrown out of work.

In *The First Eighty Years: History of the Huntington Beach Police Department*, Lt. Michael Biggs reports that with the Depression came new problems. Because so many people were unemployed, there was a significant increase in thefts and burglaries. The *Huntington*

The new Huntington Beach Grammar School, built in 1934, was considered earthquake proof. The rectangular block massing, tall narrow windows and vertical-scored decoration above the entry are all typical of the Zigzag Moderne style. *Courtesy Huntington Beach Historical Society*

Beach News pointed out that there were several instances in which burglaries occurred in broad daylight when the occupant was at home. The chief of police blamed the situation on out-of-work oil workers and tourist hobos. Because there were no new oil wells drilled during the early 1930s, the oil industry was at a low ebb. The population of the city dropped to 3,690 residents.

It would take Huntington Beach and the rest of the nation a long time to recover from the Depression. As a result of those trying times, however, President Roosevelt inaugurated several programs to bring the country back to economic health. The Social Security System, begun in 1935, brought retirement plans for the first time for those over 65. The State Emergency Relief Agency provided funds through local organizations. The Works Progress Administration (WPA) provided jobs in a variety of fields, including those requiring skilled workers, office personnel, artists, historians and other special occupations. Large public works projects such as storm drains, buildings, roads, park improvements and landscaping were paid for by the federal government's WPA program. The Civilian Conservation Corps, which provided young men with job training, established training camps all over the country. The National Industrial Recovery Act (NIRA) that was designed to revive business activity, introduced the first minimum wage agreement.

THE EARTH SHAKES AND SHAKES AND SHAKES

For those living in Orange County in the 1930s, the earthquake of March 10, 1933, and the great flood of 1938 will bring back vivid memories. Almost everyone who was above the age of three when the earthquake occurred can remember exactly where they were and what they were doing when the earth started to shake. Most can even tell you that the quake began at 5:54 p.m.

The Long Beach Earthquake, so called because that city suffered the most damage, was centered in the ocean about three and one half miles southwest of Newport Beach. Of the four deaths resulting from the trembler, three occurred in Santa Ana and one in Garden Grove. The chimneys of hundreds of homes throughout the county were damaged or destroyed.

Huntington Beach received some of the worst damage in Orange County. The front walls of several brick buildings collapsed and the structure of many of the oil derricks destroyed. The fire station was rendered unusable and the men had to sleep outside in tents for about a month while the building was being repaired.

94

THE TIDELANDS

One of the biggest and most important issues of the early 1930s was the battle over the oil in the tidelands of the ocean. Dramatic photographs from the 1920s depict rows of tall wooden oil derricks standing like motionless soldiers along the sea wall. The derricks and wall were so close to the water that at high tide waves would smash against the sea wall.

Few know that there were millions of dollars of black gold under the beach and ocean. Great quantities of gas bubbles constantly came to the surface of the water. Those who lit matches and held them to the bubbles were rewarded with a series of small explosions. During stormy days clumps of asphalt and oil were torn from the ocean floor and deposited on the beach, creating a mess that fishermen and swimmers did not like at all. In the 1930s, geologists claimed that there was probably in excess of seven million barrels of oil in the offshore tidelands area.

In 1934, another big oil boom began when a well at the corner of 22nd Street and Walnut Avenue brought in 1,000 barrels a day. Once again, houses were moved to other parts of the city and oil derricks were built as closely as possible to each other.

According to Floyd G. Belsito, in his article "The Huntington Beach Tidelands Controversy,"

the Standard Oil Company had acquired land along the beach and set up operations for straight down drilling. A sharp change in the picture was created when McVicar invented a removable whipstock drill that enabled a company to slant-drill instead of the standard straight down method. A group of three men, McVicar, McCallen and Rood, sent their pipes down under the Standard Oil wells and out into the ocean.

Before they were discovered, they had succeeded in taking a large amount of oil from under the sea. The Standard Oil Company challenged them over the right to drill under Standard's wells, and the fight was on. Belsito goes on to say:

"The *Huntington Beach News*, who assumed the position of advocate of the independent operators, held that oil was a migratory mineral which, in the case of the billion-dollar oil pool, had been placed there not by Standard Oil, but by God."

The Huntington Beach City Council sent a request to the state legislature for the granting of the tidelands to the city. The Standard Oil Company protested against the acquisition of the tidelands.

On April 7, 1931, the Assembly voted 66-0 to grant the city the tidelands rights. Immediately afterward, the State Senate, unanimously agreed with this decision. All that remained was for Governor Rolph to sign the bill. After several delays, meetings and other ways of stalling the signing of Assembly Bill Number 4, the Governor vetoed the bill.

Huntington Beach officials proudly pose with the city's first street sweeper in 1935. Fritz Wenka is the driver and (left to right) Street Superintendent Henry Worth, City Councilman Anthony Jovatt, and City Engineer Harry Overmeyer are standing in front. *Courtesy Huntington Beach Historical Society*

One of Huntington Beach's famous Fourth of July Parades heads down Main Street around 1940. *Courtesy Arline Huff Howard Collection*

This was the first time in the history of the state that a governor vetoed a bill unanimously passed by both houses of the legislature.

Next, by initiative petition, the proposition was placed on the ballot, but the voters turned the measure down. Again, when a bill was passed by the State Assembly and Senate, Governor Merriam vetoed it.

Tom Talbert takes the credit for the compromise that settled the problem. In 1935, he devised a plan that would grant percentages to the Huntington Beach Company, Pacific Electric Company, the City of Huntington Beach, the State of California and the oil companies.

ORANGE COUNTIANS TROOP TO HUNTINGTON BEACH'S PARKS AND BEACHES

As the Great Depression drew to a close, Orange County residents once again began to seek out recreational facilities. It was time for the nation to relieve the seriousness of the economic stress felt by almost every family. Huntington Beach, already home to three parks totaling nine acres, was on the brink of great strides toward an era of tourist and recreational expansion. It was not only the 5,000 or so residents of the 3.57 square miles of the city proper, but also the residents of Orange County that needed these expanded facilities.

In 1938, the city was able to take advantage of the labor provided by the Works Progress Administration (W. P. A.) and build the Lake Park Clubhouse and the Pavalon next to the pier at little cost to the community.

Community leaders in 1938 made the wise decision to back a bond issue that would acquire and improve substantial frontage along the sandy Pacific Ocean shores. The sale of $100,000 in bonds, to be used for the acquisition and improvements of public parks, was placed on the ballot for an election held on April 12, 1938. The voter's enthusiasm can be measured by the passage of the bonds by more than the required two-thirds majority. The 1,630 feet of beach-front property, was purchased for $85,000, an unbelievable bargain at today's prices. The city used the remaining $15,000 for labor and improvements for the new beach park. Restrooms and a caretaker's cottage were built, the Huntington Beach Trailer Park expanded and additional parking installed.

Shortly thereafter, a 49-acre strip of land from Lake Street to Beach Boulevard, across from the beach, was purchased for $25,000 from the Mills Land and Water Company. Because the nation was pulling out of the Depression, the property was purchased for an unbelievably low price of $700 an acre. Now valued in the millions of dollars, the land that was purchased in 1938 was, indeed, a wise investment.

THE GREAT FLOOD OF 1938

In February and March of 1938, torrents of water rushed out of Santa Ana Canyon and quickly spread over most of Orange County. It was the worst flood in the region in over 70 years. A series of heavy rain storms, producing several deluges, extended along the coast from San Diego to San Luis Obispo, and inland to the Mojave Desert.

The heaviest rainfall was recorded in the San Gabriel and San Bernardino Mountains, producing a flood discharge in excess of any previously recorded. From February 27 to March 3, 1938, records indicated that from 20 to 30 inches of rain fell in the mountain during the six-day period. An additional problem was created when years and

The flood of 1938 was said to have been the worst since the floods of 1861-62. This photo is taken from above the Santa Ana River. Huntington Beach, punctuated by hundreds of oil derricks, can be seen to the north. *Courtesy Huntington Beach Historical Society*

96

years worth of debris was washed down the gullies and into the Santa Ana River.

The United States Army Corps of Engineers reported that 87 lives were lost and damage amounting to $78,603,000 was incurred. Taking into account that those were 1938 dollars, the amount of damage must have been phenomenal.

During the six days of flooding, houses both large and small, were destroyed and highways, bridges and many other public improvements were damaged. Citrus ranch owners incurred large losses when the rivers overflowed and their groves were flooded. More than 290,000 acres of land in several counties were covered with the swiftly flowing water. Because of the rapid rise in the flood waters, many people could not be warned in time. As a result, 87 lives were lost. Particularly hard hit were the small towns to the west of the mouth of the Santa Ana River where it flows out of the Santa Ana Canyon near Olive. Such communities as Atwood, La Jolla, Fullerton, Brea and the northern half of Anaheim experienced the most devastation.

The flood waters swirled over the farmlands surrounding Huntington Beach, causing much more damage than the flood of 1916. The flood not only devastated the farmers' crops, but also left behind miles of land covered with a sticky gooey coating of smelly clay-like mud.

The disastrous flood inspired many officials and government staff members to seek a solution to the flood control problem. President Roosevelt, on May 23, 1938, approved funding for the Geological Survey Department of the Department of the Interior to prepare a survey report which would provide the data needed to proceed with a flood control plan. Additional field and office workers were provided by funds from the National Industrial Recovery Act. As a result, the construction of Prado Dam, located near Corona, was begun in 1938. Completed in 1941, it was designed to control a flood two-and-a-half times as large as that which occurred in 1938.

THE PIER IS DAMAGED BY A RAGING STORM

Mother Nature was not finished with Orange County. On September 24, 1939, a heavy and violent rainstorm, accompanied by strong winds, damaged or washed away several piers along the ocean front. A 300-foot section was torn from the Huntington Beach Pier, while a 400-foot length of the Newport Pier and 100 feet of the Balboa Pier disappeared. The Laguna Beach Pier was entirely destroyed. The Seal Beach Pier received little damage; however, several homes in the Sunset Beach area were demolished.

Meanwhile, clouds of war again were hovering over much of the nation. As Huntington Beach prepared to meet the decade of the 1940s, there would be even more surprises to come.

The Huntington Beach Arch, located at Main Street and Ocean Boulevard, is gaily decorated and lighted for Christmas in 1938. The beach is in the distance and a glimpse of the pier can be seen on left side of the photo. *Courtesy Huntington Beach Historical Society*

Chapter Five

WORLD WAR II – DRAMATIC CHANGES FOR OUR NATION

World War II was a dramatic turning point in the lives of all Americans and in the history of the United States. For the 45 months Americans fought abroad to subdue the Nazi and Japanese aggressors, Americans did all they could to aid the cause.

The war worries began in earnest when Nazi storm troops attacked Poland in September of 1939. Two days later, faced with the reality of the situation, Great Britain and France declared war on Germany. The sympathy of the United States was with them. The open threat that this country could become involved at any time produced a dark cloud over the entire nation.

Sunday morning, December 7, 1941, while most Californians were getting ready for church, the radio abruptly announced, "The Japs have bombed Pearl Harbor!" Americans expressed shock and disbelief. Two hours and 55 minutes later, Japan declared war on the United States and Britain. President Franklin Delano Roosevelt, in a speech before Congress the next day, urged the members to make a formal declaration of war.

The war situation for the United States grew progressively worse when on Thursday, December 11, Hitler and Mussolini declared war against the U.S. Mussolini told cheering crowds in Rome that "it is an honor to fight together with the Japanese." Hitler claimed that the war would determine history for hundreds of years to come. The *Los Angeles Times* of December 11 reported that Washington already had discounted both declarations with the official comment of "so what?"

The Japanese wasted no time assaulting every main United States and British possession in the Central and Western Pacific. The U.S. garrisons at Tientsin, China, Thailand, the island of Guam, Shanghai, Hong Kong, Wake Island, the Philippines, Singapore, Bangkok and Northern Malaya were bombed immediately. Meanwhile the war was coming to the west coast. According to Leo J. Friis in *Orange County Through Four Centuries*, on December 20, the Japanese attacked the tankers *Emidio* and *Agriworld*, sinking the *Emidio* near Eureka, California. Three days later another oil tanker, the *Motobello*, was sunk near San Luis Obispo. Friis reports that on Christmas day a crowd of beachgoers at Redondo Beach watched as an American bomber sank a Japanese submarine a short distance from shore.

CALIFORNIA HAS SPECIAL WORRIES

Under the direction of Brig. Gen. William O. Ryan, Commanding General of the 4th Enterceptor Command, all air guards and chief observers had been activated to their observation posts. On December 10, California experienced a gigantic blackout from 8 p.m. until 11:03 p.m. because a yellow signal had been received indicating the approach of enemy air raiders. However, the approaching planes turned out to be friendly so nothing came of the incident that caused California's first real black-out. For Americans living on the west coast, World War II was made more real because of the proximity to Japan and the long, exposed and vulnerable coastline. The danger of Japanese subs and planes bombarding the west coast contributed to a constant climate of fear among

FROM VACANT LAND TO A SEA OF TRACTS

Courtesy Huntington Beach Historical Society

The Army and the Navy march proudly down Main Street during World War II. In the background are the Red and White (Grocery) Store and Eader's Bakery. *Courtesy Huntington Beach Historical Society*

Southern Californians. According to many people who lived in the region during that time, there as a sense of an almost daily concern that the enemy was planning an invasion on the coast.

On February 24, 1942, the *Times* had a four-inch-high headline reading "Submarine Shells Southland Oil Field; Japanese Make Direct Hit North of Santa Barbara." Luckily, no lives were lost and little damage was inflicted at the Elmwood oil field, approximately 12 miles north of Santa Barbara.

Shortly after midnight on February 25, American radar posts picked up an unidentified object about 120 miles west of Los Angeles. By 2:27 a.m. it was within three miles of the city. Air raid sirens in Los Angeles and Orange County blared in warning. According to historian Leo J. Friis, who was very active in the Civil Air Command, residents of much of Orange County could hear the explosion of bursting shells and see vivid red-orange balls of fire popping from tracer bullets. The following day, according to Friis, Secretary of War Stimson announced that "as many as fifteen aircraft, probably commercial planes, caused the air raid alarm." He theorized that they were flown by enemy agents in an effort to discover the location of anti-aircraft batteries and to frighten the civilian population. Secretary of the Navy Knox dismissed the whole affair as a false alarm. Called "The Battle of Los Angeles," the mystery was never explained. Orange

Old Glory, shown in this 1945 photo, is raised on Hill 1700 by soldiers from Orange County. *Courtesy First American Title Insurance Co.*

100

County residents claim to have made actual sightings of attacks along the shores of Orange County, but, because of the secrecy required, there was nothing in the newspapers to substantiate these incidents. A constant climate of fear and anxiety pervaded California and rumors abounded.

JAPANESE SUBMARINE, TORPEDOES AND AIRPLANES

Huntington Beach played an important role in the program to arm the west coast. The Bolsa Chica Military Reservation, constructed between 1941 and 1944, was one of the 30 west coast locations built by the military for protection from air and submarine attacks.

Begun in the late 1930s, the coastal rearmament program was designed to provide facilities for long-range guns to protect the lands along the Pacific Ocean. However, previous to that fateful day when Japanese bombed Pearl Harbor, there were no military defenses located south of San Pedro.

One of the Army's most important and immediate assignments after the declaration of war in December of 1941 was to protect Los Angeles and its surrounding shoreline. Several portable 155 mm and 75 mm guns were brought in immediately to guard against a possible invasion by the Japanese.

The Bolsa Chica Gun Club, located on a high flat mesa to the north of Huntington Beach proper, was immediately pressed into service. Two 155 GPF tractor-drawn guns were installed there and were ready for action by February of 1942. The Army made plans to build more permanent armaments along the coast.

The construction of the Bolsa Chica fortifications, known to the military as Battery 128 and Battery 242, began on April 17, 1943. They consisted of huge concrete bunkers designed to support twin 6-inch long-range guns, twin 16-inch long-range guns, ammunition storage magazines, Panama mounts with 155 mm guns on circular concrete mountings and an underground Plotting Survey Room. The structures, designed to be bomb proof, had concrete floors and walls several feet thick. A deep blanket of earth that was used to camouflage the fortification, was spread over the top. A large tower, disguised as an oil rig, was built above the underground plotting room and radar equipment was installed.

When the war ended, the structures were stripped of all equipment, plumbing, wiring and scrap metal and left to the elements. The monolithic concrete hulks, which remained for over 40 years, represented our country's efforts to defend itself against a frightening enemy that was fortunately defeated before it could actually invade our shores.

THE SOLDIERS AND SAILORS ARRIVE

Prior to World War II, Orange County was a predominantly agricultural area with a population of 130,820. Few could imagine the big changes that were looming on the horizon for the peaceful country. Even before the United States entered the war, the military was preparing to expand its forces. In June of 1941, the Army established the Santa Ana Army Base on 409.49 acres, five miles south of Santa Ana. First called the Air Corps Cadet Replacement Center, it was a much-needed facility for the pre-flight training of new air force cadets. In addition, when war was declared six months later, the Orange County Airport was commandeered by the Army and was renamed the Santa Ana Army Airdome.

A 1,300-acre tract near Tustin became the Lighter-Than-Air Base which was built to house Navy blimps. Commissioned on October 2, 1942, it was officially named the United States Naval Air Station. The huge hangars, now used to shelter helicopters, are visible for miles.

The Marines entered the picture on July 14, 1942, when the Navy selected a site near El Toro to train Marine flyers. Called the United States Marine Corps Air Station, El Toro, the base was built on what was, before the war, the largest lima bean field in the world.

On November 23, 1942, the Army took possession of Irvine Park and used it as an emergency training center for infantrymen. The next year Camp George E. Rathke was established on land adjoining the park.

This photo was taken from the corner of Main and Ocean, directly across from the pier. Main Street was lined with substantial two-story brick buildings. Courtesy First American Title Insurance Company

Vacation cottages and small inviting bungalows lined the streets of Huntington Beach when this photo was taken in the 1940s. *Courtesy First American Title Insurance Co.*

102

In January of 1944, the Navy unveiled plans to build an ammunition depot on 5,000 acres of land that included Anaheim Landing. Approximately 2,000 residents were required to move and the Pacific Electric tracks and Pacific Coast Highway was rerouted around the facility. In November of 1944, the new base was commissioned as the United States Naval Ammunition and Net Depot at Seal Beach.

After the new military centers were established, soldiers and sailors from all over the country arrived in Southern California to prepare to go to war. The military had indeed taken over much of Orange County.

KNOW YOUR AIR WARDEN!

A pamphlet titled "Know Your Air Warden" was given to residents. It advised them to let the warden know the details concerning the number of people in the family, where one could be reached in an emer-

The countryside surrounding Huntington Beach was still primarily agricultural in the 1940s. This photo was taken at the corner of Harbor and Edinger. *Courtesy First American Title Insurance Co.*

gency, if there are any disabled in the household and where the gas and electric shut-off switches are located. The pamphlet gave these instructions in bold letters:

KEEP CALM AND COOL, STAY HOME. PUT OUT THE LIGHTS, LIE DOWN, STAY AWAY FROM WINDOWS, DON'T TELEPHONE. The directive also requested no screaming or running.

THE AIRCRAFT WARNING SERVICE

The Aircraft Warning Service was serious business for towns on the west coast. It mapped the flight of all aircraft, identified them and reported the details to an information center. The information was placed on a huge map called the filter board. The hundreds of volunteers who were active in this organization were called plotters and filters.

Observers often worked as partners, in order to make sure the lookout posts were manned on a 24-hour basis. Classes, lasting eight weeks, were held to teach residents how to identify different kinds of aircraft. The plotters and filters played an important part in the war effort.

THE RELOCATION OF THE JAPANESE

Although the subject is one that does not make our nation proud, any discussion of World War II is not complete without the inclusion of the subject of the relocation of the Japanese. Leo J. Friis reports that in 1940 there were 112,353 persons of Japanese ancestry living in California, Oregon and Washington. 93,717 of these lived in California, with 1,855 residing in Orange County. Of this group, 1,178 were citizens and 677 were aliens. Within one week after the Pearl Harbor attack, 595 Japanese and 187 Germans were interned.

On January 11, 1942, almost 200 members of the Japanese-American Citizens League gathered at the Santa Ana City Hall and pledged their allegiance to the United States. The group, mostly second and third generation Californians of Japanese descent, adopted a resolution that asked Congress to disenfranchise any persons advocating the principals of a foreign government or the overthrow of the country's democracy. Several prominent businessmen and local officials were the guests of the Japanese organization at a luncheon

under any circumstances to evacuate American citizens. President Roosevelt, when asked to make a decision, signed Executive Order No. 9066 giving the Secretary of War the power to remove persons from certain military areas.

On March 27, 1942, General DeWitt proclaimed a curfew requiring all German and Italian aliens and all persons of Japanese descent to stay at home from 8:00 p.m. to 6:00 a.m. Shortly thereafter, he issued an order directing all Japanese to be moved out of Orange County. The German and Italian aliens were allowed to stay.

Huntington Beach was the location of one of the two registration centers established in the county. All residents of northern and central Orange County regis-

Some of Huntington Beach's most influential men pose in front of Vic Terry's Drug Store in the early 1940s. From left: Vic Terry, Earl Irby, unknown, Tom Talbert, unknown, Marcus McCallen, unknown and Vernon Langebeck. *Courtesy Arline Huff Howard*

held that day. Friis observed that most Orange County citizens were willing to let the FBI decide about the loyalty of their Japanese neighbors.

There were many opinions regarding the Japanese. Lt. Gen. John H. DeWitt, commander of the Western Theatre of Operations, wanted to round up all alien subjects 14 years or older and remove them to the Zone of the Interior. He did not think it feasible to evacuate those Japanese who were citizens. He was of the opinion that they could be watched by their friends and neighbors and the FBI.

Attorney General Biddle informed the Secretary of War that the Department of Justice was not authorized

tered there on May 11 and 12, 1942. By the end of the week all Japanese who had registered at Huntington Beach, except for a few hospital cases, were loaded onto buses and sent to the Poston Relocation Center in Arizona under military escort. The conditions at the camp were crude and uncomfortable.

In his oral history, J. Sherman Denny remembers many of the Japanese well. He tells us in his oral history interview:

"The Japanese were active here. They had extensive agricultural holdings. They raised peppers, beans, and various other products. They had considerable land under cultivation, including goldfish farms...When it

104

A typical day at the beach in the 1940s is enjoyed by everyone from young children to seniors. The Golden Bear can be seen near the top on the left. The Macklin Building is the large building to the left of the center. *Courtesy First American Title Insurance Co.*

looked as if we might become involved with Japan during World War II, everybody was worried about Japan what they were going to do, and some of the American Legion men felt that a lot of these pepper dryer plants here were places where guns were stored and that we'd really be in trouble if war broke out and the rumors happened to be true. There were two big fisheries out here owned by Japanese. Asari owned one of them and I think the other was the Orange County Fish Hatchery, both located north of Huntington Beach. When the Pearl Harbor attack finally happened, the police, FBI and military groups seized the Japanese and and searched these places. Well, of course there were no guns or any type of war equipment found here. Mr. Sasaki used to take a lot of pictures of business affairs, chamber of commerce members and individuals at flower shows, and of course, rumor had it that the pictures were being sent to Japan and probably used against us later. (At this point Mr. Denny laughed.). Well, as far as we could ever learn, nothing like that ever happened. The Japanese were quickly bundled up and sent to the camps maintained for "aliens" in other states, and many of them almost lost their homes. One

home was burned down, unfortunately. Nobody was left to represent the Japanese effectively and care for their property, but some of the Mexicans took over and tried to protect their interests."

Many of the evacuees would remain in the camps for the entire time while others were allowed out on work leave. In October 1944, Gen. Harry Pratt, acting commander of the Western Defense Command, announced that after January 2, 1945, all Japanese evacuees who had proved their loyalty would be permitted to return to their homes.

With so many men away fighting the war, there was a need for citrus pickers that could not be fulfilled. In 1945, over 500 German prisoners of war were brought to Orange County to help pick the orange crop. The German prisoners were headquartered at the Santa Ana Army Air Base. The growers paid the government the same rate per box for the oranges picked by the prisoners of war as was paid to civilian laborers. The Army gave each prisoner 80 cents per day in canteen coupons if he had reached his daily quota of oranges picked. More than a million boxes of fruit were picked by the prisoners.

THE HOME FRONT

As soon as World War II began, Americans rallied to the cause, giving their wholehearted support to the defeat of the enemy. Among civilians, the American Red Cross, church groups and business leaders participated in organized efforts to provide bandages, knitted wear and needed items for the men in the service. Most residents did their best to cooperate with a complicated rationing system, going without necessities to help the soldiers and the war effort. Strong feelings of patriotism, war bond drives and parades encouraged every citizen, from small children to seniors, to contribute to the war effort.

ROSIE THE RIVETER

Unprepared for war when it began in Europe on September 1, 1939, the United States made a valiant effort to catch up by producing nearly 60,000 planes a year during the war. Southern California was particularly active in the aircraft industry, and many county residents played a vital role in its early development.

Rosie the Riveter, a pin-up that symbolized the contributions of the women who went to work in the shipbuilding and aircraft industries, appeared on posters in an effort to inspire women to enter the work force.

THE IMPACT OF RATIONING – EVERYONE PULLS TOGETHER

Any product containing rubber or oils, including tires, automobiles, bicycles, boots, shoes, stoves and gasoline, was rationed. In addition, foods such as meat, sugar, cheese, lard and butter were also on the list. Anyone labeled a "hoarder" (someone who stockpiled rationed goods) was despised and treated like an outcast.

UNITED STATES OF AMERICA
OFFICE OF PRICE ADMINISTRATION

THIS IS TO CERTIFY THAT

Nevada Staines

has fulfilled the necessary requirements, and by reason of service to our country is hereby designated a

MEMBER

of War Price and Rationing Board No. 82.5.33 of Los Angeles, California

DATED 8/6/45 DISTRICT DIRECTOR *Frank X. Balthis jr.*

Local ration boards were organized to handle the process. In May of 1942, residents were required to register at their local elementary school in order to obtain Ration Book No. 1. Each book contained 28 stamps, good for the purchase of sugar, coffee and shoes.

A few months later, in December of 1942, special coupon books were issued for the purchase of gasoline. In the days before refrigerators had large freezers, many grocery items were processed in tin cans. Canned meats, fish, vegetables, fruits, soups and prepared foods were rationed, using a point system. The sale of all processed foods was halted in February of 1943, so that stamp books could be issued. Anyone who can remember World War II will remember Spam, the canned processed ham-based loaf that was one of the few meats available during the duration of the war. Every housewife knew at least a dozen ways to prepare Spam. For more detailed information about rationing, Leo J. Friis, in *Orange County Through Four Centuries*, gives important details of that unique time in our nation's

The Rexall Store, on the corner of Pacific Coast Highway and Main Street, in the late 1930s. *Courtesy First American Title Insurance Co.*

history. Mr. Friis, a prominent historian and attorney, was very active in the civil air patrol.

THE END OF THE WAR

On Monday, May 7, 1945, the headlines of the *Los Angeles Times* screamed "V-E DAY!" At 2:41 a.m. the Nazis had surrendered unconditionally to the Allied Powers. The surrender took place in the little red schoolhouse which was the headquarters of General Eisenhower. The war was half over. The *Times* went on to say:

"Organized resistance by Germany has ended. Allied lives have paid the terrible price of suppressing the mad terror unleashed by Adolph Hitler. Germany herself is paying the awful penalty of having been led into a depravity of cruelty almost unequaled in the world's history."

Approximately two months later, on August 15, 1945, the headlines, with four-inch-high letters, proclaimed "*PEACE!*" The Japanese had accepted without qualifications the surrender terms set forth by President Truman. The president proclaimed a two-day holiday, and America celebrated with parades, tears of joy and celebrations.

A NEW DOOR OPENS

As is often true, the closing of one chapter opens the door to another. During the war, thousands of soldiers had seen Southern California for the first time. The balmy weather, the beaches, the mountains, the small towns and cities, and the friendly people made a big impression on many servicemen. They liked what they saw and resolved to return some day.

GUARDING LIVES AND FIRE DIVING

They came by the thousands in the summer. Beachgoers armed with blankets, picnic baskets and towels, stepped off Pacific Electric Red Cars from Los Angeles and Santa Ana or arrived by automobile.

Delbert "Bud" Higgins, in his oral history, vividly remembers what it was like to be a lifeguard in Huntington Beach. Higgins served as a part-time lifeguard during the summers from 1924 to 1932, while working full time for the Southern California Edison Company. In 1933, he quit the Edison Company and went to work for the city as a full-time lifeguard. Beginning in 1933, Higgins also worked as a volunteer fireman. In 1950 he was offered the job as Fire Chief and immediately transferred from the Lifeguard Department to the Fire Department. Retiring as chief in 1967, Higgins devoted his retirement years to the history of his beloved city.

The Higgins family's presence in the area goes back to before Huntington Beach was born. His mother's parents moved from Valley Center to the Westminster area about 1885. In 1903 they moved into Pacific City (Huntington Beach) where his grandmother, Mary Reed, opened the first hotel and eating place in the new town. His grandfather, Jacob Reed, was one of the first deputy constables in Huntington Beach.

Bud's father, who moved to Talbert in 1898, moved back to Los Angeles in 1899, returning in 1905 to settle permanently in Huntington Beach. Although Bud was born in Los Angeles (August 27, 1907), he grew up in Huntington Beach.

Higgins' first experience as a lifeguard was in June of 1924. He gained the knowledge and experience while working for Harry Lee. Between 1921 and 1925, Lee, an expert boxer and boatman, was the head lifeguard as well as an oil field worker. Bud Higgins, then a teenager, worked weekends and holidays. As part of his training for the job, he learned how to row an 18-foot-long dory through the heavy surf. Higgins recalled that the early-day lifeguards, who used either the breaststroke or sidestroke when they swam, were not very good swimmers. They did not know how to do the less-cumbersome American or

The Huntington Beach Pier, as it appeared in the 1940s. Ornate Zigzag Moderne shops had been added to each side of the main thoroughfare. *Courtesy Marsh Collection*

106

Huntington Beach's
lifeguards, shown here in
1942, were headed by Bud
Higgins. Note the female
lifeguard in the back row.
*Courtesy Huntington Beach
Historical Society*

A lifeguard station and rescue jeep in the Huntington Beach State Park. *Courtesy Geivet Collection, Old Courthouse Museum*

if there were adequately trained lifeguards available. Sadly, early records show that there had been as many as one or more victims per week. On July 4, 1931, there were three drownings before 10 a.m. After Higgins instituted the new program, there were no drownings from July of 1931 to September of 1939 — a remarkable record. The Huntington Beach Saltwater Plunge, located next to the ocean near Main Street and Ocean Boulevard, was a center for swimming and diving events. Bud, at 10 years of age, joined the swimming team and also had his first experience with competitive diving. The Los Angeles Athletic Club held swimming and diving events at the Plunge, as well as in the ocean near the pier. Competitive diving challenges between teams from several beach cities were often held at the Plunge.

Bud Higgins was also a fire diver. In addition to performing in competitive diving events, Bud thrilled the crowds at special celebrations with his fire dives. He would douse himself with alcohol, light his clothes with a match, making himself into a flaming ball of fire as he dove into the water. Sometimes as an extra thrill, he would add a summersault or spin to his dive. What an awesome sight that must have been!

In 1927, Higgins was there to witness the introduction of surfing to the United States by the legendary Hawaiian surfer, Duke Kahanamoku. Higgins and his friend, Gene Belshe, ordered a slab of redwood lumber and made their own boards, using a block plane and a drawknife to shape them. That first year, they were two of only four men in Southern California who had surfboards. By 1929, Higgins estimated that there were a dozen or more so boards in Orange County.

In the mid-1930s, the lifeguards' first rescue vehicle was a motorcycle, with sidecar, that was given to them by the police department. Before receiving the

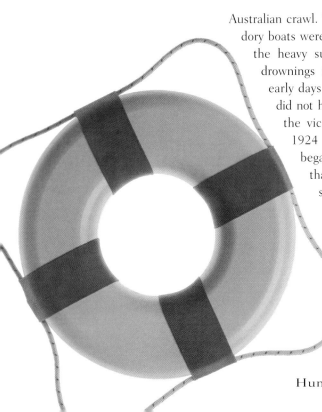

Australian crawl. Therefore, the wooden dory boats were needed for rescues in the heavy surf. There were many drownings in the riptides in the early days because the lifeguards did not have the skills to rescue the victims. It was not until 1924 when the Red Cross began to teach lifesaving that the easier swimming styles and lifesaving skills were introduced.

After Higgins became a lifeguard, he and his friends decided that there was no excuse for a person to drown

motorcycle, the lifeguards sometimes had to run five or six blocks before jumping into the ocean and swimming 300 to 400 yards to rescue the victim. The motorcycle greatly improved their speed and efficiency. A few years later, the lifeguards were given their first pickup truck. In 1935 the lifeguard headquarters was moved to a building on top of the pier.

In 1937, the men recognized a need for a communication system. The telephone company put in a switchboard, installed poles and strung wires, while the men mounted a telephone on their truck. When an emergency arose, they would pull the truck up to a telephone pole and plug into the switchbox.

Higgins saw many startling changes in the beaches of the city. During the early years, when most people came to swim only in the summer, about 50,000 visited the beach each year. As transportation improved, swimming became a year-round activity, and dedicated surfers began using their boards in all kinds of weather. By the middle of the 1930s, approximately 100,000 people were coming to the beach every year. By the 1960s, the number had expanded to as many as 100,000 per day.

Bud Higgins was interviewed extensively by Harry Henslick as part of the very significant oral history program at California State University at Fullerton. His interviews are well worth reading and rereading because of Higgins' memory for details and because of his involvement with the city. Several years ago, he donated his large collection of historic local photographs and memorabilia to the Huntington Beach Historical Society.

THE POLICE DEPARTMENT GROWS

Major events triggered important changes in the duties and scope of the Huntington Beach Police Department: the discovery of oil in 1920, the Great Depression of the 1930s, the beginning of World War II in December of 1941 and the tremendous growth of the 1960s.

Lt. Michael Biggs, in *The First Eighty Years; History of the Huntington Beach Police Department*, tells us that the oil boom brought with it "people who were in a hurry to make a fortune, and in so doing, disregarded the traffic and speed laws." By the end of 1921, in the previously quiet little town, more than 300 people were arrested for various offenses, including drinking, gambling, bootlegging and vagrancy. Previous to that time, traffic and speeding were the principal focuses of the department.

When oil was discovered in 1920 there were 1,687 people living in Huntington Beach. Cardboard shacks and tents were erected on the beach to house the newly arrived oil workers. City Historian Alicia Wentworth notes that the situation was so bad that as many as three people would sleep in the same bed, and rooms were often rented by shifts.

Ed Manning, the city's first mayor in 1909, became the mayor for the second time on February 17, 1919, exactly 10 years to the day of the city's

The tram driver looks back at his load as a man with a fishing pole prepares to climb aboard. The popular Pier Café was located next to the pier and served, among other things, hamburgers, jumbo shrimp, fish dinners and hot dogs. *Courtesy Huntington Beach Historical Society*

Members of the Huntington Beach Police Department pose with Chief Keller in about 1933. Standing from left are: Bill Hunter, Les Grant, Chief Vern Keller, G.W. Cox, Owen Mosier and Vern Mohn. George Gelzer (left) and Howard Robidoux (right) are shown on motorcycles. *Courtesy Huntington Beach Historical Society*

incorporation. To him fell the arduous task of controlling the city during the first days of the oil boom.

On April 1, 1921, the city council appointed Jack Tinsley to serve for the second time as marshal. Two months later, the official title of "Marshal" was replaced by "Chief of Police." Chief Tinsley was also authorized to hire a special policeman to handle the increasing police duties and to buy a new police car. Chief Tinsley had several important jobs. In addition to his position as police chief, he also served as street superintendent, fire chief and head of the life-guard system.

Chief of Police Donald Blossom is sworn into office on May 15, 1941, after the death of Chief Les Grant. Shown from left: Tom Talbert, Blossom, Arthur Morehouse, Fred Grable, Marcus McCallen, Lee Chamness and City Clerk Charley Fir. *Courtesy Huntington Beach Historical Society*

By the 1930s, when the nation was in the depths of the Great Depression, the police department problems increased as many oil workers lost their jobs and hobos from other states moved into Southern California in search of jobs and a warmer climate. Because there was no new oil drilling projects in the early 1930s, the population dropped to 3,690 people. Theft and burglary became the greatest problems faced by the police department. In 1940, just before the beginning of Word War II, the official census lists 3,738 people living in Huntington Beach, an increase of only 48 residents in 10 years.

In April of 1937, Lester Grant, who had joined the police department in 1930, was appointed as the sixth chief of police. In August of that year, residents of the city voted to make the chief of police an elected position. Grant, who won the election, had the honor of being the first elected chief of police in Orange County. Sadly, Chief Grant was involved in a motorcycle accident in 1939 and never recovered sufficiently to go back to work. Don Blossom, who was appointed assistant chief in July of 1940, was given the job of running the department. Chief Grant died on May 12, 1942 at the age of 42.

Chief Donald Blossom, elected to the office in April of 1942, had the increased responsibilities of the war years on his shoulders.

In anticipation of having to defend Huntington Beaches shores, the police force was required to take target practice three times a day. In order to obtain the needed bullets, the Belshe family made them in a shop in the basement of city hall.

The population of Huntington Beach, estimated at 4,912 persons in 1942, increased to over 5,000 residents in 1943 (5,048). By 1950, there were 5,871 living in the city. Still, the city still had the intimate feel of a small town, and everyone still knew the members of the 17-man police force by name. The average salary for an officer was $250 per month.

In 1945, the installation of FM radios in the city's police cars, improved the efficiency of the police department. Patrol cars could contact each other as well as the police station.

By 1966 the police department had grown to more than 60 personnel, and the average salary was more than $600 a month. A Vice and Narcotics Unit was created with Gene Pool as head of the department. Drugs, for the first time, were becoming a real problem. A system was initiated to investigate the increasing traffic of runaway teenagers who were drawn to the beach scene. By 1961, when Clinton Wright was chief of police, there were 15,850 persons living in Huntington Beach. The city would continue to grow by leaps and bounds from the early 1960s to the present.

The carnival rides on the ocean side of Pacific Coast Highway, at Main, were a popular summer attraction. This photo was taken in the 1940s. *Courtesy First American Title Insurance Co.*

J. SHERMAN DENNY AND THE HUNTINGTON BEACH COMPANY

J. Sherman Denny remembers well the day in 1923 when he came to work for the Huntington Beach Company. It was the stepping stone toward his becoming the local manager of the influential company. Active in the Rotary Club and Chamber of Commerce, he could usually be found helping out in numerous civic activities that made Huntington Beach such a special place to live. In 1953, he was chosen "Man of the Year" by the

The Huntington Beach Fire Department is ready for action in this 1962 photograph. *Courtesy Geivet Collection, Old Courthouse Museum*

112

Chamber. That same year he served as chairman of the countywide beautification committee. He became interested in the Tuberculosis Society through his collection of Christmas Seals. In addition, he was a rock hound and a gardener interested in the propagation of succulents. He was also fascinated by psychic phenomena and archeology.

An intelligent man, Denny, who had moved from the Imperial Valley to Long Beach in 1914, was hired by Mr. James S. Lawshe, then manager of the Huntington Beach Company, to take charge of oil records. Because Mr. Lawshe's office was in Los Angeles and he could only get to Huntington Beach once or twice a week, he needed someone on a full-time basis to run the office, go out to the oil fields, collect information from the leases, track the oil production and prepare reports. The office, located at 474 Ocean Avenue, was shared with the Huntington Beach Water Company.

During 1936 and 1937, the firm, which was primarily a land-holding company, decided to invest in the cattle and agricultural products business. At that time, the company owned approximately 1,400 acres, most of which was leased out for oil production and pipeline easements. The new headquarters for the farming operation were at 2110 Main Street. In addition to the dairy cattle and few horses, the company had 800 or 900 sheep grazing at various locations on the mesa. The company also experimented with peasants and turkeys, but those endeavors were not a commercial success.

After Mr. Lawshe died suddenly in 1947, the company decided to give up the farming activities and concentrate on the land leases. To his surprise, the company directors gave Mr. Denny a promotion to general manager.

J. Sherman Denny is particularly remembered for his efforts in increasing communications between the Huntington Beach Company and local residents by suggesting that company officials come to the city from San Francisco for regular luncheon meetings with civic leaders. The luncheons were held monthly for 12 years.

Mr. Denny's successful career as manager of the local Huntington Beach Company office lasted from 1947 to February of 1962. He retired at that time so his successor, Ed Hartsock could take over.

It is obvious when reading Denny's series of interviews by Harry Henslick, in *Huntington Beach, An Oral History* (Cal State Fullerton, 1981), that Mr. Denny was a highly intelligent, although modest, man who was very involved in the life of Huntington Beach.

EL GENERALISSIMO

William Gallienne, known to his friends as "El Generalissimo," was involved in almost every civic endeavor held in Huntington Beach during his 30 years as secretary-manager of the chamber of

commerce. He was known for his out-going pleasant personality, his ability to get others to compromise, and the many celebrations he planned and directed. In addition, he had a strong singing voice, a flare for showmanship, and loved to play the cornet and trumpet.

Born on the Isle of Guernsey, between England and France, Gallienne was 15 when he came to Huntington Beach with his parents and a group of friends in 1910. Huntington Beach was a small town with no street lights, no gas, no paved streets, no sewer and only one café.

When he first came to town, Gallienne, who had apprenticed as the Caldonia Nurseries in his native land, worked in the plant nursery of the Huntington Beach Company. He went on to work for Eader's Bakery for a few years before becoming a grocery delivery person for the W.L. McKinney and Company.

After six years working for the Standard Oil Company, delivering gas and oil to customers in the area, Bill with a partner, Lynn Cobb, opened a Standard Station at the corner of Main and Olive. It was after he sold the station that he became secretary-manager of the chamber of commerce at about age 40.

Gallienne's true love was the Huntington Beach Municipal Band, both as a promoter and performer. Old timers recalled Sunday afternoon band concerts on the beach. Bill would bring tears to people's eyes when he played solos such as "Till the Sands of the Desert Grow Cold."

Gallienne was the choir director of the First Christian Church for a number of years. With his fine tenor voice and love of music, he sang in many Orange County musical productions and appeared on almost every stage in the county, earning the title "Impresario."

While serving as secretary-manager of the chamber of

commerce, he planned and orchestrated the annual Christmas Parades and the Twin-O-Ramas that brought thousands of people to the city. In addition to his membership in the Elks Club, he served as secretary of the local unit of the Urban Land Institute and a term as president of the California Chambers of Commerce Managers. Governor Edmund G. Brown appointed him to the Orange County Fair Board. When Gallienne died in November of 1965 at the age of 70, his funeral was one of the largest such gatherings ever held in the county. Many dignitaries from throughout Southern California attended and all 25 chamber of commerce directors acted as honorary

William Gallienne poses with Minnie Higgins (left) and a smiling bathing beauty, in 1949. Bill, who worked as secretary-manager of the chamber of commerce for 30 years, organized many of the city's major events, including the Christmas Parade, the Twin-O-Rama, and the Fourth of July Parade. He loved to play the cornet and trumpet, and was a big supporter of the Huntington Beach Municipal Band. *Courtesy Arline Huff Howard*

113

During the 1940s and 1950s, twins from all over the country came to Huntington Beach to participate in the annual Twin-O-Rama. *Courtesy Huntington Beach Historical Society*

PROOF ONLY
PRINTS $2.00 MAILED
TAX INCLUDED
ORDER NOW
Picture No.

114

pallbearers. George Putnam, well-known Los Angeles newscaster, delivered a eulogy to Mr. Gallienne on the 10:00 News.

FLYING HIGH AT THE MEADOWLARK AIRPORT

In the late 1940s, a handful of small airports were established in Orange County because many county residents who had become fascinated with flying were buying their own airplanes.

The 65-acre Meadowlark Airport, founded in 1946, offered pilots a place to tie down their planes for $55 a month and a landing fee of $3 for each flight. Located at Warner Avenue and Bolsa Chica Road, the airport was operated out of a group of corrugated metal buildings and World War II Quonset huts that had been moved to the site. A 320-foot long landing strip ran along the west side.

By the mid-1970s, homes and businesses were crowding closer and closer to Meadowlark. Residents worried about crashes and lobbied to close the airport. Additionally, the land, leased from the Nerio family of

Talbert Stadium, built in 1946, is the ring shown in the middle of the photo. Pacific Coast Highway runs diagonally across the bottom corner. In operation from 1946 until 1959, the stadium was the site of popular jalopy races held on Friday and Saturday nights. *Courtesy Geivet Collection, Old Courthouse Museum*

Westminster, was becoming more and more valuable. In 1974, developers Bartoli and Stelbrecht made plans to put up 25 homes, using the landing strip section for an access road. After going to court and failing to get an injunction to stop the development, the airport owner, John Turner, finally gave up and closed the airport. Homes and businesses now occupy the site.

THE HUNTINGTON BEACH WOMAN'S CLUB

In 1958, the members of the Huntington Beach Woman's Club celebrated 50 years of dedication to the city. They are the unsung heroines of the major civic, educational and cultural movements in the community. The Woman's Club did much more than provide an intellectual outlet for its members. It gave them a chance to participate in the development of the community, educate themselves and meet together to solve problems.

As in many other communities, the Woman's Club was instrumental in establishing the public library, raising the consciousness of women in civic matters and providing healthy social events for the community.

After the first meeting in January of 1908, held at Florence Blodget's home, the seven members quickly went to work cleaning up the town for the tourist season. On April 3, they sponsored a Municipal Cleaning Day that was to become a tradition. In addition, the organization bought several much-needed trash containers for the business district. On the social side, the first event was a Martha Washington-themed party held one month after the club's formation.

Active in politics from the beginning, in February of 1909 the Woman's Club came out in favor of the city's incorporation, contributing to the success of the ballot measure. As politically-minded women who could not vote, the campaign for women's suffrage was an important issue. The organization publicly favored a proposal to place the matter on the ballot in 1911, and continued to campaign for the cause until women's suffrage was passed in 1919.

Members of the Woman's Club were quick to recognize and identify problems within the community. For instance, they took the lead in organizing the Red Cross Auxiliary and conducted philanthropy projects for the needy. During the oil boom, which began in 1920, one of the women's main civic interests was the conditions of the dance halls. They lobbied for a law which would govern the operation of those facilities.

Concerned about the municipal playgrounds, particularly along the beach, they worked toward more supervision of the popular attractions.

A good example of the organization's tenacity and problem-solving skills involved the successful establishment of a club house in which to hold meetings and events. In June of 1912, they began their building fund with $14 they had earned from projects during the year. The first of many events to raise money for the building fund was a musical production which netted $39.22. Proceeding ahead with determination, the women had, by 1915, saved $275 toward making their dream of a club house a reality.

A committee consisting of Mrs. Vernon Shank, Bertha Heffner, and Florence Blodget was formed to investigate the details of the purchase of a piece of property. In June of that year, the Huntington Beach Company offered to sell adjoining 25-foot-wide lots on 10th Street for half the market value. Still needing additional funds to make the purchase, the women held a banquet and asked for donations. They were successful in raising the funds that allowed them to become the successful owner of the lots with a bid of $479.90.

The next month they bought a surplus board-and-batten school house and moved it to the lot. The club house rapidly became an important gathering place for the community.

The many significant contributions of the Woman's Club to the community involved dedication, hard work, sacrifice, intellect, strength and ability. For excellent detailed information and in-depth research on the Huntington Beach Woman's Club, see Dr. Barbara Milkovitch's article "Influences of the Woman's Club on the Development of Orange County, 1900-1930," in the *Proceedings of the Conference of Orange County History, 1988*. In addition, an article by Mikel Garcia titled, "Federated Women's Clubs Through the Nation," in the same publication, provides an early history and general information on the women's club movement.

The Huntington Beach Woman's Club, founded in 1908, was the primary influence behind many important civic projects. The occasion for this photograph was the organization's Golden Jubilee in 1958. *Courtesy Geivet Collection, Old Courthouse Museum*

Chapter Five

An oil geyser erupts near Pacific Coast Highway in 1955. The Sea Breeze Café, which advertised "Home Cooking," is shown in the foreground. *Courtesy First American Title Insurance Co.*

beneath the ground for thousands of years. Oil would continue to be discovered in the Huntington Beach fields for decades to come.

In 1946 and 1947, interest was renewed in the Tar zone at the corner of 20th Street and Orange Avenue, and 136 new Tar zone wells were drilled in 1949. In August of 1953, Clark Peterson redrilled an abandoned well called "Brower" No. 1 near the corner of Huntington Avenue and Chicago Street. The well "Huntington" No. 5 was brought in by Jack Crawford on January 1, 1955. Within a very short period of time, 216 wells were drilled. Because they were placed very close together, the oil and gas were withdrawn rapidly and production declined.

Two oil platforms, built in the ocean, contain drilling equipment that plunges from 4,000 to over 12,000 feet into the floor of the sea. They were christened Emmy (owned by the Signal Oil Company) and Eva (owned by the Union Oil Company). Helicopters flew the Emmy's crew to its platform from a launching pad near 22nd Street.

THE HUNTINGTON BEACH OIL FIELDS

When the Huntington Beach "A" No. 1 oil well was brought in on May 24, 1920, it signaled the beginning of the billion-dollar oil industry, which would bring an economic boom to the city. However, no one dreamed of the vastness of the riches that had lingered

In 1965, there were 2,270 wells in Huntington Beach, with 1,712 of them pumping oil. Approximately 19 million barrels, at an average price of $2.25 a barrel, were produced that year, yielding a total of more than $45 million. More than 500 whipstock wells were producing approximately 11 million barrels of oil annually. The oil industry had not only grown and endured through four and one-half decades, but also continued to be the major economic force in the community.

THE GOLDEN BEAR

The Golden Bear, a stucco-clad monolithic nightclub built in 1926, faced Pacific Coast Highway, one block south of Main Street. The club's eclectic fare offered a wide variety of musical talent and included blues, heavy metal, folk, western swing, jazz and punk. The Golden Bear was known for booking artists that didn't try to please everybody.

There was something about the Golden Bear that inspired musicians to do their best. Some praised the

Huntington Beach created a unique Christmas tree by decorating one of the metal oil derricks with fir branches and lights. *Courtesy First American Title Insurance Co.*

acoustics, others the atmosphere, and still others the club's staff and responsive audiences. Sometimes performers such as Los Lobos or David Lindley would continue to play long after it was time for the club to close. For many artists who traditionally played more well- known venues, it was a good place to develop new material or begin their national tours. The audience at the Golden Bear was known as one that had an intuitive sense about what would be successful. The Golden Bear was a natural stepping stone on which new artists could share their dreams and aspirations.

Huey Lewis, Linda Ronstadt, Bob Dylan, Stevie Ray Vaughan, Jimi Hendrix, Leo Kottke, David Grisman, Lenny Bruce, Janis Joplin, Chris Isaak and Silverstone are among those who have made their mark at the Golden Bear. The Knitters, the Blasters, the Neville Brothers, the Fabulous Thunderbirds and Los Lobos are among the groups starring on the Bear's stage. Well-known blues artists such as B.B. King, Muddy Waters, John Lee Hooker and Albert King appeared frequently. The Golden Bear served as a second home for many musicians.

According to the January 30, 1986, edition of the *Orange County Register*, things have happened at the Bear that wouldn't have happened other places. For example, the night comedian, Steve Martin, took the whole audience down to the pier to razz the grizzled fisherman there. One night while improvising at the Bear, the Spirit came up with their hit, "I Got a Line on You." The British progressive missionary Peter Gabriel was such a hit that the audience inside was still applauding long after he walked out the back door for a swim in the ocean.

Hollywood stars such as Errol Flynn and John Barrymore frequented the restaurant that once occupied the building. By way of contrast, in 1933 the undamaged building gave shelter to the homeless after the earthquake of March 10 when the Red Cross set up an emergency soup kitchen and shelter.

The Golden Bear met its demise on January 30, 1986, and closed down with little fanfare and few chances to say goodbye. Rick and Charles Babiracki, who had owned the club for 12 years, hoped to have a chance to present several farewell concerts with proceeds to go to the saving of the Bear. However, there was no time left and, after giving the Babirackis a week to move, the owners went through with their plans to tear down the Bear. Robin Thrower, Phoebe Snow and the Taj Mahal were the last acts to appear there. For lovers of live music in Orange County, the end of the Golden Bear was very sad.

The Golden Bear, built in 1926 on Pacific Coast Highway, near Main, was a popular nightclub that played host to artists such as Linda Ronstadt, Bob Dylan, Jimi Hendrix, Lenny Bruce and Janis Joplin. It closed its doors in 1986.
Courtesy Huntington Beach Historical Society

THE 1950s

(Far right top) Golf was becoming a popular sport in the 1950s. Shown here is the clubhouse for the Municipal Golf Course on 17th Street. *Courtesy Geivet Collection, Old Courthouse Museum*

The 1950s were good years for the city of Huntington Beach. At the beginning of the decade the town had 5,258 residents, and the community still had a small-town atmosphere. At the end of the decade, in October of 1960, the population had doubled to 11,492 persons.

(Far right bottom) In the 1950s and 60s it was possible to find farms still operating in the area. *Courtesy First American Title Insurance Co.*

Fairgoers admire the Huntington Beach display at the South Orange County Fair in 1954. *Courtesy Geivet Collection, Old Courthouse Museum*

118

Members of the Huntington Beach Professional Woman's Club are shown here in the process of picking out a turkey in 1951. *Courtesy Geivet Collection, Old Courthouse Museum*

Beauty queen Carol Huff, wearing a fashionable bathing suit of the 1950s, poses with the Huntington Beach sign in March of 1952. *Courtesy Geivet Collection, Old Courthouse Museum*

HUNTINGTON BEACH CALIFORNIA'S *Finest* BATHING BEACH

119

Chapter Six

HUNTINGTON BEACH FACES PHENOMENAL CHANGES

Beginning in the 1950s, Huntington Beach began to grow at a fast pace. Several annexations between 1957 and 1960 swelled the boundaries of the city from 3.57 square miles to over 25 square miles.

In the 1960s and 70s, as residents by the thousands moved into the city, the rate of growth accelerated even faster. As tract after tract was built, Huntington Beach became the fastest-growing city in the continental United States.

THE ARRIVAL OF THE DOUGLAS SPACE SYSTEMS CENTER GIVES THE COMMUNITY A NEEDED INDUSTRIAL BOOST

Most of the industry of the early days, represented by the Holly Sugar Factory, the Bolsa Tile Company, the Broom Factory, canneries, the Pacific Linoleum and Oil Cloth Company and a handful of other companies, had disappeared by the 1940s. Huntington Beach was in need of an industrial base to match the mushrooming residential growth.

The community was excited when the Douglas Space Center moved to town in the early 1960s. The facility was devoted to aerospace research and development and occupied 312 acres in the northern section of the city.

In 1965, Douglas began production on the Saturn S-IVB upper stage missile and the third stage of the huge Saturn V booster that would send a team of American astronauts to the moon. At that time, the company employed approximately 6,800 persons, providing the largest payroll in the city.

The Southern California Edison Steam Plant, with 350 employees, was credited with having the second largest local payroll. The lights on the huge Southern California Edison plant were visible for miles and became a landmark for airplanes and ships.

Other notable employers in the city during the 1960s included the City of Huntington Beach, Signal Oil and Gas Company, Standard Oil of California, the Gemco Department Store, the Alpha Beta Meat Packing Plant and the Orange County Ceramic Tile Company.

NEW CITY CHARTER ADOPTED

In 1966, as a result of the adoption of a new city charter, two new members were added to the five already serving on the city council. The job of chief of police, an elected post since August of 1937, became an appointed position once again. Council salaries were increased from $125 to $175 a month.

Huntington Beach had been a Special Charter City since 1940. After determining that changes needed to be made in that Charter, the council appointed a Citizens Charter Review Committee. After working for seven months, the committee produced a 52-page document to present to the voters. The new City Charter was approved by a vote of 3,255 to 1,108. In February of the next year, the Charter was approved by both the State Assembly and the State Senate. The city quickly made the needed changes.

HUNTINGTON BEACH PRESERVES ITS UNIQUE PAST

A day at Huntington Beach State Park is a treat for the whole family. Two families share a day of swimming, fishing and marshmallow roasting in July of 1952. *Courtesy Geivet Collection, Old Courthouse Museum*

122

(Bottom right) Apartments and condominiums also experienced a building boom in the 1950s, 60s and 70s. *Courtesy First American Title Insurance Company*

The early 1950s marked the beginning of a huge tract-building era for Huntington Beach. Shown here in June of 1952, this early tract was a predecessor of the hundreds of tracts that would spring up in the 1950s, 60s and 70s. According to Historian Dr. Barbara Milkovitch in *A Hundred Years of Yesterday*, Huntington Beach was given the distinction of being called the fastest-growing city in the nation during the 1970s. *Courtesy Geivet Collection, Old Courthouse Museum*

THE POLICE DEPARTMENT GROWS TO MEET THE NEEDS OF THE COMMUNITY

From the 1920s to the 1940s, roughnecks employed in the oil fields were a big problem for the police department. By the 1960s, youthful beach rioters and members of the hippie generation created new and complicated concerns in the city.

Chief Smeltzer appointed a task force, called "Smeltzer's Sandmen," from members of the department. Pulled from the regular force to patrol the beaches, the Sandmen wore beachwear, making them less conspicuous.

They did much to keep the problem under control. The events that made Huntington Beach such a magnet for those wanting entertainment also created additional special concerns for the department. The traditional Fourth of July and the All Southland Salute to Santa Claus parades brought thousands of spectators to the city. In addition, each September the city played host to the United States Surfboard Championships.

Chief Smeltzer presided over five major divisions. One of only a few police departments in Orange County to book and record its own arrests, the department also maintained its own fingerprint files. Sgt. Henry Archer was in charge of that program.

FIRE DEPARTMENT

In the 1960s, with Chief Delbert "Bud" Higgins at the helm, the Fire Department was growing with the city. To meet the new demands of expansion, the department increased to 54 full-time and 72 part-time employees. At that time, the department had the use of six pumpers, one ladder wagon and two rescue units spread among its fire stations.

The new heavily residential areas that had been added to the city created a complexity of fire problems. Chief Higgins was particularly concerned because the old oil wells that were previously steamed out were producing sulfide gas. He felt that the situation could raise fire and rescue problems.

Chief Higgins, who had grown up in the city, had served as a volunteer with the department since 1932. In August of 1950, after Chief Sargent had retired, Higgins was appointed fire and lifeguard chief. He worked to improve the department during the heavy period of growth, and retired in 1967.

A jib-foot grader, shown here in August of 1952, prepares the roadbed for one of the hundreds of new city streets which were created in the 1950s, 60s and 70s.
Courtesy Geivet Collection, Old Courthouse Museum

TWO NEW LIBRARIES

On Sunday, September 30, 1951, the city's new international-style library located at 525 Main Street, opened its doors for the first time. Dedicated by Mayor Vernon Ragenbeck, it was built at a cost of $140,000. Lyle Mossinger, who served as head librarian for about 20 years, was in charge of the new facility.

Beginning in the 1960s, the city sensed the urgency for more library space. In 1967, the city selected a 10-acre site on Talbert Avenue which included part of Talbert Lake. During the elections on November 5, 1968, a bond issue which was placed on the ballot received the support of 62 percent of the

123

The stylish Pacific Sands Homes, constructed in 1966, were typical of the many tracts being developed in Huntington Beach.
Courtesy Arline Huff Howard

The highly popular 3 bedroom Chanticlaire, with Spanish available in 4 exterior designs from $29,950

See this exciting Private Beach Community in Huntington Beach

deane Homes

PACIFIC SANDS

The second Huntington Beach Public Library building opened on September 30, 1951. Located at 525 Main Street, it cost $140,000 to build. When the new main library opened in Central Park in 1973, this building became a branch library. *Courtesy Geivet Collection, Old Courthouse Museum*

124

voters, barely failing to get the required two-thirds majority. The city council, looking for other avenues by which to finance the needed library, formed a Public Facilities Corporation to obtain the funding. A five-man board was appointed to run the corporation.

The next task was to choose an architect for the new library. After reviewing the work of 35 architects, the field was narrowed to 17 candidates. After considerable thought and investigation, the father and son team of Richard and Dion Neutra was chosen to design the facility. Shortly thereafter, Richard Neutra died, leaving Dion to complete the work.

The groundbreaking was held on October 28, 1972. The library and its lovely natural setting are a source of continuing pride to the community.

GOLDEN WEST COLLEGE IS FOUNDED

In 1965 the new Golden West College, located on a 122-acre campus between Golden West, Edinger, McFadden and Gothard avenues, held its first classes. The 15 original buildings included a 370-seat lecture hall and labs for business, science, math, technology, fine and applied arts and the humanities. The centerpiece of the campus was a multi-purpose student center. The new school library began its life with 21,000 volumes.

Dr. R. Dudley Boyce was chosen in 1964 to lead the college in its first years. The establishment of Golden West College expanded the opportunities for residents to obtain further schooling, greatly benefiting the community.

HUNTINGTON HARBOR POSSESSES A TRUE MAGIC

Huntington Harbor, a $200 million development created in the 1960s, ushered in a whole new lifestyle to the public when it was built on 900 acres at the city's north end. Fishing, swimming, boating and a chance to view some truly awesome scenery were a few of the amenities offered by the new development.

The land on which the community was built had problems with unclear land titles, the remnants of oil wells and derricks, no supply of fresh water, environmental eyesores and the lack of civic backing.

When the true potential was discovered, the land was developed to include 620 acres of buildable land and 258 acres of waterways. When the project was finished it allowed for 18 miles of waterfront property. Tennis courts, swimming pools and a variety of special events, such as sailing races, made Huntington Harbor especially attractive. Shopping centers, schools, parks and mooring facilities were developed for the residents' convenience.

THE NEWLAND HOUSE IS RESCUED

In May of 1898, when Mary and William Newland moved their large family into their new Victorian home on a bluff overlooking a tree-shaded ravine and miles of lowlands, it was the only house in sight.

Today the stately house has been restored in remembrance of the Newland family and as a symbol of the unique history of Huntington Beach. The Huntington Beach Historical Society, a hard-working and dedicated organization, has completed the major restoration tasks needed to make the house look as it did when the Newland family lived there.

The lowest and most discouraging point in the house's restoration history came when vandals set fire to a mattress in the vacant boarded-up house, burning a hole in the roof and causing serious damage to the second floor. In addition, the water used to put the fire out ruined the plaster walls throughout the house. The Historical Society members went to work repairing the damage and restoring the house to its former beauty.

As long as Mary Newland was alive the house was in good condition. After William died in 1933, she managed the ranch and cared for the house by herself for many years. In addition to running the ranch until the mid-1940s, she tended the vegetable garden, fruit trees, berry bushes and rose garden. Mary Newland was undoubtedly a hard-working and remarkable woman.

developer's requirements for park land. The empty boarded-up house, surrounded by a chain-link fence, was rapidly deteriorating and had been vandalized several times.

In 1974, the City of Huntington Beach and the Huntington Beach Historical Society came to an agreement that would allow for the restoration of the Newland House as a house museum that would serve as a centerpiece in the newly-established park.

The organization, with over 200 eager volunteers, held several fundraisers to finance the beginning of the herculean restoration task. They tackled the badly damaged house with energy and vision.

As the restoration work progressed, the Historical Society opened the house for periodic tours. The society collected historic photographs, memorabilia, furniture and artifacts for use in the house. The spacious first floor contained an entry hall, formal parlor, dining room, master bedroom, guest room, nursery, boy's bedroom, kitchen, pantry, bathroom, office, back porch and sunroom. The sun-

In 1952, after Mary died, the house was leased to the Signal Oil Company who rented the home to its employees for about 20 years. When development was completed on another section of the property, the house and site were dedicated to the city as part of the

125

The classic oak fireplace front in the dining room replaces one that was stolen when the house was empty. The tile surround and hearth, however, are original.
Courtesy Huntington Beach Historical Society

126

changed to leave some areas free of plantings to allow for future archaeological work. The Newland House Rose Garden was dedicated in June of 1987.

On October 24, 1985, the Newland House was honored by its placement on the National Register of Historic Places, our nation's list of significant historic properties. In addition, it has been designated both as an Orange County Historic Site and a county archaeological site.

The Huntington Beach Historical Society continues to maintain and preserve the Newland House. Artifacts and memorabilia are still being collected. The archive of Huntington Beach history is located on the second floor of the barn that was built behind the Newland House in the 1980s. Organized by Dr. Barbara Milkovitch, the archives contain a variety of materials and photographs relating to the history of Huntington Beach.

The Huntington Beach Historical Society is an active group which holds monthly meetings in the large meeting room on the first floor of the barn, as well as conducting special events and activities. In addition, they present awards to citizens who have contributed significantly much to the history of the city. The organization staffs the Newland House and conduct tours on a regular basis.

room and second floor sleeping porch were added in 1915. The second floor features the playroom, sleeping porch, hall, alcove and octagonal tower room.

As the interior began to take shape, plans for the authentic landscaping that would set off the house were made. However, the Pacific Coast Archaeological Society became concerned because of the potential value of excavations on the land surrounding the house. In the 1930s, an ancient Indian village dating back to as far as 5000 B.C. had been discovered by archaeologists from the W.P.A. Even before that time, the Newlands had discovered and collected a variety of Indian artifacts on the property.

When the P.C.A.S. began digging test sites, a ramp had to be built over the test sections so people could get into the house, and booties had to be worn over people's shoes so the dirt would not be tracked inside. After the tests were completed, the garden plans were

THE HISTORIC RESOURCES SURVEY

In the spring of 1985, the Historical Society requested for the city to conduct a survey to identify historic buildings in the city's historic core. Led by Dr. Barbara Milkovitch, the Society pointed out the value of researching, mapping, recording and identifying the historic buildings significant to the history of the city.

Six members of the Historical Society formed the Heritage Committee to guide and direct the survey. In October of 1985, Thirtieth Street Architects was hired to train the volunteers, oversee the field work and prepare the final report. The committee consisted of Arline Howard, Guy Guzzardo, Dr. Barbara Milkovitch, Jerry Person, Maureen Rivers and Susan Worthy. The survey area was laid out with Clay Avenue as the northern boundary, the Pacific Ocean and Lake Street on the east and Golden West Street on the west. The committee members, who were active during the

Mr. and Mrs. Newland's bedroom featured an old-fashioned high-backed Victorian double bed, a rocker and a side table.
Courtesy Huntington Beach Historical Society

127

The sun porch, added to the south side of the house in 1915, featured the typical informal-style wicker furniture that was so popular in the 1910s and 20s.
Courtesy Huntington Beach Historical Society

One of the finest Colonial Revival houses built in the city between 1904 and 1912, this home was rescued from the wrecking ball and moved to 1211 Olive in the mid-1980s. *Courtesy Marsh Collection*

regulations designed to preserve sufficient historic resources to evoke the distinctive character and important stages in the history of the city;

• To promote community awareness of local history and historic architectural styles.

The members of the committee and volunteers spent hundreds of hours performing tasks required to complete the survey. The first such task involved a complete drive of the historic section of town, making a list identifying all architecturally significant buildings within the survey boundaries. A list of 554 buildings built before 1946 was compiled.

entire course of the survey, supplied much of the labor and recruited volunteers to conduct field work, take photographs, check city records, prepare maps, research historic records and conduct oral histories. The consultants prepared the final report, organized inventory forms and designed a public relations brochure.

The committee listed the following goals:

• To identify the historic and cultural resources of the city in order to provide a base of information for future planning;

• To identify buildings within the commercial core of the city which should be preserved and protected in conjunction with redevelopment;

• To develop recommendations for city policies and

Next, basic architectural styles were identified and categorized. Each building was given a preliminary rating reflecting its architectural and historical importance. Significant buildings were researched and the history recorded. Three sections: the Downtown District, Ninth Street District and Wesley Park District were outlined as potential historic districts.

The Historic Resources Survey Report recommended that the city adopt a special Historic Preservation Ordinance and establish a Historic Resources Commission to work with the city on matters concerning its significant buildings. A brochure was designed to reflect the importance and character of the city's historic structures.

128

This typical beach cottage was one of hundreds of this style built in Huntington Beach during the first quarter of the 20th century. First used mainly as vacation cottages, almost all of them have been converted to full-time residences. *Courtesy Marsh Collection*

POPULATION GROWTH

During the decade of the 1970s, Huntington Beach was the fastest growing city in the nation. As more and more land was annexed during the late 1950s and early 1960s, large tracts were built to house the city's new residents.

Year	Residents
1910	815
1920	1,687
1930	3,690
1942	4,912
1946	5,173
1950	5,258
1953	5,871
1965	70,053
1966	87,646
1967	94,377
1968	104,124
1969	112,021
1970	115,960
1971	137,000
1972	143,500
1973	146,300
1976	151,500
1977	157,800
1979	167,419
1980	172,200
1983	176,370
1985	176,156
1987	178,788
1990	181,115
1992	184,962
1995	189,159

Charming single-storied Spanish Colonial Revival houses, built in the late 1920s and early 30s, are sprinkled throughout the older section of the city.
Courtesy Marsh Collection

During the years 1910 to 1925, many high-quality Craftsman Bungalows were built in the city. Several still survive on Main Street.
Courtesy Marsh Collection

129

The Boy Scout Cabin at 934 11th Street, was dedicated as a Huntington Beach Historic Landmark in 1974. The plaque reads: " This rustic cabin was erected in 1924 by the Lion's Club, local Carpenter's Union, and Edison Company as a center for scouting in Huntington Beach and has been in continuous use by Troop I, Boy Scouts of America, ever since. The cabin was completely renovated."
Courtesy Marsh Collection

The Huntington Beach High School Auditorium was saved from demolition by the outcry of the city's residents. It was built in 1926 by the firm of Alison and Alison and was designed by famed architect, Frederick Eley.
Courtesy Marsh Collection

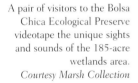
Visitors pause on the sturdy wooden bridge that leads from the parking lot to the Inner Bolsa Bay at the Ecological Preserve.
Courtesy Marsh Collection

EXPERIENCING THE BOLSA CHICA WETLANDS

The Bolsa Chica Ecological Preserve, the largest coastal sandmarsh in Los Angeles and Orange County, is a vivid and beautiful reminder of the way the vast Bolsa Chica wetlands looked when the Indians roamed the land and collected clams on Shell Beach. Today the sense of peace, beauty and quiet still pervade the air as visitors walk casually along the trails.

Home to a wide variety of birds, animals and plants, the 185-acre wetlands preserve is known as one of the best bird-watching stations in the country. Visitors are invited to park in the lot across from the Bolsa Chica State Beach or at the nature center on the corner of Warner and Pacific Coast Highway. The one and one-half-mile trail is designed in a loop pattern. A sturdy wooden bridge leads from the parking lot back into the Inner Bolsa Bay. Visitors can be seen leaning over the railing, watching crabs, fishes, sea slugs, horn snails, small sharks, stingrays and other marine life move about in the water. Other watchers train their binoculars on the herons, egrets, stilts, wrens, avocets, terns, sandpipers, geese, ducks, pelicans and a host of other water birds as they sail through the air or walk along the bank.

Because the wetlands are situated on the Pacific Flyway, it attracts thousands of birds migrating between North and South America. In the fall and winter you can see an enormous number of waterfowl busily feeding on the rich products of the preserve. The spring and summer brings birds that nest in the marsh grasses along the shore.

The Bolsa Chica Conservancy, established in 1990, has as its mission the preservation, restoration and enhancement of the wetlands. The Bolsa Chica

Interpretive Center, on the corner of Warner and Pacific Coast Highway, features an exhibit room with many interesting educational displays. Free bird watching inventories, listing the 336 kinds of birds that have been seen at the wetlands, are available. The Amigos de Bolsa Chica assist in staffing the center, leading tours and conducting special projects.

The California Department of Fish and Game manages the Bolsa Chica Ecological Preserve. The 185 acres of coastal marsh have been restored, with plans for an additional 600 acres in the future.

Tom Talbert, who visited the wetlands often during his lifetime, recalled seeing "birds by the thousands so thick in flight as to almost eclipse the sun. The hours-long flight of ducks patterned against the blazing sunset sky was amazingly spectacular and beautiful. When startled, great flocks arose to circle around and return to their beloved heaven." Although there are not as many birds to see, Tom Talbert, if he were alive today, would undoubtedly enjoy visiting the Bolsa Chica Wetlands Preserve, and enjoy the sights, smells, colors and sounds of this very special place.

A pair of visitors to the Bolsa Chica Ecological Preserve videotape the unique sights and sounds of the 185-acre wetlands area.
Courtesy Marsh Collection

131

An egret walks along the
shore north of the bridge,
in search of a morsel of food.
Courtesy Marsh Collection

THEN & NOW

We like to sit around over dinner with friends and talk about Orange County history. Each person has his or her unique memories. Sometimes the discussion gets into a spirited, but friendly argument. We always agree on one thing, however. For those of us who have been here since the 1940s and 50s, Orange County has grown and changed beyond our wildest dreams.

Richard Vining, who was brought up in Costa Mesa and worked for the Monarch Oil Company in the summer of 1957, remembers that there was only one house on Adams Street from Brookhurst to Beach. It was a white Craftsmen Bungalow that belonged to the Bushard family. Richard also remembers the hot rivalry between the sports team from his school, Newport Harbor High, and Huntington Beach High School, especially the basketball teams.

Many long-time residents remember the huge thresher that sat along Newport Boulevard during the harvest season. For weeks the machine would run both day and night. It regularly spewed beans on the ground, and the company allowed the public to glean the beans and take them home.

As a young child in the 1950s, Dennis Johnson went to Huntington Beach each summer with his grandmother. She would rent a tent with a wood floor and spend the season on the beach. Dennis remembers that he and other children were taught how to dig for clams to use in the clam chowder his grandmother had simmering on the back burner of the cook stove each day.

The idea behind the "Then and Now" section is to illustrate the changes to the physical environment in Huntington Beach by comparing each historic photo with a present photograph. In 1950, the city looked much as it had during the previous 30 years. It was only in the mid-1950s that dramatic changes began to take place.

Some of the photos represent marked contrasts, while other show little difference between "then" and "now". It's fun to examine the old photos and say "I remember that!"

THEN1912

A popular destination for many Methodists and G.A.R. members was the tent city at the Methodist campgrounds. Revival meetings and encampments were held every summer at the site, bordered by Orange and Acacia, 11th and 13th streets.

Courtesy First American Title Insurance Company

NOW

The corner of Orange and 13th Street as it looks today.

Courtesy Marsh Collection

THEN1914

The concrete pier, constructed in 1914, has been a popular spot for fishermen, strollers and beachgoers for more than 80 years. The Streamlined Moderne shops were added in the 1930s.

Courtesy Marsh Collection

Pier - Huntington Beach, Cal

NOW

Volleyball is a popular sport at the beach these days.

Courtesy Marsh Collection

THEN1916

Long-time residents have found memories of the Carnegie Library, built in 1912 at the corner of Eighth and Walnut. It closed its doors in July of 1951, when the new library on Main Street was finished.

Courtesy First American Title Insurance Company

NOW

Apartments now occupy the corner where Carnegie Library stood.

Courtesy Marsh Collection

THEN 1920s

Shown in the 1920s, the pier area at the end of Main Street featured changing booths, a Saltwater Plunge and a dance hall.

Courtesy Marsh Collection

NOW

The pier entrance and promenade in 1998.

Courtesy Marsh Collection

THEN1930

This photo of the family and friends of Matthew Helme (seated at left with the white beard) was taken in front of the Helme House Furnishing Company on Walnut Avenue in about 1910.

Courtesy First American Title Insurance Company

NOW

The Helme Furniture Company building, now listed on the National Register of Historic Places, as it appears today.

Courtesy Marsh Collection

THEN1930

Looking up Main Street from the Pacific Coast Highway during the l930s, it is evident that Huntington Beach had become a well-established city.

Courtesy First American Title Insurance Co.

NOW

New buildings were constructed on each side of Main Street in the 1990s.

Courtesy Marsh Collection

THEN1936

This scene, on Harbor Boulevard, was typical of the thousands of acres of rich farmland that surrounded Orange County cities and towns. It was taken in 1936.

Courtesy First American Title Insurance Co.

NOW

The same scene, as it looks today.

Courtesy Marsh Collection

THEN1930s

The entrance to the pier, as it appeared in the 1930s. The dance hall is located on the right and the Pacific Electric Depot on the left.

NOW

A new restaurant has been built on the left and interlocking paving now covers the wide pier entrance.

Courtesy Marsh Collection

Partners in
Huntington
Beach

145

Patron — Unisource

(Photo on opposite page) Courtesy Marsh Collection

Building a greater Huntington Beach

147

Huntington Beach real estate, construction and
visitor service industries shape tomorrow's skyline,
while providing working and living space for people.

PCS Associates

Founded in the summer of 1992, PCS Associates rose up amid the rubble of the Los Angeles riots. Accompanied by armed guards, Patrick Howell and Chuck De La Mater walked through the ashes of burned buildings and devastation, rolled up their sleeves and began to rebuild a community.

From those early days in a one-room office in Westminster, California, where Patrick and Chuck sat face-to-face across two small borrowed desks, to the corporate office currently located in Huntington Beach, PCS Associates has experienced consistent growth. Year by year, careful planning and attention has allowed PCS to find and select its expanding personnel. The company now has branch offices in Canoga Park, Visalia and Dixon, and it is supported by a sales, marketing, accounting and administrative staff of approximately 120.

As a builder in the U.S. Navy Seabees, Patrick Howell received invaluable training under the strictest

PCS Associates rose up amid the rubble of the Los Angeles riots of 1992.

Patrick Howell learned much about construction from his stint in the U.S. Navy Seabees.

set of eyes. His early days in construction exposed him to all of the varying trades, which would remain separate in today's construction world. After being honorably discharged in 1976, he continued his career in construction throughout the country. By the close of that decade, he chose Huntington Beach as his home base and focused his efforts in the insurance restoration industry. He fine-tuned his management skills during the 1980s working as an estimator and project manager and lending his expertise as a construction consultant.

Today as owner and general partner, Mr. Howell develops the company's strategic business plan and oversees project design and development, sales, and project cost analysis.

Chuck De La Mater, also principal and partner, is a lifetime resident of Orange County. He attended Orange Coast College, California State University at Fullerton and the University of St. Louis. His educational knowledge in business and environmental issues is complemented by a diversified construction background, which includes experience in insurance restoration and the construction of multi-family residential complexes, commercial retail facilities, residential housing tracts and shopping centers.

With the establishment of PCS Associates, this marriage of talent combined more than 30 years of construction experience. Initially the firm focused its

attention toward the highly specialized field of insurance restoration of residential and commercial property.

What is insurance restoration? The term "restoration" has been adopted by the fire repair industry over the years to describe the techniques required for removal of smoke residue, odor, water damage and the treatment of personal property or building contents. When disaster strikes due to water, wind, fire, or other man-made and natural disasters, PCS Associates is able to provide full-service capabilities. It continues to develop and strengthen a special niche in the insurance restoration arena.

David Kasen, owner of the Key Drug Shopping Center located at the heart of the Los Angeles riots, had this to say about PCS Associates:

"I am certainly pleased with the recent work you performed. The quality of work was superb and the price was certainly reasonable. As you know, I have always been pleased with the super building that you constructed after the riots. Thank you for your service and friendship."

Following the riots and the rehabilitation of those damaged areas, Howell and De La Mater guided the growth of PCS Associates when it helped property owners with fire damage restoration in the Malibu and Pasadena areas. The Northridge earthquake of 1994 and the rains of El Niño during the spring of 1998 continued the company's rapid growth pace. Insurance carriers and adjustors consistently called upon its services to restore and rehabilitate distressed properties.

Inherent of its specialization, PCS Associates often enters the lives of property owners at very stressful times. Through a variety of emergency services, it can provide security, protect property from weather or

mitigate immediate damage. Estimators can then create a written scope of work identifying what it will take to restore the property to its original condition. Finally, specialized construction services are provided to accomplish the restoration, maintenance or repairs.

Essentially a full-service general engineering/building contractor, the company soon began to function as a one-stop turnkey solution for its residential and commercial clients. With multiple licenses in engineering, building, flooring and other specialty trades, PCS Associates consistently delivers performance, commitment and service to its construction clients. In addition, the company is an authorized dealer for Wedgcor, Inc., recognized as a world leader in steel building systems. It is staffed for the sale and construction of custom-designed steel buildings.

The leadership of PCS Associates envisioned a company composed of several stand-alone divisions. Today, each division operates with its own staff, equipment, technical expertise and specialization. Not

PCS Associates was instrumental in remodeling the Bushard fire station.

149

Patrick and Chuck cooking for the PCS staff at a company picnic

only is there an insurance restoration division, the original area of emphasis, but now there are also divisions for homeowners' association reconstruction, environmental, public works, consulting, and demolition and housemoving.

Fifty-foot holes were bored into bedrock to strengthen this foundational structure, which was weakened by storms and beach erosion.

with the insurance companies. Patrick Howell and Chuck De La Mater have built a company with in-house professionals capable of fixing the worst that Mother Nature can deliver from the roof to the foundation.

Jan Groshan, treasurer of the board of directors of one of PCS Associates' large building projects, offered these accolades when its construction was completed: "...The Board of Directors of Hazelwood Homeowners Association would like to take this opportunity to commend PCS on the work which it provided to us. During the difficult times of the project, it was comforting to know that all possible efforts were being made to minimize the disruption in the lives of our 48 homeowners. We want to thank you for the time you took to listen to each one of us and address our concerns."

Its homeowners association division is responsible for construction defect, deferred maintenance and

The insurance restoration division is responsible for 24-hour emergency services, negotiation of insurance claims, and the rehabilitation of damaged property. Emergency services can be accessed by call-in 24 hours a day, seven days a week. These services include loss mitigation and immediate repair/restoration services for the residential and commercial sectors. This division will tarp damaged roofs, provide water extraction services and demolish or shore up unsafe structures. With trained personnel and proper equipment, immediate efforts are made to minimize the loss of property and restore the victim's peace of mind. PCS Associates has successfully negotiated fair and impartial settlements for thousands of clients ranging from single-family dwelling homeowners to large condominium associations. It has the experience and sensitivity to fully understand the client's needs and the professionalism to talk directly

general maintenance. PCS Associates provides professional services to construction defect attorneys during the litigation process, which consists of expert witness testimony and forensic testing. Deferred maintenance includes putting together comprehensive estimates and financial packages to lessen the economic impact on the HOA. General maintenance consists of ongoing day-to-day service.

The environmental division and its affiliates are able to provide asbestos and lead abatement services. The public works division has been involved as a prime contractor at all jurisdictional levels of government work, including federal, state, county and municipal construction. PCS's team is an ideal candidate for minority or joint venture partnering.

This residential roof system was replaced after it was damaged by fire.

151

various committees and trade shows not only contributes to the promotion of these organizations but also gives the company opportunities to assist homeowners residing in properties managed by members of these organizations.

PCS Associates also co-sponsors "Construction Affairs," a weekly radio broadcast, on behalf of the Contractor's State License Board and the California Department of Consumer Affairs.

What are some of the goals and objectives for the future? With the visionary guidance of Patrick Howell and Chuck De La Mater, PCS Associates is consistently broadening its scope of activities for the 21st century. Mr. Howell speaks enthusiastically of working to develop opportunities for low-income housing in the United States and Third World countries, and the firm works hand-in-hand with affiliates of the company to create inventive and unique new products designed to reduce material and labor costs.

With a little financial creativity and imagination and a solid foundation of rehabilitation expertise, the Demolition and House Moving Division has literally made "the American dream" a reality to future property owners in the Central California Valley under the direction of American Dream Homes, a division of PCS Associates.

Through the efforts of its marketing staff, PCS Associates is an active participant in various trade organizations, such as the Community Associations Institute (CAI) and California Association of Community Managers (CACM). Its participation in

PCS Associates is much more than two contractors brought together in 1992 by the devastation and hardship experienced by a Los Angeles community. It is a concept that has come to fruition, a belief that has come to reality that a whole host of talented, dedicated men and women comprise the dynamic synergy of PCS Associates. All of those faces make up the true image of builders striving to pour firm foundations and raise sturdy walls that support the lives and futures of those who hand over a priceless commodity - their trust.

Huntington Beach Conference and Visitors Bureau

A spectacular ocean, a surfer poised on a board riding the curl of a wave and a long, sandy shoreline is a vision synonymous with the total California experience: Huntington Beach. It provides a paradise for surfers, swimmers and sun-soakers, yet was omitted from maps for years. The Huntington Beach Conference and Visitors Bureau, founded in 1990, turned that omission around with successful marketing putting Huntington Beach, Orange County's third largest city, on the map as a destination resort.

The city was known as a small ocean resort in the 1920s and 1930s, but when surfing became a California sport in the late 1940s and early 1950s, it attracted young surfers who came to experience riding the great rollers. The building boom of the late 50s further expanded Huntington Beach. Funded by the Transient Occupancy Tax added to the cost of motel and hotel room rental, the bureau answers thousands of inquiries each year. The use of brochures and well-placed media advertising has elicited a great response in selling the city and the entire region to travelers. The bureau feels there is no better place to stay when one wants the total California experience.

The bureau, working closely with city agencies and businesses, is instrumental in the development and building of the artfully planned Pier Plaza which features a 300-seat stone amphitheater accented by a stunning tile mural depicting the past and present of the city. Sporting competitions are a part of the seasonal events, and famous surfing legends are honored at the Surfing Walk of Fame on Main Street at Pacific Coast Highway. Great moments in the history of this sport are captured forever at the International Surfing Museum.

The bureau draws leisure travelers and tour groups by promoting all the attractions in the area. Guests can stay at the beach and take delightful side trips to exciting attractions like Disneyland, Knott's Berry Farm, The Queen Mary, Long Beach Aquarium of the Pacific and the Getty Museum. World-class shopping is close at South Coast Plaza in Costa Mesa and Fashion Island in Newport Beach, while a number of fine restaurants are within close proximity. Those who are nature lovers can observe more than 300 species of rare and endangered birds at the Bolsa Chica Ecological Reserve.

The Huntington Beach Conference and Visitors Bureau assists meeting planners and coordination of accommodations at local hotels. According to its statistics, the average attendee spends around $186 a day, a boost to the local economy during the winter months.

The Huntington Beach Conference and Visitors Bureau not only put Huntington Beach on the map, it has brought to light the city as a cultural and artistic center where guests and residents alike can bask in the unique heritage of this engaging city.

This tile wall mural designed by Terry Schoonhoven at Pier Plaza creates a memory of place. *Courtesy Robert Kinsler, City of Huntington Beach Public Information Office*

Pier Realty

Pier Realty takes its name from — what else — the famous Huntington Beach Pier. The business began in November 1982, founded by Tom Van Tuyl, Natalie Kotsch and Phil Benson. All three had many years of experience in the Huntington Beach, Fountain Valley real estate market and because of their love of the beach area and foresight into the changes that would be happening there, they decided to establish their own realty company.

Pier Realty is a well-known landmark of downtown Huntington Beach.

Originally, Pier Realty was located two blocks from the Huntington Beach Pier in the original Water Department Building. When it was torn down in 1988 or 1989, it set-up temporary quarters in the old health clinic and finally, moved into its present quarters in 1990. It is right downtown, in the center of the downtown area.

Since its inception, Pier Realty has seen many changes in downtown Huntington Beach. The real estate market has paralleled the changes in the city's history from an oil town to a surf city to a destination resort community.

In the early 1990s Pier had a brief association with ERA but when this ended in 1994, Jan Shomaker came into the business as an owner. Shomaker and Von Tuyl had known each other as past board presidents of the Association of Realtors and worked together quite well. At a Mayor's Dinner, Kotsch told Shomakler that they were terminating their association with ERA and asked if she would be interested in joining them. She jumped at the opportunity.

Shomaker brings to Pier Realty a wealth of local background. When she and her husband were married 31 years ago, they established their home in Huntington Beach and have been here as residents ever since. Their two children were born and raised in Huntington Beach, and they have been involved in the city's activities as a family for over 30 years.

At the time Pier Realty was established, it became a sort of pioneer in selling the downtown area. As a result, Van Tuyl, Kotsch and Shomaker are all respected by the city's movers and shakers. Kotsch is responsible for instituting the Surf Museum, and Shomaker is past

Planning Commissioner and chairman of the Planning Commission. Pier Realty is well-known by the city building people, planning people and administrative officials. It is actively participating in the downtown improvements and working to establish Huntington Beach as a destination resort city.

A unique feature of Pier Realty is its "walk-in" business. For example, Shomaker tells the story of a couple walking in one day when she was in the office. They said they were from back East and were here on vacation. They were having lunch across the street and decided to see what sort of properties were available for a second home. Shomaker joined them for lunch, and two days later, they bought a vacation home.

"This happens all the time," smiled Shomaker. "Working at Pier Realty is like working in a vacation resort. I walk out the door of my office, and I see the Pacific Ocean. What a great place to have fun, play in the sand and even work!"

Walk-in business is common at Pier Realty.

TEAM Construction Management

owntown Huntington Beach has undergone a significant transformation during the last 20 years. Once a sleepy surfing community with a handful of tourist shops and aging buildings, the entire Main Street shopping district has been revitalized. Old, unsafe structures have been structurally retrofitted or replaced with newer buildings, helping create the village atmosphere and a new sense of community. TEAM Construction Management has been there since the beginning of this renaissance.

TEAM … [provides] a single source for designing and constructing buildings.

TEAM designed and built its corporate offices downtown in the building many locals identify with its Starbuck's Coffee tenant. This popular corner landmark building helped establish TEAM's presence in Downtown Huntington Beach.

In addition, TEAM has worked on and built many other Main Street buildings, including 24-Hour Fitness, Perq's, George's Surf Shop, Rocky Mountain Chocolate Factory, Huntington Beach Beer Company, Candy Baron, Huntington Beach Art Center, Westbay Cafe and many others.

TEAM Construction Management is a design-build company based on the idea of the "master builder" providing a single source for designing and constructing buildings. Principals Jeff Bergsma and Michael Fein believe this has given their company a competitive edge, a more efficient operation, and greater accountability and control over the outcome.

With in-house architects and engineers, TEAM has been able to express its ideas in noteworthy structures that dot the landscape of this eclectic coastal community. Fein and Bergsma have influenced the city's environment in a way that demonstrates a sincere concern for its future.

With several exciting and challenging projects in the works, TEAM's legacy should endure well into the next century.

154

TEAM's Main Street Huntington Beach office

Jeff Bergsma, founder and president (top), and Michael Fein, chief executive officer

Peter's Landing

Situated along the scenic stretch of the Pacific Coast Highway that separates Huntington Harbor from the city of Seal Beach, Peter's Landing is undoubtedly one of the region's most unique retail and entertainment destinations.

A weekend visit to the long-standing J. Dee's Landing Bar & Grille only reinforces Coulter's assessment. The restaurant was once largely a popular retreat for boat owners to gather and recount their adventures on the high seas at the end of the day.

Office spaces, specialty retail stores and restaurants reside in the two-story, L-shaped structure that embraces a picturesque marina populated by sleek seafaring watercraft and recreational vessels of all shapes and sizes.

Although there are many other marinas in the area, boaters have long recognized Peter's Landing and Huntington Harbor as a preferred dockside locale.

"Peter's Landing is a place where people can come to enjoy the water and retail environment that epitomize the Southern California experience," says John Coulter, owner of California Property Management, which manages the waterfront landmark's office and retail spaces.

Since its inception in 1980, the site has served as home to a number of popular restaurants, bars and nightclubs. Although Coulter admits to a high turnover in the retail space during the mid-1990s in response to a fluctuating economy, he adds that Peter's Landing has since emerged as a major entertainment and dining destination.

Today, the marina fixture is often filled to capacity with locals and tourists alike who flock to the informal eatery for good food and drink, the live entertainment of jazz musicians, pop bands or even karaoke performers, and an atmosphere infused by the gentle rocking of boats in the harbor and the salty sea air.

Business & Finance

Investment banking and securities brokerage,

insurance and diversified holding companies

provide a financial foundation for a host of

Huntington Beach companies.

Fabian Financial Services and Fabian Investment Resources

The Fabian Plan is the story of a family legacy, two generations pulling together to attain one dream. For the Fabians, the dream was to develop a simple investment plan for any American who wanted to build wealth over the long term. Not only has the Fabian family achieved this goal, but made it possible for many others.

It began when Dick Fabian discovered that most individuals who invested in the market for long periods of time made little or no money due to their emotions, bad advice and bad investments. Believing that the investor was more important than the investment, his goal was to teach people how to successfully grow their money, without the help of commissioned salespeople. To that end, Dick researched, wrote and self-published *How to Be Your Own Investment Counselor* which explained a simple, two-rule plan he called the Fabian Compounding Plan. As an experiment, on the last page of this book, he wrote that interested parties could send $79 for a year's subscription of his newsletter. Needless to say, the book touched a cord among the investment public, and after receiving hundreds of checks, Dick launched Telephone Switch Newsletter in April, 1977.

Dick based the newsletter's original name, "Telephone Switch Newsletter," on a revolutionary concept in 1977: the investor's ability to move money between various mutual funds simply by making a telephone call. This new tool allowed him to put his investment plan to work since investors could easily switch money in and out of the market as needed for profit and safety.

Using Dick's plan, investors buy and sell no-load mutual funds following the market's trend. When the trend is up, a "Buy" signal is generated, and investors move their money to stock mutual funds. When the market is in a downtrend, a "Sell" signal is generated, and investors move their money to the safety of money market funds. In addition to the monthly newsletter, Fabian subscribers can receive these buy and sell signals by phone, fax and e-mail.

For those who didn't wish to direct their investments, Dick established a money management company called Fabian Financial Services in 1981 which executes trades following his simple approach. Today the company manages over $150 million for individuals and corporations.

Dick's son Doug joined the family business in 1978, working for his parents in downtown Huntington Beach. In those days, the whole family pitched in, including Dick and Doug, Dick's mother, Mickey; his wife, Marie; his daughter Mary Jayne; and his son, Gary. Marie made lunch while they sat around the dining room table preparing the newsletter to mail.

In 1989, Doug succeeded his father as president of Telephone Switch Newsletter, and in 1991, his sister Mary Jayne Fabian Barnett joined him as co-editor. As the industry grew, so too did the business

Fabian's original manual from 1977

How To Be Your Own Investment Counselor

Through The Use Of "Telephone Switch" Mutual Funds

EASY to Understand
SIMPLE to Operate

The Fabian Family:
(Top) Doug, Mary Jayne
Barnett, Gary; (Bottom)
Marie, Mickey, Dick

which eventually moved from Marie's dining room table to larger Huntington Beach offices. In 1993, the monthly newsletter was expanded to 12 pages as more how-to and educational articles were added. To reflect this broadened editorial scope and additional investment plans, its name was changed to Fabian Premium Investment Resource. An estimated one billion dollars in individual investors' money now follows the Fabian Plan, and the Fabian Investment Resources company has grown to include four lines of financial services products.

In 1994, Mary Jayne left the newsletter to become vice president of Fabian Financial Services, and today is a writer and popular investment speaker along with Dick and Doug at Money Shows across the country.

Dick and Doug can be seen on numerous financial programs including *Wall Street Week*, CNBC, CNN-FN and Fox Cable News. They are also regularly featured in the *Wall Street Journal, Barron's, Money* magazine, *USA Today, New York Times* and *Forbes*.

When the original "How to be Your Own Investment Counselor" went to press in 1977, it introduced a unique investment philosophy and lifestyle, one that would have turned a $100, investment in April 1977 to $2.7 million as of March, 1998. Today, the newsletter reaches over 30,000 subscribers worldwide and was rated number one on a timing-only, risk adjusted basis over the long term by *Hulbert Financial Digest*, a publication which tracks the performance of invest- ment newsletters. Fabian investors have attained their financial goals. But more than that, they have peace of mind, investment simplicity and compounded growth working for them which together form the foundation for building wealth the Fabian way.

Mulligan's Properties

Gary Mulligan, owner of Mulligan's Properties, is a man who wears many hats. He is also a man who has looked into his own private crystal ball and predicted tremendous growth and redevelopment in the city of Huntington Beach, to which he has contributed no small part.

In 1974, Mulligan purchased a business called Gospel Swamp. It was a beer bar located at 117 Main Street, and it took its name from the first historic name for Huntington Beach, Gospel Swamp. Everyone told Mulligan he was crazy to purchase a rundown business like this and, at times, he wondered if perhaps they were right. Main Street was far from a picturesque street at that time. Three or four of the buildings were boarded up. At night the 40 watt light bulbs in the street lamps did little to light up the street. It was so dark you couldn't see two feet in front of you.

However, Mulligan stuck to his guns and changed the name of the bar to the Main Street Saloon. He worked hard, and the business did well. The next year, with the assistance of Dr. Loren Johnson (who had helped him with the saloon purchase), Mulligan and Johnson purchased the building itself. Later research revealed the building to be one of the oldest on Main Street, constructed in 1909.

Once the bar was a success, it was only one more step for Mulligan to become actively involved in the redevelopment of the city, an action long overdue in the minds of many residents and businessmen. He worked on the Redevelopment Project Committee from 1976 to 1977. Redevelopment was the key word during this period, and one and all advised him that in five years, Huntington Beach would be a really great town.

Mulligan worked with the staff of the Redevelopment Project and with city officials and helped develop a coastal plan which was then submitted to the Coastal Commission. Once approved, the plan was returned to the city as Huntington Beach's Coastal Plan and officials went to work to implement it.

Now Mulligan was running a bar, working with redevelopment and city officials, and as if that wasn't enough, he became vice president of Fox Development, a company which built houses and apartments throughout Huntington Beach.

In the early 1980s Mulligan became involved with the Maid/Pieu Project Committee and was active in the downtown redevelopment planning. In 1981, he opened his own real estate office, Mulligan's Properties which is still going strong today.

In 1983 when he obtained his hard liquor license, Mulligan changed the name of the bar to Perq's. The word is taken from the French "perquisites" meaning rewards or gratuities.

Perq's underwent a retrofit in 1998. The old building has been brought up to standard for seismic requirements. All new electrical, plumbing, flooring and bathrooms have been installed. Although the building has been basically gutted and redone, the original bar remains. The upstairs now includes a front balcony with a view of the pier and another balcony in the back where customers can relax, enjoy a drink and take in a view of the fabulous sand, white water and sunset for which Huntington Beach is renowned.

Mulligan has seen the plans he worked on for the redevelopment of Huntington Beach come into being. He has maintained and prepared an historical building and watering hole to move into the 21st century. He has made a big difference in Huntington Beach. But as he modestly puts it, "It's been scary, but fun!"

Courtesy Debbie Stock

161

Manufacturing & Distributing

In addition to providing and distributing an astounding variety of goods for individuals and industry, area manufacturing and distributing companies also provide employment for Huntington Beach residents.

Budnik Wheels

A golden yellow 94 Chevy C1500 Extended Cab truck, transformed from an ordinary truck into an extraordinary vision, is one of Alan Budnik's latest creations at Budnik Wheels where he owns the business which produces top of the line rims, steering wheels and trim accessories and is now expanding into truck/SUV grills and other accessories.

Alan Budnik cannot remember a time in his life when he wasn't fascinated by cars, hot rods, motorcycles, virtually anything on wheels. When he was a 17- year-old high school student in Texas, he got a part-time job after school working at a machine shop where he learned to machine parts out of steel and aluminum. It was at this small shop that Budnik was introduced to computer controlled machinery, and from this beginning, he has progressed to designing all his wheels using CAD-CAM technology.

Budnik worked his way up the ranks but soon realized if he continued doing job shop work, producing other people's designs for them, he would never be in control of his own destiny. The shop was mainly doing oil field work, and when the oil industry crashed the shop was heavily hit. Budnik had been attending the University of Texas studying for an engineering degree. But in his heart, he was yearning to start his own business. He knew if he just had the opportunity he could use his experience in machining and fabricating to start his own product line.

In July, 1986, Budnik moved from Texas to California to help someone else start another wheel company. He worked there for two years and when he

left, he began his own company machining aircraft parts. By 1989, however, he was ready to make the big leap, and he started Budnik Wheels, originally located in Fountain Valley. By 1992 he needed more space and moved Budnik Wheels into Huntington Beach. Initially, the business occupied half the building but grew rapidly and took over the other half. Today, Budnik is looking for quarters large enough to double the current space.

Budnik Wheels offers over 35 road wheel designs and 17 split grip steering wheel designs, with new designs always in the works. In the copycat custom wheel business, Budnik Wheels has never copied designs. Alan does most of the designing personally. He has come a long way from doodling cars and designs on his school notebook covers to the high level of technology he utilizes in his business.

Alan Budnik cannot remember a time in his life when he wasn't fascinated by cars, hot rods, motorcycles, virtually anything on wheels.

Alan has always relied on creating new designs. The customer is the start of the design process, and this customizing sets Budnik apart in the industry. The customer can choose any combination of style, diameter and offset, making almost limitless combinations. Budnik himself likes to do difficult parts because they present more creative challenge. His expertise in design combines many years of knowledge about cars and machining. "I try to design wheels that look good, that are strong and that can be readily machined, polished and easily maintained," Budnik explained.

Budnik Wheels also produces steering wheels. Traditionally steering wheels were covered with wrapped leather stitched around the outer rim. However, if a thread breaks and starts to unravel, it is the death of the steering wheel. Budnik

164

Budnik Wheels transformed this golden yellow 94 Chevy C1500 Extended Cab truck into a real beauty.

Budnik Wheels is proud to
make its home in
Huntington Beach.

designed the Split Grip® steering wheel. The back of the product is aluminum and the front is leather. The leather actually tucks into an attached ring so there is no stitching to unravel. Following the success of the Split Grip Steering Wheel, Budnik created the Budnik oval horn button for which he received a U.S. patent.

Budnik Wheels attends many trade shows, car shows and street rod events all around the country. The business advertises in national magazines such as specialty automotive and hot rod magazines, and truck and sport utility magazines that cater to the truck and sport utility market. Budnik products are sold to individuals and to dealers all around the country, including dealers who purchase for export to such places as Japan.

The most recent development of Budnik Wheels is its Project Vehicle division which Budnik began to make a truck that would showcase the wheels. In the process, his came up with some new product ideas, and the end product was the evolutionary C/K Ducati Hauler, featured on the cover of the May 1998 issue of *Sport Truck Magazine* and the Budnik Camaro on the cover of the June, 1998 issue of *Popular Hot Rodding*.

Alan Budnik is a man who is as proud of his company as he is of his family, who has a passion for success and a desire to maintain an equal balance in life coupled with service to his customers and to his staff. The Budnik Wheels facility is maintained in a state of almost hospital cleanliness and efficiency.

"I try to design wheels that look good, that are strong and that can be readily machined, polished and easily maintained."

In 1989 when he was just starting out on his own, Budnik went to the NSRA Nationals with his first four original wheel designs, along with a wheel rack he designed and built to make his mark. Today, he is a man in control of his destiny, a man who has met his goals by insisting on quality — quality which keeps the doors open to customers who know the difference.

Ezernet, Inc.

Founded in 1993 by Huntington Beach residents Seiji Steve Oyama and his wife Katharine, Ezernet Inc. embodies the dream of this couple to establish a firm that facilitates business relationships across cultures. It enjoys a sterling reputation within the exporting industry.

The Huntington Beach company initially focused on shipping American and European motor vehicles customized for the Japanese market. It diversified its product line to include sporting goods, clothing, institutional seating, and home and giftware items. Whatever the need or request, Ezernet is committed to servicing the client.

Currently, Ezernet has developed direct distribution agreements with several U.S. manufacturers to further broaden its product line to include after-market auto parts, auto care parts, gourmet kitchen products, crafts supplies and religious giftware items.

Company founders Seiji Steve Oyama and his wife Katharine

"We believe our first responsibility is to the individuals who use our products and services."

Given the backgrounds of the founding partners, this is indeed an amazing business venture. Steve Oyama earned a master's degree in divinity from Tokyo Graduate School of Theology and a master's degree in theology from Fuller Theological Seminary in Pasadena. His intent was to devote himself to the Christian min-

istry. He served as an associate minister at a Japanese church in downtown Los Angeles and did preparatory work toward starting a church in Torrance before commencing his current entrepreneurial endeavor.

His wife and business partner, Kathy, majored in Japanese studies at Washington University in St. Louis and worked with a student ministry group for two years after graduation. Upon relocating to Southern California, she taught cooking classes and ran her own tutoring company until she joined forces with her husband to make Ezernet a reality.

Although the venue has changed, the couple's commitment to living a life of faith remains the same. They strive to run their business according to biblical principles, characterized by honesty and integrity. Both Kathy and Steve feel strongly that their primary mission is to bring a Christian dimension to all that they do. They highly value the relationships they have with their clients and vendors and seek to make each person feel that he or she is precious to them.

With the international heritage of its founders, the firm is uniquely qualified to serve as a two-way ambassador between the marketplaces of the United States and Japan.

"We're essentially serving to build a bridge between American and Japanese companies and economies," say Steve and Kathy. "We want to help facilitate North American firms that desire to do business in Japan and assist them by not only translating the language, but also the culture of the

The Ezernet Team (L to R): Sandra, Susan, Brock, Steve, Mari, Shoji and Fumi

Seiji and Kathy Oyama say their company mission is to "build a bridge between American and Japanese companies and economies."

167

country. We work as a kind of international marriage counselor as we bring American and Japanese firms together in business relationships, bringing out the best in each as they partner together. We named our company 'Ezernet' from the Hebrew Ezer, which means 'helper, protector' to portray our desire to facilitate business relationships across cultures."

The Oyamas are quick to attribute the growing company's success to its personnel, who possess "a long history of efficient administrative and innovative marketing skills, as well as an unparalleled level of customer service, state-of-the-art technology, and cutting-edge product development." Each employee is a valued member of the company's team, working toward the shared goals and values that define the firm.

For the long term, Ezernet's founders envision continued development of the firm's distribution network in Japan and protection of the reputation and integrity of the manufacturers and products it represents. Ezernet intends to pursue exclusive distributorships of high quality products that the Oyamas feel will succeed in the Japanese marketplace. Also in development are plans to begin importing and distributing products from Japan that they feel will find a place in the American market.

"We will achieve our mission by providing innovative, practical, and top-quality products. We believe our first responsibility is to the individuals who use our products and services. In carrying out our day-to-day business, we strive to treat our employees with respect, dignity and encouragement and we follow the philosophy that our customers come first and deserve our best service."

Through its long-term commitment to this philosophy, Ezernet will undoubtedly continue to earn its reputation as a company that works hard to ensure that its products are of the highest quality, delivered in a timely fashion at a fair price.

House of Batteries

When customers visit the House of Batteries they realize immediately there's a lot more to the world of batteries than just the pink Energizer Bunny. A lot more! Not only can House of Batteries provide the usual batteries, but its inventory includes over 5,000 different batteries such as those for concert halls, portable dental equipment, freeway call boxes, missile launch/tracking equipment, robots and skydiving instrumentation to name only a few of the more esoteric items in stock. It has batteries that go into clones which are dragged behind airplanes for the Air Force to shoot down with their missiles and they have batteries that go in the buoys out in the ocean. In fact, the motto at House of Batteries is "Batteries for Every Electronic Application."

House of Batteries is owned by Don West, president, and Maggie West, chief executive officer. The business is a family endeavor, with Maggie's father and sister also on staff. Serving as "vice president" (complete with business card) is the family's pet dog, Kelsey.

Initially, Don became involved in the field when he joined his father's manufacturer's representative company in 1971. It evolved into a fairly large manufacturer's rep company and is still flourishing today as West Electronic Sales Team. About 20 years ago, West Electronic Sales Team represented Yuasa, a Japanese manufacturer of batteries. West represented one segment of their product, sealed lead acid batteries which are used in emergency lighting and uninterruptible power supplies such as in battery backup systems and security equipment.

> *"...the goal of House of Batteries is not to be the largest battery distributor, but the best."*

At that time, House of Batteries was a customer of West Electronic Sales Team. The business began in 1965 in Costa Mesa. In the course of his business dealings with them, Don got to know the owner fairly well. House of Batteries was primarily a storefront retail business, a sort of mom-and-pop operation. However, because of Don's experience in the electronics industry with the rep business, he knew there was a real growth opportunity with House of Batteries. It was a gamble, but in 1989, Maggie and Don decided to take the plunge and buy it.

Batteries! Batteries! Batteries! More than anyone can imagine.

168

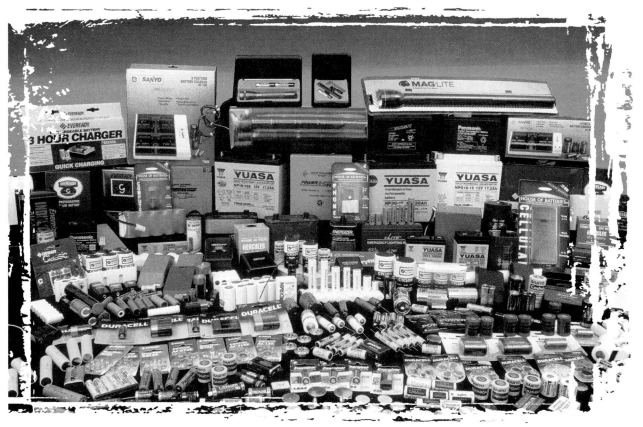

The Wests launched their new endeavor on January 1, 1990. The 1989/1990 holiday season was quite hectic for the Wests what with handling the paper work involved in the purchase as well as doing an inventory of the stock. Although the inventory they acquired was quite large, they discovered a lot of the batteries were either dead or obsolete and had to be disposed of.

Maggie West and her father started working for House of Batteries immediately, supported by about six employees. The business was still primarily retail. The facilities had no heating and no air conditioning. They were dependent upon kerosene heaters for warmth (which affected the staff's breathing) and open doorways for cooling (which meant the breezes blew dirt into the store). The Wests felt the facility was archaic and there was no room for growth.

In early 1991, the Wests found their current building and moved in on April 1, 1991. A month later, Don moved the manufacturer's rep company to a building down the street. West Electronic Sales Team now represents 18 different companies and continues to grow.

House of Batteries provides the batteries for such companies as Disneyland, Knott's Berry Farm, Warner Brothers Studios, movie and TV studios for their portable camera equipment, Hughes Aircraft and the City of Los Angeles. All the Huntington Beach police and Huntington Beach firemen buy their batteries from House of Batteries. West estimates they have about 50 city contracts.

Not only does it sell its stock locally but also nationally to the tune of about 6,000 customers all over the United States. The business has a national 800 numbers as well as a Web site from which orders are received almost daily. It is a source for hard to find batteries which are not stocked in retail stores such as Circuit City and because it is a high volume distributor, it can also offer very low prices.

The Wests, who make their home in Huntington Beach, are active participants in local affairs including Orangewood Charity for abused children, Orange County Alzheimer's Disease chapter and Huntington Beach First Christian Church. Don is a member of Huntington Beach Sunrise Rotary Club, is past president of the Electronic Representatives Association, past president of the Electronic Distribution Show, past chairman of the Board of Wescon show (the largest electronic components show in the U.S.) and past president of Radio Pioneers. The Wests have been involved in electronic organizations for many years and are currently members of the National Electronic Distribution Association. They are also members of RBRC (Rechargeable Battery Recycling Corporation) which is a recycling program. Customers who buy

Don and Maggie West are the powerhouse team that owns House of Batteries.

nickel cadmium and lead acid batteries from the House of Batteries can bring back their spent batteries which are then sent for recycling.

House of Batteries provides the batteries for such companies as Disneyland, Knott's Berry Farm, Warner Brothers Studios, movie and TV studios for their portable camera equipment, Hughes Aircraft and the City of Los Angeles.

Don and Maggie West are enthusiastic about the future growth of House of Batteries. In 1997, they opened a sales office in Northern California and they opened an office in San Diego in 1998. They have manufacturer's reps selling for them all over the United States and do quite a bit of exporting to South America, Europe, even Africa and Asia.

Since those early days, their staff has expanded to about 36 employees. As Maggie emphasized, "Our staff are very important to us. We have some very loyal people who have stayed with us through the years, and we appreciate them very much." Both Maggie and Don West point out that the goal of House of Batteries is not to be the largest battery distributor, but the best.

Lulu's Dessert Factory

If you happen to be driving on the freeway you might see an attractive truck featuring the silhouette of a little girl holding out a plate of dessert and the name LuLu's Dessert Factory. If so, you have received your first introduction to a unique manufacturing company in the city of Huntington Beach.

LuLu's Dessert Factory produces a tasty dessert in the form of ready-to-eat cups of flavored gelatin. These cups, filled with jewel-like colors of gelatin, can be found in the deli-refrigerated section of nearly every major market in California as well as in 28 other states. In fact, LuLu's is the first company in California to manufacture ready-to-eat gelatin.

The company is the result of hard work and a very bright idea by its owner, Maria de Lourdes Sobrino, known to her family and friends as "Lulu." Maria immigrated to the United States from Mexico and was determined to start up a business of her own. After some market research, she was amazed to discover that there was no gelatin dessert product available in the Los Angeles area, a very popular dessert in Mexico. Using her mother's gelatin recipes, Maria made a batch of gelatin desserts and distributed samples to neighbors and friends. The overwhelmingly positive response convinced her that this was the product for her, and she began production in a 700-square-foot retail store in Torrance, making everything by hand.

At first, Maria's gelatins were made in large ring molds and were sold primarily for parties and to families. However, after three months, she began making individual cups and distributed them in independent "mom & pop" stores in Hispanic neighborhoods where gelatin desserts were already known and desired. She was still making the cups by hand, pouring the liquid from jars.

In building LuLu's, Maria faced several challenges, not the least of which was making her gelatin desserts well-known. Also, she had no contacts to purchase ingredients wholesale so she was incurring unnecessary expense by buying sugar and other needed items at the grocery stores. But she was determined this would be a successful business. She sold her desserts on consignment, delivering her product in the morning, and very soon discovered they were sold out by the afternoon.

At the end of her first year in 1983, Maria connected with Concept Food Brokers who agreed to broker LuLu's, and the business began to expand. Maria developed her gelatin formulas with chemists and food processing people and within five years, she had attained the high quality and long shelf-life (upwards of 120 days) that exist today. From that first year of making 300 cups a day by hand, the company has grown to today's more than 50 million cups a year using state-of-the-art equipment.

By 1985, LuLu's had outgrown its location and moved to a 3,000-square-foot industrial building in Gardena. At this time, the company was also making other items such as roasted peanuts and carrots spiced with jalapenos. However, the demand for the gelatins was so strong, these other products were dropped. In 1988, Maria was approved for an SBA loan for a new location and to expand. Maria found the exact building she had in mind in the city of Huntington Beach, a 15,000-square-foot building with refrigeration.

LuLu's has grown so rapidly, with over 13 brokerage companies and distribution nearly nationwide, that

Maria is again looking at the need to expand. However, this time she is designing her own plant, which will have all the space LuLu's needs to continue to develop new products for the millennium.

As if running this successful company was not enough, in 1990 Maria started another company, along with Salvatore Titone, called Fancy Fruit Corporation. Fancy Fruit are frozen fruit bars or "Paletas" as they are commonly known throughout Mexico and South America. They are currently available in 14 delicious all-natural flavors. Fancy Fruit is sharing the Huntington Beach facility with LuLu's Desserts and is marketed worldwide. Some of the countries that already carry it are England, Australia, New Zealand, Chile, Canada and Korea. They can be found in single servings through convenience stores and small markets as well as in four-pack boxes through supermarkets and larger stores.

LuLu's has achieved a national reputation for gourmet gelatins, over 40 different varieties in sizes and flavors. Included are items for children's portions and tastes to meet more sophisticated adult requirements. In 1999, flan, pudding and ringmolds were introduced. Just as she did in the early days, Maria counts on taste tests of new products to ensure her companies put out the freshest-tasting products available.

Maria states "Our success is due to the support and enthusiasm from our employees, family and

friends." She would like everyone to try her products and discover that they truly are "More Fun For Your Spoon."™LuLu's products are available in Vons, Ralphs, Albertson's, Food 4 Less, Wal-Mart and Stater Bros. as well as in many other small independent markets. Just look for LuLu's Desserts in the deli section.

Mepco/Huntington Beach Machining

Dean and Lauretta Madsen

T oday, stepping out the front door of Mepco/Huntington Beach Machining one can see the vast industrial centerpiece the area has become. Back in 1975 when Mepco/Huntington Beach Machining opened its doors there was only one other machine shop in town. At that time, barren dirt fields surrounded the shop. Like Huntington Beach, the machine shop has grown and prospered in a nurturing technological environment.

Small family-run businesses are the heart of industrial Huntington Beach and this father and son machine shop epitomizes that axiom. Two enterprising men, Dean and Bob Madsen saw the need for good quality products produced to exact company specifications and opened their own shop to fulfill that shortage.

Dean worked for Northrop Corporation for many years. Bob, having graduated from Whittier College with a physics degree, worked awhile for both Northrop and Lockheed Aircraft. He decided to try a different approach to production and went to work for his uncle, Glenn Madsen, who owned his own machine shop.

Glenn trained Bob in the essential elements of machining. With that knowledge, Bob attacked each assignment looking for an improved production method. Bob enjoyed the challenge of taking a customer's problem and designing a component to fill that need. He learned how to take the process to its conclusion by manufacturing the product. That experience would help him make a success of his own business.

After deciding to open their shop, Bob and Dean began to search for equipment. With a limited budget, they heard about some used machinery for sale in Aguanga (Riverside County). When they arrived, the man walked them out behind his house to the barn. Amidst the mice and cobwebs, old lathes and mills sat unused, waiting for some imagination and ingenuity. They loaded and trucked the machines up to Huntington Beach. Huntington Beach Machining was ready to open.

They started business with one employee, a part-time high school student, and 1,750 square feet. Their first customer needed a valve cage for use in a steam cleaner. A month after opening, their big break came when a friend had a problem at his restaurant. Gordon Nichols could not get his five gallon plastic pails of sour cream open. Dean, in conjunction with Bob, searched for a product with the proper design capability. Nothing existed. So they set to work and after extensive research, developed the "Lid-Off," an opener specifically designed for the pails.

They patented "Lid-Off" and Mepco was born. To this day, it remains at the cornerstone of their business. Huntington Beach Machining became the job shop. They hired experienced machinists who could take engineering plans, interpret them and manufacture the product. Working with lathes and mills, the Madsens designed and produced components for aircraft, hydraulic fittings for water pumps and rivet pullers for repairing government aircraft and tanks.

Word-of-mouth advertising proved successful and their business grew and prospered. But because of the complexity of operating the machinery, they were finding it harder and harder to find qualified people. In 1981, they began buying new computerized machines that would change the way they did business. Now, a skilled set-up man could keep several people busy operating different machines. The Madsens began investing in equipment as well as paychecks.

A business that began by hand-making every part had progressed to a variation on mass production. The birth of computers improved quality, increased output and reduced costs. The industry evolved from "turning handles into pushing buttons."

Productivity went up and, along with it, customer satisfaction. They could now manufacture a better product in less time often cutting costs for the client and ultimately the end user. Huntington Beach Machining regards each product with a pride of ownership stemming from attention to detail, cutting unnecessary costs and making products reliable.

In 1986 Dean passed away leaving Bob to carry on the traditions he and his father had worked so hard to support. Along with the growth of the town, Huntington Beach Machining strengthened its base by including Bob's son, Erik. In 1989, they moved to their present location and enlarged their shop space to almost 12,000 square feet.

Carrying on the traditions of the past two generation, Erik expanded the business and developed products in new areas. Utilizing his math and computer science degrees, he began by automating data collection and providing better control of finances. Erik's expertise as a musician prompted him to fashion components for guitars and drums.

Mepco/Huntington Beach Machining in Huntington Beach

earthquake-prone California homes are honed and refined in the shop.

Mepco/Huntington Beach Machining is not just about products. People have played an important role in its progress. Treating their company like a ministry, the Madsens have helped rehabilitate people recently released from jail. The satisfaction of being able to help others is their true reward. And, sometimes, it comes unexpectedly as the former employee who came back five years after leaving his job just to thank Bob for giving him the time to get his life back together.

To counteract the industrialization of the business, Mepco/Huntington Beach Machining focuses on helping the area's youth understand and learn about the business of machining. They contact local area high schools and colleges and offer an internship program for any person interested in engineering. They also give local area young people, uncertain of their future goals, direction and guidance by hiring them and providing them with an opportunity to decide what path they want to take.

The humanitarian efforts of the family-run business nourish loyalty from their employees. Of the 21 people presently employed, many have been there 10 to 20 years, preferring to stay with the unique company.

The owners of Huntington Beach Machining opened their business with the concept of a team effort where everyone could derive benefit. They give people an opportunity to be part of and to reinforce a positive work ethic. They continue to strive to meet their goals and contribute to their town. They have more than met their expectations.

In turn, Huntington Beach has seen a stable and reliable machine shop offer secure jobs, provide dependable products and lend support to its community environment.

The shop continues to broaden its product line with dental hand pieces and air bag units. Today, roller blade components, carbon fiber products, motorcycle parts, hydraulic fittings for aircraft and water pumps and monthly output of 10,000 gas shutoff valves for

The "Lid-Off" grabs the lids off plastic pails that contain everything from sour cream to fertilizer.

173

Realys

In 1985, when Lisa Crowther, her friend Zoe Falley, and Zoe's husband Mikey Falley told people they were going into the nail abrasives business, people said "Really? You're really going to do that? Really?!" This happened so frequently, that finally Lisa, Zoe and Mikey decided to name their new business "Realys," an acclamation to their endeavor. Now, some 13 plus years later, if the same "Really?" spouters could be told of the enormous success of this business, their "Realys!" would be 10 feet tall.

Zoe Falley was a licensed cosmetologist when she and friend Lisa began discussing what kind of business they could go into together. At the time, Mikey had just finished working for another company that was in a similar business. Not only was he familiar with this type of business, but he liked it. He suggested that Lisa and Zoe open a manufacturing company, and he would come to work for them. They agreed, and Realys, Inc. was launched.

Realys has always been located in Huntington Beach. It first opened its doors in a small 1,700-square-foot office on Slater Avenue. It had one machine, and Lisa, Zoe and Mikey were the employers and the employees. It started making parts, and soon they started growing. The owners purchased a second machine, then a third machine and before they knew it, they had outgrown their little office space. The company moved to a 4,000-square-foot building on Gothard Street, but after adding more machines and more employees, it was ready to expand again after three years. This time Realys moved up the street to Gothard Street, and in no time, it added the adjoining building for more space, giving them a total of 17,000 square feet. Soon the company had to expand so it added the adjoining building on Gothard. Three more years passed and once again, Realys was shopping for more space. The owners found their current location on Woodwind Drive, and decided it was perfect. When it moved, it had 29,000 square feet, but with the company growing every day, soon it was cramped. Another building was found, just a few doors away, adding 11,000 square feet. Now Realys has 90 employees to work in its 40,000 square feet, and it just keeps on growing.

Realys' primary products are tools for the professional manicurist, including nail files, buffer sticks and buffer blocks. The convenient 4-way buffers have the advantage of a 3-way buffer plus a file in one tool, making manicures easier and more efficient. Each buffer comes with directions for usage printed on each part for added simplicity. There are also 3-way buffers with a side for filing nail edges and removing ridges, another side for smoothing the nail surface and a third side for a super shine. The files are for use on acrylic or natural nails. Round sanders are also available for contouring all natural and acrylic nail surfaces.

In addition to files and buffer sticks, Realys produces foot files for smoothing rough skin and removing calluses. A cuticle treatment made from all natural ingredients and enriched with Vitamin E, jojoba and coconut is also available. The ointment's quick-penetrating formula promotes healthier cuticles. Realys also makes toe separators and distributes items such as nail tips and nail glue. No product manufactured by Realys is tested on animals.

One unique feature of Realys' products is that they are washable. When the files are not shining the nail any longer, it is an indication that the tiny holes are filled up with nail filings. Realys' files can be placed in water, brushed lightly, and they will be good as new again. In professional nail salons, they can be placed in a sanitizer or disinfectant wash, a great advantage in an industry which has to guard against infection producing tools.

Realys' products are manufactured for private label companies, although it does put its own label "Tropical Shine" on products sold as the house brand. But primarily, it sells to beauty supply chains.

Realys' products are sold through distribution to beauty supply houses who, in turn, sell the nail grooming imple-

ments to professional manicurists. They received appreciation awards from 1993-1996 from Sally Beauty Supply, one of the largest distributors in the United States. The company is known in the industry for the highest quality available and because of its reputation, it continues to expand throughout the United States and worldwide.

In addition to products for the beauty salon industry, Realys produces sanding blocks for hobby shop distributors featuring washable sandpaper. It sells some abrasives to hardware distributors, guitar stores and distributors for motorcycle manufacturer Harley-Davidson.

The Realys' success story is a tribute to the city of Huntington Beach which has always made sure that the business was well taken care of. Realys has been featured on "Made in Huntington Beach" a local television program. Most Realys employees live in Huntington Beach and walk to work. It is also a measure of the hard work of the Falley and Graziano families. In addition to Mikey and Zoe Falley, their daughter Calli, Mike's brother Steve and son Sate work at Realys while Lisa Crowther's father, Jimmy Graziano and sister, Gina Graziano also contribute their skills to the business.

In the future Realys plans to sell branded names in the retail industry through chain drug stores and supermarkets and the company is growing in that direction. Lisa, Zoe and Mikey see no boundaries to their expansion. After all, as Mikey put it, "Anybody who has fingernails is our customer!"

SolderMask, Inc.

From cellular phones to satellites, SolderMask, Inc. is a national technological leader in both solder mask processing and stencil manufacturing. Founded by the Kurisu family in 1986 as a service bureau to the printed circuit-board industry, the company has grown from its 6,000-square-foot location in Costa Mesa to its current 10,000-square-foot Huntington Beach location, which was built in 1988.

The company's early focus was on the application of conventional, thick, dry film solder masks (DFSM) for high-end circuit boards. The company evolved with the industry, and its services now include the application of liquid photoimageable solder masks (LIPSM). Now the only service bureau in the United States that applies liquid photoimageable solder masks in a Class 10,000

Clean Room, SolderMask, Inc. provides defense-industry businesses and other commercial clients such as Boeing, Cray Research, Hughes Space & Communications,

SolderMask, Inc. has a reputation for being a "can do" company in a sometimes "can't do" world.

Motorola, Texas Instruments, Raytheon, Honeywell, 3M and other Fortune 500 companies with solder mask protection services usually within 24 hours.

As the needs of its clients evolve with advances in technology, SolderMask, Inc. continues to rise to the challenge with its commitment to excellence and technology. It is currently the only Department of Defense solder mask facility in the nation.

Whatever the end product — computer motherboards, Patriot or MX missile components, weather and communication satellites, telephones, Boeing 777s, or automobile-door pod switches — the bare printed circuit boards require an application of one of a wide variety of liquid photoimageable or dry film solder masks to protect them from solder shorts during the assembly process and against environmental extremes.

Either a dry film process, which uses a plastic-like film, or a liquid photoimageable process similar to silk-screening is necessary, depending on the end use. Both processes encapsulate the copper circuits and prevent solder shorts during assembly.

The processes are "simple but complex," as each step in the solder-masking process must be completed successfully or the entire process will not yield good product. Because of this SolderMask, Inc. employs highly skilled technicians who have many years of experience. Many of the crew members have been with the company since it was established.

In 1994, SolderMask, Inc. diversified and now manufactures custom-made stainless steel solder paste and epoxy stencils. This stencil is used by manufacturers to

"Our strength is our dedication to developing processes tailored to specific customer requirements and attention to quality."

(Opposite page) Solder paste stencils can be manufactured with lines and apertures of less than 0.005 of an inch, which is essential to assemblers working with fine-pitch devices.

deposit a solder paste used to "solder" the components to the boards. The stencils are manufactured by chemical etching, which produces features with a tolerance of less than 0.001 of an inch, essential to assemblers working with fine-pitch components.

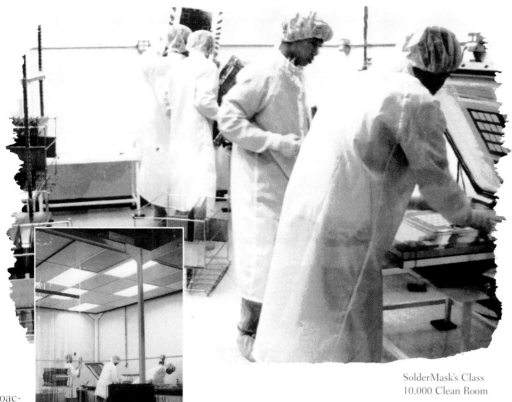

As the complexity of the circuit boards increase, the size of the components decrease, allowing for more of the components to be placed on the board. This miniaturization of boards and components will soon exceed the limits of chemical etching so once again SolderMask, Inc. will rise to the challenge by manufacturing stencils with a laser cutter capable of producing much finer features.

As a service bureau for a very time-sensitive industry, SolderMask, Inc. has to be "reactive rather than proactive." Customers from all over the United States send boards to SolderMask, Inc. and the boards then must be processed quickly yet perfectly and then returned by same-day or next-day delivery. Along with a sincere concern for customers' boards, SolderMask, Inc. also has a genuine interest in protecting the environment. All in-house wastestreams from solder mask processing are treated

SolderMask's Class 10,000 Clean Room

to ensure that outgoing wastewater is ultimately more pure than the incoming water, protecting the community and its residents from environmental pollutants.

SolderMask, Inc. has a reputation for being a "can do" company in a sometimes "can't do" world. When approached with a bizarre or unusual request it turns to its creative family of employees to seek out solutions to the problem.

"Committed to Excellence ... Committed to Technology" is SolderMask's motto, which will continue to drive the company in the next millennium.

TRUWEST, Inc.

In 1984, only four years after its beginning, TRUWEST, Inc. was so highly thought of that it was given an order to make custom parkas for the 1984 Olympic swimming and diving teams. In addition, the team honored Lee Westwell, founder and CEO of TRUWEST, by inviting her to be in the team picture. She is the only manufacturer who was allowed to be in a picture with an Olympic team wearing the manufacturer's product.

TRUWEST, Inc. is a company that makes athletic wear such as parkas, warmups, banners, water polo caps, lifeguard outfits and swim suits. Its specialty is custom athletic wear. Primarily, it sells through its catalogs and directly to the teams although it does make some products for scuba diving stores and for some specialized swim stores. Some of its products are also sold to major sportswear companies.

The company sells its products all over the world, primarily to colleges, universities, high schools and sporting teams. All of TRUWEST's huge variety of items are made from its own patterns and designs.

The Westwells have been swimmers all of their lives. Husband Gil was a highly successful competition swimmer in Portland, Oregon, where he grew up. Winner of junior national championships in individual medley, he also swam distance and swam for the armed forces in Europe. Lee was raised in Medford, Oregon and was also an avid recreational swimmer. The two met in Long Beach where Gil was going to college and working as a lifeguard at the old Pike Plunge. Lee was working in Long Beach but spent her spare time swimming at the Plunge. Soon they were married. Their reception was at a swimming pool and, instead of the groom leading the bride out on the dance floor for a first dance, they had a first swim together.

Although they first lived in Long Beach, the Westwells moved to Huntington Beach and raised two sons, Norm and Gary, who were also swimmers and are now part of TRUWEST, Inc. Both sons were on the swim team for Huntington Beach High School, and Gary also played water polo and was on the surf team.

The Westwells developed a parka for swimmers to replace the sleeping bags that were used to keep swimmers warm and dry between events. At the time, Gil was vice president of promotions for Arena Swimwear, a division of Adidas. He dealt with coaches all

over the United States and internationally. He knew the market, and Lee had the know-how on manufacturing and sales.

As Lee described it, "We saw a need and knew how to produce and market it. We had the know-how so we plunged into business." In 1980, she quit her job and started selling a product they would have in six months. Because so many of the coaches around the country knew the Westwells, they were willing to give orders sight unseen. TRUWEST contracted with Hind, a big company at that time, to do the manufacturing. Working from her home, Lee took orders from coaches, kept the books and ran the business. It didn't take long for TRUWEST to outgrow the Westwells' home. Lee rented a small section of a building and hired two employees — one for the office and one for production. A week later, they already needed a second production employee, then another and another, etc. The original two production employees, Rodel and Ronel

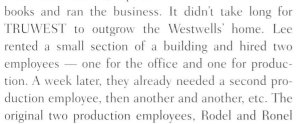

TRUWEST's catalog has a dizzying array of items from parkas, customized warmups, bags, suits and much more.

Angeles, are still with TRUWEST today. TRUWEST is a family-oriented business, and there are several husband and wife teams working there.

In 1985, Gary Westwell joined the company in sales, research & development, and promotion. Later in 1987, Gil joined the company when it began growing by leaps and bounds. Norm Westwell was drafted by the rest of his family when his experience in sales and operations was needed in 1991.

The company has expanded tremendously in its 18 years in business and continues to grow at the rate of approximately 20 percent per year. There are now 48 employees working in a 12,000-square-foot plant. Its catalog has a dizzying array of items from parkas, which can be custom designed, to customized warmups, to bags, to suits and much more. A customer can even order a water polo rink (demarcation area) if so inclined.

Gary Westwell developed a water polo cap, complete with ear guards, which has swept the country. As a water polo player, he knew very well what was needed.

The cap is offered in custom colors whereas the competition offers only blue & white. Because of the explosion and acceptance of the custom-colored caps in the United States offered by TRUWEST, the international water polo community took notice and changed the international rules to allow multicolored caps for a more colorful game.

Recently, the company produced a new rubber suit for women's water polo, a rapidly exploding sport. TRUWEST had the fabric developed specifically for this sport. In the future, the company expects to spread out into other sports as needs arise. Coaches let the TRUWEST people know what their needs are, and TRUWEST develops new items from those expressed desires. The company's bag line was developed from coach suggestions, and now more than 30 different bags are available.

Another unique feature of TRUWEST is that unlike most companies, it never discontinues an item. If a team decides on a uniform they want to have as its team suit, that suit will always be available at TRUWEST. This is one of the reasons customers always come back to TRUWEST, along with the fact the company is uniquely responsive to their needs and desires.

The Westwells are active participants in the Huntington Beach community, and TRUWEST supplies uniforms for the city lifeguards, colleges, high schools and various sport teams. When Lee and Gil took their first swim as a couple, they had no idea how far that first plunge would take them.

Vicki Marsha Uniforms

Beautiful plaid, striped and solid fabrics carefully sewn together to make perfectly matched school clothes is the focus of Vicki Marsha Uniforms' product line. An industry leader, Vicki Marsha Uniforms provides outfits for nearly 100 private and parochial schools in Southern California and manufactures and sells skirts and jumpers for other school uniform companies in Northern California and other states. Considered the "Cadillac of uniforms," Vicki Marsha has conducted business in exactly the same fashion for over 50 years.

Arriving from Mississippi in 1945, Wallace and Camille Crook never dreamed they would own a clothing company. Renting a furnished house in Long Beach, Wallace worked in the plastics industry while Camille was involved in substitute teaching and raising their daughter, Sherry.

across the country including Marshall Fields, Neiman Marcus, I. Magnin and Bullocks Wilshire.

Following the Crooks' takeover, all of the employees stayed with the business including talented fashion designer, Melva Bostrum. With help and guidance, the "team" taught the couple everything they needed to know for continued success; and with their second child on the way, Wallace and Camille instilled a sense of family within the company.

The factory was located behind Fashions in Miniature, a retail clothing store. Each dress was made individually by a team of ladies, mostly homemakers, who loved to sew and took pride in their work. When ready for the final touches, the dresses were funneled down to Lulu Carpenter who expertly finished them off with satin bows, silk flowers and quality lace. Wallace used his accounting skills to balance the books with

Camille Crook with daughter Sherry and son Buck, who have taken over the company's operation

In 1947 they read that a business named Vicki Marsha Originals was for sale. The economy was questionable following World War II but the Crooks, a cautious and conservative couple, decided to take a risk anyway and purchase the business. Looking back, Camille said, "We must have been crazy." The original owner manufactured a line of little girls' frilly dresses which she named after her daughter, Vicki Marsha. The popular label was purchased by high-end stores

timely payment of the bills his top priority. Changing hats, he was also the only "shipper" packing dresses with care to arrive at their destination, no matter how far away, without a wrinkle. With the designer's help Camille learned to select and purchase fabrics, many of them imported. Close attention was paid to recent trends in fashion, staying up-to-date with their little customers' preferences. Camille enjoyed working with different mills and vendors and became friendly with them all, her warm Southern accent easily identifying her on the phone.

The focus of business at Vicki Marsha changed in 1952 when nuns from a nearby Catholic school came to them seeking a more attractive uniform for their female students. Creating a balance between fashion and practicality, the Crooks chose an imported gingham plaid for the girls' jumpers and skirts. This new look made quite a stir in the Catholic communities and, before they knew it, Wallace and Camille were being contacted by other schools in the surrounding area. The trend in uniform manufacturing continued to grow and for nearly 10 years the company kept up with orders for both their original fashion line as well as uniforms. With lace and frills declining in popularity by the early 1960s the decision was made to manufacture the uniforms exclusively and the company's name eventually became Vicki Marsha Uniforms.

Vicki Marsha Uniforms is still family owned and operated. When Wallace passed away in 1976, son, Buck began working with Camille and took over his father's duties. Their daughter Sherry, having worked there for years during busy seasons, joined the business full time in 1990. The company outgrew three buildings in Long Beach before settling into a 10,000-square-foot facility in Huntington Beach in 1977. Despite its growth Vicki Marsha Uniforms is run with the same values and practices set in the early days. The fabrics used are of the highest quality and each batch is cut and packed in bundles to be passed on to the seamstress sewing that particular style of jumpers and skirts. There is no piece work sewing done there — each outfit is started and finished by the same operator. Similar to matching patterns when wallpapering, the plaid fabrics are also matched so that the uniform looks the same front to back.

Just as the company's uniforms are made with special care, the steady growth of the business has been accomplished conservatively and conscientiously.

A new phone system with a hold button was finally added in 1991 as well as a fax machine.

A tour through the warehouse finds only the necessary modest furnishings. Rows of clothing racks filled with the company's product line are organized by size and style. Boxes cut out to resemble storage bins hold colorful knit shirts, sweaters, socks and accessories to match each school's uniform. This merchandise is purchased from the finest suppliers of school uniforms in the country, constructed from durable, high-quality wash and wear fabrics that resist fading and shrinking.

The lobby serves as a waiting room lined with cushioned benches. During the busiest time, parents take a number from the dispenser and sit while staff members with tape measures dangling around their necks search for the next child waiting to be fitted. Keeping with the company's original policy, and without specific titles or job descriptions, everyone does whatever is needed at the time to get the job done — teamwork is the key.

In 1996 Sherry and Buck saw the need for more space and purchased the building behind them, expanding the company's manufacturing operation. Looking to the future, their priority is to maintain the best service possible to their existing schools and be able to deliver what they are committed to. They have chosen to turn away new business rather than sacrifice quality and service. Nearly 100 percent of the company's growth has been without advertisement or sales representatives, only by word-of-mouth and a solid reputation.

The original staff at Vicki Marsha consisted primarily of homemakers who loved to sew.

181

Birdhouse

Skateboarding has come a long way since the 1960s, when boards were little more than wood planks, and wheels were solid metal. Now, skateboarding is an international sport with custom boards and specialty products. One of the most recognized company names in skateboarding is located in the skating mecca of Huntington Beach: Birdhouse.

Formed in 1992 by champion skater Tony Hawk and Per Welinder, Birdhouse designs and sells a variety of skateboarding products, including boards, wheels, silkscreened t-shirts, pants, jackets, shoes, stickers, grip tape, hats and other assorted items. About 40 percent of the company's business is international; the company focuses on smaller, high-end retailers for its domestic business.

Manufacturing is done offsite, and then brought into the large warehouse for distribution. Most of the skateboarding products are not sold as complete skateboards. Buyers prefer to assemble their own skateboards, so most of the company's products are components. There are two basic types of boards sold by Birdhouse. The most popular board is made of seven layers of maple wood. The other type is also seven layers of maple, with a layer of plastic designed to make the board last longer.

One element that sets Birdhouse apart from the competition is the variety of silkscreened designs on the boards and wheels. The colorful designs are often named after the pro skaters who skate for Birdhouse in

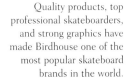

Quality products, top professional skateboarders, and strong graphics have made Birdhouse one of the most popular skateboard brands in the world.

Owners Per Welinder and Tony Hawk in the Birdhouse warehouse are surrounded by skateboard products ready for shipment to destinations worldwide.

international and domestic competitions and exhibitions, including Andrew Reynolds' "The Reaper," Willy Santos' "The Crusher," Steve Berra's "Pumpkinhead," Heath Kirchart's "Gravedigger 2," Jeremy Klein's "Demon Child," Bucky Lasek's "Lasek Park," and Tony Hawk's "Fulgore" and "Full Skull."

Many skateboarders identify with the various pro skaters and their products, but a product is usually in production for only four to six months before it is retired and a new design is introduced. Two designers and a team of illustrators are constantly at work, creating new artwork for the three board divisions: Birdhouse, which features a gothic comics theme; Flip, which offers a Star Trek meets The Grateful Dead motif; and Hook-Ups, which focuses on Japanese animation characters such as Electra, Killer Bee and Devilman 13.

After an initial base of about 200 stores, Birdhouse is now available in nearly 1,500 stores across the United States. And with the continued growth in skateboarding popularity, Birdhouse is poised for even greater things. Co-founder Tony Hawk is constantly on the move, promoting Birdhouse throughout the world wherever he skates and helping to keep Birdhouse's pulse on current skateboarding trends. Of course, the fact that a majority of Birdhouse employees are in their 20s also helps keep the focus on the youth market. Looks like Birdhouse isn't just looking to the future — it's skating toward it in style.

California Faucets

Among residential neighborhoods, schools and shopping centers, a large portion of Huntington Beach is designated for manufacturing and light industrial firms. This thriving business community, with its roll-up doors and product showrooms, employs many of Surf City's residents and shares a friendly exchange of merchandise and services. Among the neighborhood entrepreneurs is Fred Silverstein with his company, California Faucets, manufacturer of decorative, high-end plumbing fixtures.

Having worked in the plumbing industry all of his life, Silverstein believed he was ready to relax, retire and play as much golf as he wanted. He sold his plumbing distribution business and had no intention of starting another company. Deciding he wasn't ready for retirement after all, Silverstein returned to plumbing. He was accustomed to and successful in the distribution phase of the industry but thought he'd try the manufacturing side this time around. "In distribution we have people to answer to from all sides but, in manufacturing, there's the opportunity to be up at the top and everything trickles down from there." He opened California Faucets in March of

Silverstein takes care in purchasing the highest quality materials available, including 24K gold-plated metals, custom-blended colored finishes to match any decor, and handles made by Swarovsky ...

1988 at the same Huntington Beach location it currently occupies.

California Faucets has done more than just keep owner Silverstein from becoming bored after retirement. Business is brisk with a national sales force and projects as far away as Asia and South America. The company brings in raw materials from suppliers and the final product is assembled and shipped from its Huntington Beach factory. Silverstein takes care in purchasing the highest quality materials available, including 24K gold-plated metals, custom-blended

colored finishes to match any decor, and handles made by Swarovsky, a manufacturer of fine European cut crystal. Other finishes include polished brass, pewter, satin nickel and many others.

At California Faucets, quality control is crucial. Each faucet undergoes a stringent battery of tests prior to packaging and delivery. In addition to frequent inspection of finished surfaces at each stage of manufacture, all valves are checked for proper operation by company technicians and then pressure tested for leaks in the company's in-house testing lab.

California Faucets has recently become a family operation with the addition of Silverstein's son, Jeff. After graduating from high school in Huntington Beach, attending the University of California, Berkeley and settling into a position directing a summer camp in the Poconos Mountains, it seemed as if Silverstein was not going to be able to pass his company on to one of his children. With a little prodding and a lot of patience, however, Jeff decided to return to Huntington Beach and join his father in running the company. Silverstein is pleased and very proud that Jeff will eventually take over entirely. "I'm just glad that one of my kids decided to come into the business," he says, smiling.

When asked about future plans, Silverstein shrugs his shoulders and grins. He's very happy with his enterprise. He has good employees, good customers and a son interested in carrying on after he decides to retire — for the second time.

Coatings Resource Corporation

What do Ed Laird and Huntington Beach have in common? That's an easy one. They both have had humble beginnings, both grew up in a world of often-conflicting ideals, and today they are both icons of how to marry environmental consciousness with sound business concepts.

First, there is leadership. In the case of Coatings Resource's founder and chairman of the board, Ed Laird, he had a dream — if not a passion. As a trained chemist, Ed was confronted in the early 1960s with the challenge to replace environmentally harmful solvents with water and still produce paints that would adhere and protect and would help consumers enjoy long life out of the products they needed.

Ed worked in other companies' laboratories for 17 years helping them produce systems that removed heavy metals and polluting solvents from paints. In 1976, he started Coatings Resource Corporation, and he began doing this for himself. In the beginning, like Huntington Beach, Ed had to plan his future. What kind of a business did he want to own and what types

Founder Ed Laird (second from left) and sons Richard, Robert and Jeff make Coatings Resource Corporation the family business.

of employees did he want? The underlying focus was that whatever Ed did, it had to be for his family, his community and his love of the environment.

Today, Huntington Beach is the 12th largest city in California, with many accolades adorning many walls. It is a city full of families, volunteering, a strong commitment to the environment and an emerging economic base. Coatings Resource Corporation is the same. With over 80 employees, a client list that includes three of the world's largest toy manufacturers, global leaders in telecommunication and entertainment

devices, and multinational manufacturing entities, Coatings Resource Corporation has reached an important phase in its history and in the industry.

Providing lead-free and nontoxic coatings for Barbie's lips, Hot Wheels, and Sony televisions and developing simple yet complicated procedures for applying waterborne coatings to furniture parts and even venetian blinds are just a few of the ways that Ed Laird has made a difference. He has also made the world a little safer to live in, but he no longer does this alone. Robert, Richard and Jeff Laird are in the business and the business is in them. They individually head up operations, key account management and engineering. At Coatings Resource Corporation, business means family and family means business.

One of its newest ventures, AQC Environmental Engineers, helps others deal with usually well-meaning but oftentimes scientifically impossible or economically unrealistic rules, rules and more rules. Its corporate mission statement: Help others do a better job of producing their products in an environmentally sound way by understanding the law, often times rewriting it and out of need, helping the regulators deal with some of their own issues.

Is that all? Certainly not. There is Ed Laird, the philanthropist. In fact, Ed was named Philanthropist of the Year for Orange County and is chairman of the board of the Orange County Council, Boy Scouts of America. How about Environmentalist of the Year from a premier wetlands conservancy? The list is so long and the trophies so many that no one would believe the difference one man has made. The best part, it is not over yet.

Clean air and economic growth. Change, protest, consensus-building and fights. A chemist receiving an environmental award. A commitment to helping his customers, at times replacing his own products. Doing well by doing good. All oxymorons, contradictions or are they points of light and roads least taken?

Huntington Beach is a great community today because of entrepreneurs like Ed Laird. Part of Ed's success is a community like Huntington Beach where people who have ideas and dreams tend to experiment. The partnership seems to have been a success.

DeGuelle Glass

DeGuelle Glass has been providing glass and mirrored products to Huntington Beach and surrounding communities for over 30 years. When Jim DeGuelle opened his doors to the public in 1962, quality, service and integrity were important to him. Originally named DeGuelle and Sons, Jim had his boys working by his side and together they built a company that would become a fixture within downtown Huntington Beach. They provided a burgeoning building industry with windows, wardrobe doors, wet bars and more.

With the company's foundation well established, Jim turned the reins over to his youngest son Tom in 1980. Construction starts were down and the community turned its focus from buying new to fixing up existing structures. This trend continued for nearly ten years. Tom and his crew installed mirrored glass over entire interior walls, polished and beveled the edges of half and three quarter-inch thick glass for table tops and installed mirrored wardrobe doors to make small bedrooms appear larger. DeGuelle Glass was becoming busier with remodel work, and Barbara Haynes came on board to help in 1988. For nine years Barbara figured cost estimates and worked with customers and suppliers until June of 1997, when she and her husband Michael purchased the company.

The Hayneses have continued with the original family's business philosophy and plan to keep the DeGuelle name. Many of the employees are still with them, and some have been with the company more than 15 years. They continue to educate themselves on new products that might best fit the needs of their customers and they have a strong commitment to their community. As current president of the Orange County Glass Association, Barbara attends meetings and industry expos and encourages her staff to go along with her. Her spirit of camaraderie prompts Association members to refer work to each other depending on their expertise. Michael is a member of the local Masonic Lodge and Kiwanis Club, and they both are active in the Chamber of Commerce. Their policy is to purchase as much as they can from local sources and always as if they were buying for their own home. Their staff is polite, neat and well-groomed when they enter a customer's residence or business, and they are continually proud of the company's safety record. It is important to both of them to maintain the high standards set years ago by Jim and his family.

The Haynes family, Michael, Barbara and kids work together to make DeGuelle's "The Glassiest Place in Town."

185

And what are Michael and Barbara's visions for the future? As some of Jim DeGuelle's early projects begin to age, Michael and Barbara will work with these customers to renew and refurbish as needed. More than 90 percent of their work is residential with

DeGuelle Glass has been providing glass and mirrored products to Huntington Beach and surrounding communities for over 30 years.

no plan for that to change. The mainstay of their business will continue to be windows, shower and tub enclosures, glass table tops, patio doors, screens, mirrors and repairs.

Barbara and Michael have relieved the DeGuelle family of the daily responsibility of opening the shop. Walking in the door, though, one can see that not much has changed. The showroom still displays a large variety of shower enclosures and windows. The box filled with samples of glass colors and finishes can still be found in the reception area. And as they both say, DeGuelle's is still "The Glassiest Place in Town."

Gemtech Inc.

From automobile bumpers to patio furniture and from golf clubs to baby strollers, powder coating is today's choice in finishing technology. Gemtech of Huntington Beach uses this process to coat a variety of metal products. Their customers include automobile restoration artists, furniture manufacturers, builders of metal display racks and a company that makes old fitness equipment look new. A recent project was to provide the finishing touches on the bleachers for a local hockey rink. Gemtech began, however, with an idea for a different product over 25 years ago.

When Shig Shiwota moved into a home above Los Angeles, he looked for a way to transport his bicycle up and down the steep hills. Not finding anything suitable, and necessity being the mother of invention, he created and built the first hoop rack. The hoop rack enabled bicycle enthusiasts to attach their cycles to their vehicles, leaving room inside for passengers and equipment. He approached his wife, Maya, about manufacturing the product themselves. She supported the idea even though he would have to leave a lucrative engineering position. Needing to choose a colorful coating that would please the eye and be durable enough to withstand the elements, they chose powder coating and began using the services of local suppliers. Dissatisfied with turn-around time, they purchased their own equipment.

Recognizing an opportunity to expand the business, they began powder coating for others. In 1990 Gemtech moved from the Los Angeles area to Huntington Beach. With many choices in bicycle racks now available, they no longer manufacture the hoop rack but enjoy a brisk business providing powder coating for customers. Gemtech's mission to provide a high-quality product at an unsurpassed level of customer service has made it an industry leader. With Shig handling sales and Maya running the inside operation, it's a team effort. Ninety percent of Gemtech's business is from repeat-customers and word-of-mouth advertisement. Looking to the future they see unlimited potential as the industry continues its commitment to provide an expanded menu of coatable surfaces, vibrantly beautiful colors and textures all with safety to the environment.

The powder coating process is interesting to see. Finely ground particles of pigment and resin are electrostatically charged and sprayed onto a metal product. The metal being electrically grounded, these particles adhere until melted and fused in a curing oven at 400 degrees. Curing takes 20 minutes and the end result is metal with a smooth durable finish. There are no volatile organic compounds (VOCs) present so the process is environmentally clean, unlike traditional painting. Because powder coating is not solvent-based, it's also environmentally safe and the final waste product is minimal. Originally available in black, white and beige, the colors now include clear, sharp blues, shockingly vibrant reds and yellows comparable to the brightest burst of sunshine. While just about any shade comes standard, custom colors are also blended to customer's specifications. For imperfect metal surfaces, textures can be created and clean metal can even be made to imitate the look of naturally weathered brass.

The Shiwota family is proud to watch its industry grow. New powders developed can now be cured at lower temperatures enabling powder coating to finish materials other than metal, including plastics and wood. Powder coating will be tomorrow's technological choice for years to come.

Gemtech Inc.
Huntington Beach

Johnson Manufacturing

Johnson Manufacturing was a dream for A. Richard Johnson, even when he was working for Disneyland as a machinist in the 1970s. The purchase of a small, one-man machine shop in Buena Park gave Johnson Manufacturing its start. Rich Johnson, as he is known by his family and friends, continued with his full-time job and started to build the business as a second job for over two years. When injury struck, entrepreneurial seeds blossomed, and he decided to concentrate on Johnson Manufacturing as a full-time endeavor.

The patriarch of the family and Rich's father, Garlon Johnson, came to Huntington Beach when it was a tent city in 1918 at the age of nine, and settled on a five acre plot off Newland Street, now the site of the Bayshore Condominiums. The younger Johnson recalls cutting across the open fields, spending lazy days at the salt water plunge, and festive 4th of July parades followed by breathtaking fireworks over the water. No weekend was complete without a trip to the Surf Theater or the downtown drug store where his mother once worked.

Peaceful and familiar sounds of oil wells pumping are a fond memory of Rich Johnson. He remembers when Huntington Beach oil wells were constructed of wood. His father worked in those oil fields, but always farmed and planted barley on plots of land; initially for income, and later for a pastime. In the mid-1960s Rich was enjoying life as a Huntington Beach High School student, the city was growing and new schools were being built at a dizzying rate. At the beginning of his junior year he moved to a new school, Marina High School.

What ensued for Rich Johnson after the 1970s were many years of hard work, following the ups and downs of the aerospace industry. Johnson Manufacturing has contributed to this industry by supplying many of the major airplane manufacturers across the country, both domestic and military, with hydraulic flight control hardware. Although the aerospace industry has seen some dismal years, Johnson Manufacturing has always had work and estimates that 95 percent of its revenue comes from that industry segment.

Johnson Manufacturing supplies major airplane manufacturers with hydraulic flight control hardware.

In 1994 this family owned business finally relocated and returned to what the Johnson family considers its roots, the city of Huntington Beach. Now, just minutes from home, Rich Johnson often works later than he might if the business was a distance away. His wife and sons are an integral part of this manufacturing operation, each contributing their share to the success of this growing business, which was just a dream not so many years ago.

The future and continued success of Johnson Manufacturing lies with the aerospace industry and, perhaps, with other industries where pinpoint precision measured in microns is a necessity for mechanical parts. Mostly, it lies in the commitment to excellence found in this family's business.

Marksman® Products

Marksman Products has been a producer of innovative outdoor products for over 50 years. The company was founded in West Los Angeles in 1948 when it introduced the model 1010 Air Pistol, a single shot spring piston BB pistol resembling the Colt-Government issue .45-caliber service automatic. Over the years, the company grew and changed. Slingshots were added to the product line. New tooling and modifications were made to the 1010 Air Pistol, and it became a BB repeater as well as having capabilities to shoot pellets and darts single shot.

In 1981, Robert A. Eck became president of Marksman, relocated the facility to Huntington Beach in 1982, and has led the company ever since. The company introduced a new International Series line in 1985 which featured high quality, precision adult airguns imported from Europe. This expanded its customer base from the youth market to include the adult market.

In 1988 the Marksman Shooting Team was developed for research and development through field testing and competition to further guide the adult airgun category. This was the first factory sponsored shooting team in the airgun industry and is composed of full-time Marksman employees.

The new Model 1790 Biathlon Training Air Rifle was introduced in 1989, and it revolutionized the youth airgun market. The Boy Scouts of America selected the Biathlon for use at the National Scout Jamboree held every four years at Fort A.P. Hill, Virginia. During this week long event, more than 25,000 Scouts have an opportunity to use the rifles. For many, it is their first shooting experience. The United States Shooting Team gave its endorsement to this same air rifle which was the beginning of Marksman's support of Olympic shooting.

Three outstanding athletes serve as Spokespersons for Marksman Products: Bob Lilly, formerly of the Dallas Cowboys and an NFL Hall of Fame member; Kim Rhode, 1996 Olympic Gold Medalist and the youngest person ever to be on the U. S. Olympic Shooting Team; and Deena Wigger, World Class Shooter and three time U.S. Olympic Committee Athlete of the Year in the Shooting Sports.

Marksman products are sold through large retailers such as Wal-Mart, Kmart, Big 5, Sports Authority and other sporting goods stores. Products are also sold through independent sales agents and exported to longtime distributors.

More recent developments within the Marksman organization saw the acquisition of Beeman Precision Airguns in 1993. A perfect complement to Marksman's own unique line of youth airgun products, Beeman has been the recognized national leader in precision adult airguns for over two decades.

Marksman actively supports the local and national chapter of the Boy Scouts of America and is directly involved in promoting various youth and shooting sports programs. In addition, Marksman offers a complete line of controlled velocity airguns and related accessories intended to promote responsible shooting.

Marksman itself has come a long way since 1948. Its products continue to be built in the United States and the packaging proudly bears the "Made in U.S.A." slogan.

As a highly successful company that knows its market inside and out, Marksman Products is now poised for the future. In his statement on the occasion of the company's 50th anniversary, President Robert A. Eck stated, "Thank you for your support of our company over our first 50 years. We hope you'll enjoy this year's new products and celebrate the next 50 years with us as you experience the excitement of 'Shooting: A Sport for Life!'"

Robert A. Eck, president, with official spokespersons Deena Wigger and Bob Lilly

Marksman Products is a proud member of the Huntington Beach business community.

188

Reliable Wholesale Lumber

Reliable Lumber, the predecessor of Reliable Wholesale Lumber, Inc., was started by Jerome Higman in 1929 in Rosemead, California. A few years later, Higman married Anna, and they had two sons, Jerry and Dan Higman. In those early days, not only did mother and father work in the original lumberyard, but so did the two brothers as they were growing up, and they joined the company right out of college in 1959 and 1960. Although Jerry and Dan later developed their own company, Reliable Wholesale Lumber, Inc., Reliable Lumber remained an active retail yard until 1994.

The picture changed drastically in 1946, when Jerome Higman died suddenly. He left a widow, two young boys and a business in an uproar. Although it was unheard of in the 1940s for a woman to run a business by herself, let alone a lumberyard business, Anna Higman rolled up her sleeves and took over Reliable Lumber. She struggled on her own for many years, and out of sheer necessity, learned how to run a lumber business. When Jerry and Dan completed their educations, they joined their mother and shouldered a great deal of the burden.

In 1971, Dan and Jerry decided to branch out and established Reliable Wholesale Lumber in Temple City. They remain the sole stockholders to this day. By 1973 they were ready to expand and began looking for property in Huntington Beach. The commercial realtors they hired did not have much success in finding an appropriate piece of property so the Higmans put a realtor friend from Yorba Linda on the search. Since they had advised her that they needed property that was rail-served, the enterprising realtor got out a map of all the railroad lines, drove along them and one day wandered up to a guy who was taking clay off the soil. She stopped to talk to him and discovered he was the owner of the property. He finished taking off the clay and sold the property to the Higmans. The city provided a special-use permit, and Reliable Wholesale Lumber was off and running.

By 1959, Reliable Lumber Rosemead had nine employees and was doing about $500,000 a year in business. Some 47 years later, Reliable Wholesale Lumber does approximately $130 million annually in sales and has 175 employees.

Currently, Reliable has locations in Huntington Beach, Temple City, Fontana and Santa Ana. Approximately 65 percent of its sales are to large contractors and home builders. The balance comes from wholesale distribution to other yards and to home centers such as HomeBase and The Home Depot. The business has an industrial sales division which sells industrial-type lumber to cabinet shops, furniture stores, and other businesses that use lumber and plywood for commercial boxing and crating.

Jerry Higman is president and CEO of Reliable, and although he now makes his home in Idaho, he keeps track daily of the lumber yard via an extremely competent management team. Dan Higman serves as secretary and chief financial officer of the company. Dan and Jerry learned the lumber business from the ground up by driving trucks, building loads and working in the mills. Now their sons are the third generation of Higmans involved. Jerry's son Will Higman has worked at Reliable for almost 19 years, and does a great job buying and running the contractor sales. Dan's oldest son David Higman graduated in 1997 from USC, joined the firm and is serving as assistant CFO.

Because many employees of the business have been with the company for so long, Dan and Jerry consider the staff part of their extended family and prefer to promote from within, providing opportunity for their staff to grow as the company grows.

The Higmans are enthusiastic about a productive and growth-oriented future. As Jerry Higman proudly points out, "We have a wonderful company, and it's been a wonderful experience being in Huntington Beach. The city government has been very supportive of our business, and that has helped us in no small way to reach the success we enjoy today."

Jerry (right) and Dan Higman have made Reliable Wholesale Lumber what it is today.

The Marketplace

Huntington Beach retail establishments, service industries

and leisure/convention facilities offer

an impressive variety of choices for

Huntington Beach residents and visitors alike.

Jack's Surfboards

When businessman and entrepreneur Jack Hokanson saw a vacant bank building on Pacific Coast Highway, he thought it would be a perfect place for a surf shop. He was right. Forty years later, Jack's Surfboards is a household word among the many surf and water sport enthusiasts up and down the California coast.

Jack opened his first store in 1957. He had owned many businesses over the years, including laying brick and running a cafe. Knowing very little about the sport, a surf shop was something new for him. Situated next to the legendary Golden Bear nightclub and directly across from the blue Pacific ocean, Jack's stocked surfboards, wetsuits and anything else needed to paddle out and catch a wave. Since surfers lived inland, too, a second store was opened in Anaheim. Within two years, however, Jack decided to combine both locations into one, larger building along the coast.

The two-story brick structure, built in 1915, was chosen for the store's permanent home. The first floor formerly housed Obarr's Drug Store. Many of the town's lawyers and dentists occupied the second floor until residential tenants staked their claim in the 13 upper level rooms. The location was perfect. There was pedestrian activity in front along Main Street and visibility of the shop was clear for drivers and their passengers traveling in either direction down Pacific Coast Highway. The pier was only a crosswalk away, at the very gateway to Surf City.

In addition to surf clothing and equipment, Jack was receiving requests to carry Levi's jeans for the workers in the nearby labor camps. In the early 1970s,

> *Forty years later, Jack's Surfboards is a household word among the many surf and water sport enthusiasts up and down the California coast.*

he came in contact with Mike Abdelmuti, owner of Mike's Men's and Boy's retail stores, who provided him with the jeans. For years they referred customers to each other's stores, building a strong business relationship. They also cultivated a deep and lasting friendship that Jack's wife, Clara says spread to include their families.

In 1972, when Jack wanted to retire from his business, it was only natural that he would offer it to his long time friend and business associate and Abdelmuti agreed to buy him out. He closed all eight

Completed in 1992, Jack's Surfboards now resides in this multilevel Mediterranean style structure located on the same legendary corner.

of his own retail stores with the goal to take his new venture to a higher dimension. He soon opened a second Jack's in Huntington Beach and added larger stores in Newport Beach and Dana Point. Carrying a complete line of top quality surfboards, wetsuits, accessories and clothing such as O'Neil, Stussy and Billabong, Jack's was a one-stop shopping experience. Through involvement in local and global surf contests, they became internationally known, with customers as far away as Japan, Brazil and throughout South America. Business was brisk with no sign of slowing down.

December 1990, however, marked a turning point for Jack's Surfboards. Racks were filled with merchandise ready for a busy holiday season when Abdelmuti was faced with the largest challenge in his professional career. The historical brick buildings of downtown Huntington Beach were showing signs of deterioration. By this time he had purchased the structure housing Jack's but a wall was beginning to bulge and swell, making it unsafe. It was going to be condemned just in time for Christmas. The original Jack's building across the street had already been leveled and a large Mediterranean style structure was erected in its place. City officials had redevelopment on their minds and suggested Abdelmuti conform with the project on the opposite corner. They were urging demolition. The decision was made to tear down and rebuild rather than attempt to render the historic building structurally safe.

More than a year later, spring of 1993, Jack's reopened in magnificent style. The 50,000-square-foot building boasts a fully stocked surf shop once again. Offices and conference rooms on the second and third floors are positioned to take full advantage of the ocean air. Hungry surfers can have it their way with a view of the ocean at the Burger King adjacent to the retail store. The sidewalks along Pacific Coast Highway are extra wide to accommodate increased foot traffic during busy summer months. A surfing walk of fame with 68 slots commemorating the notables of the sport is built into the sidewalk and serves as one of Abdelmuti's most treasured projects. The building even won the prestigious Pacific Coast Builders grand award in its class, with entries coming from all over the world.

Sitting in his upper floor office, sliding door open with the afternoon sea breeze threatening to rustle the papers on his desk, Abdelmuti believes the frustration of recent years has been worth it. He takes Jack's Surfboards very seriously. Jack Hokanson passed away in 1997 but his legacy will live on. With two stores in Huntington Beach and one in Newport Beach, Abdelmuti says that Jack's Surfboards is an owner occupied enterprise. On any given day a member of the Abdelmuti family is on the premises keeping the business running smoothly. With a solid commitment to clientele and community contributions are regularly made to the local school's sports programs. Abdelmuti views this downtown area as the central business district of Surf City, surpassing neighbors to the north and south, Seal Beach and Newport Beach. Looking forward, Jack's will continue to grow in international recognition as it hosts surf competitions and surfers from around the world. Huntington Beach has found its place on the map as the official Surf City, USA and Jack's Surfboards continues to ride the wave right along with it.

Best Value Tire & Automotive Centers

"If it rolls, we can put tires on it!" proclaim Mike Maxwell and Steve Abersold, owners of Best Value Tire & Automotive Centers. "We work on every kind of wheel and do every kind of tire from trailer tires to forklift tires to backhoe tires to you name it."

Best Value Tire & Automotive provides service to a wide variety of customers from the Rod Millen Race Team, the B.F. Goodrich Race Team, the Terrible Hebrst Off Road Race Team, to the ordinary person. They have worked with approximately seven race teams, fitting Indy race tires and doing custom alignments.

The two partners met when they were in their teens. Fortuitously, Mike's cousin was president of Mark C. Bloome Tires. Both Mike and Steve went to work there, starting as tire mounters, and have remained in the tire business for the past 16 years. Steve's career followed the retail line while Mike went into the wholesale end of the business. When a chance for a store of their own opened up, and with the blessing of several vendors, Steve and Mike launched Best Value Tire & Automotive Centers in March, 1994. Although it was at a time when businesses were folding up right and left, they toughed it out, made it through the first couple of hard years and have made a success of their endeavor ever since.

One of the lessons Mike and Steve learned through their careers was how to establish long-term relationships with their customers. This way, they know the customers' needs and the customers can depend on quality service from Best Value. It's a formula that never fails.

"It's real simple. Treat people right, do quality work, sell quality products, make a fair profit but don't gouge people and people will find you."

The partners pointed out, "It's real simple. Treat people right, do quality work, sell quality products, make a fair profit but don't gouge people and people will find you."

When Best Value first opened, the employees consisted only of Steve, his wife, Cindi, Mike, one

194

Mike Maxwell and Steve and Cindi Abersold are proud owners of Best Value Tire & Automotive Centers.

Everyone at Best Value Tire & Automotive Centers strives for excellent customer service.

The experts at Best Value Tire & Automotive Centers will work on any type of wheel and provide any type of tire.

195

mechanic and one tire mounter. "We mounted a lot of products ourselves and still do," said Mike. Today, there are seven employees, mostly trained fully by Mike and Steve. Their site encompasses 4,000 square feet, and they are scouting Orange County for another retail location and additional storage space.

Mike and Steve have weathered tremendous changes in the tire business. When they started, there were about eight sizes of tires which fit 90 percent of all automobiles. Today, every time a new vehicle hits the street, there's not just one new tire, but option tires available for every model. Stocking inventory is really a challenge.

Mike and Steve are active in the Huntington Beach Chamber of Commerce, a wide variety of local networking groups, Kiwanis and the Southern California Tire Dealers Association.

Best Value Tire & Automotive Centers is an outstanding example of how hard work, persistence and a desire to excel can create a successful business. "We do a lot of things most tire shops have never done and never will do," say Mike and Steve proudly.

Express Valet Cleaners

In 1972, Ezra Schley immigrated from Israel to the United States to carve out his share of the American dream. Like the majority of immigrants, Schley spoke no English and had no family in Southern California. He had been raised on a kibbutz in his homeland and had fulfilled his military obligations as a lieutenant with the Israeli paratroopers. Ezra was a hard worker and soon found employment with a corporation which owned 21 dry cleaners. Little did he know that he had found his share of the dream.

Express Valet Cleaners vans can be seen all around Orange County.

After several years of experience, Schley decided to launch his own cleaning service. One of the cleaners he worked for provided cleaning service for guests at many Orange County hotels. Schley borrowed $5,000 from his mother and used it to purchase two of the cleaners which already had 17 employees. As the hotel business blossomed in Orange County, so did Schley's business until he had nearly doubled the number of employees.

By 1982, Schley owned two retail establishments and one large wholesale establishment which serviced the hotels. He fell in love with one of his employees, Lucretia, and they were married. Lucretia worked at the retail establishments. Within six years, the Schleys began to open retail stores throughout Orange County. They would purchase a cleaners, build it up and then sell it. As they bought and sold cleaners, they began to notice an interesting phenomenon taking place. Clientele from a particular cleaners they had sold would search them out and drive to their new location.

They finally realized the customers liked them because they were always available whereas most owners were not.

Both Ezra and Lucretia place great importance on customer service, and their customers know the Schleys will go the extra mile for them. As Lucretia expresses it, "It is really very simple. We just treat our customers and their things as we would want to be treated."

Ezra and Lucretia carved out a niche for their services — hard to clean items. They consider their customers to be discerning people who are concerned with how they present themselves, people who want quality service and cleaning. Through his many years of experience in the cleaning business, Ezra has developed a unique understanding of the chemistry of the dry cleaning business, and this stands him in good stead with the customers.

The Schleys' cleaners specialize in hard-to-clean garments, items with suede, leather, sequins and beads, antique or heirloom fabrics, problem stains and even wet cleaning. They have a whole program for servicing exquisitely designed gowns such as wedding, christening or confirmation garments which require experienced handling because of the delicate laces, appliques, pearls and fine fabrics involved. Once a special garment

> *"It is really very simple. We just treat our customers and their things as we would want to be treated."*

is brought in to them, they put it through an 11-step cleaning procedure which begins with a customer consultation to learn his/her needs and desires through the final stage where the garment is carefully packaged in an acid-free box with cotton muslin liner and ultra porous acid-free tissue paper to cushion the folds and maintain the delicate lines of the garment. The final step of the process is placing the box in a muslin bag.

As their business clientele grew, the Schleys recognized another characteristic of their customers. They were doing work for very busy people, people who could just barely squeeze a trip to the cleaners into their work schedule. This led to another innovation, pick up and delivery service from home or business, which they named Express Valet Cleaners. With Express Valet the customer calls and places his order, the items are picked up on the designated day for the customer's location and returned on a predesignated day. The customer need not be home so long as the cleaning is left in a designated area. An itemized bill is included with delivery of the cleaning. If the customer has special requests, a note in the laundry bag is all that is required for Express Valet to comply. Nylon bags are provided for dry cleaning and laundry. Full-time customer service staff are available for questions or special requests.

Their careful observation of their customers' needs paid off for the Schleys, and their business boomed for several years. Express Valet was so successful, they sold all of their retail stores and concentrated solely on the pickup and delivery service. Soon they were providing service to nearly all of Orange County

Their business is booming bigger than ever, and they are developing many new areas and new ways to accommodate their customers.

and as far north as Long Beach. The number of employees expanded to 60, and the future looked very rosy.

However, at this point, the Schleys hit a bump in the road. In 1994, the owner of the building they were renting went bankrupt and lost the building as part of his bankruptcy. With the other tenants, the Schleys were evicted by the new owner and faced a tremendous financial hardship to move their business and save it from being totally demolished. Lucretia, who had not been working in the family business for several years in order to concentrate on raising their family, returned to the job. Ezra let his managers go and worked 18-hour days. Friends, colleagues, equipment installers and suppliers all pitched in. With the same kind of hard work and the support of others that had launched them in the first place, the Schleys turned things around and are back on their feet again.

Today, the Schleys are busy devoting their efforts to meeting their customers' needs, to providing excellent and unique service and to the growth and development of their slice of the pie, Express Valet Cleaners. Their business is booming bigger than ever, and they are developing many new areas and new ways to accommodate their customers.

197

Lucretia and Ezra Schley — proud owners of Express Valet Cleaners

Harry's Fine Jewelry

Five brothers were working together in 1976 in Philadelphia's famous jewelers' row, when they began a wholesale jewelry business, providing design and other services to the industry. This was the beginning of Harry's Fine Jewelry, although the foundation for the business was formed many years before in Beruit, Lebanon.

Raised by proud Armenian parents, the Merdjanian brothers became jewelers' apprentices around the age of 14. They worked side-by-side with old world gold craftsmen, learning the ancient art and techniques of jewelry making, such as filigree work, a technique that produces quality not possible by modern machinery. They were raised by their parents with the greatest respect for honesty and integrity. Their roots served them well as they took their place as fine jewelers in a tight knit industry where reputation is extremely important.

By 1980 the brothers decided to open a retail location in Philadelphia and continued to manufacture fine jewelry and offer services in the wholesale fine jewelry market. In 1983 one of the brothers ventured to California, decided to stay, and opened a retail store next to the post office on Warner Avenue at Goldenwest in Huntington Beach. Slowly, one-by-one, the other brothers moved west to the Huntington Beach area.

Harry's Fine Jewelry was expanded in 1986 to showcase a wider selection of jewelry and to house a larger manufacturing area. As the retail business grew, the brothers realized it would be much more efficient if they were all in one location, where they could offer

Old world values of honesty and excellence of quality are precious gifts from the brothers to each and every customer.

the finest in jewelry design, manufacturing and retail sales. They would be able to work directly with their customers during every phase of the jewelry making process. Finally, in 1988, the Philadelphia location combined with the Huntington Beach location, and the focus of the brothers was on producing their own line of custom designs and special order pieces.

A comfortable atmosphere at Harry's Fine Jewelry is evident. Customers become personal friends and the brothers are known as the neighborhood jewelers. Clients know that their precious gems and jewelry items will be treated with respect, whether the value be

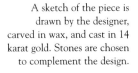

A sketch of the piece is drawn by the designer, carved in wax, and cast in 14 karat gold. Stones are chosen to complement the design.

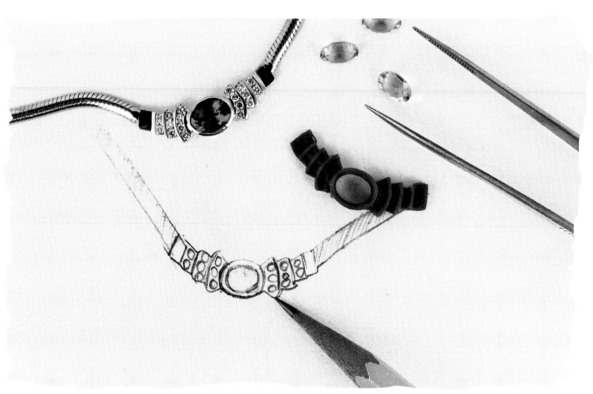

monetary or sentimental. Jewelry is an important part of the heritage of many families, and something that can be handed down as an heirloom. Families enjoy custom-designed gifts for all the memorable occasions of life. From graduation to engagement to wedding to

Customers become personal friends and the brothers are known as the neighborhood jewelers.

new baby gifts, the cycle of customer's families continues beautifully from generation to generation. It is no surprise that most new customers come from referrals of friends and family. Many consider the store a hidden treasure because the brothers do very little advertising. The brothers believe strongly in community involvement, often supporting local high school athletic programs, children's organizations, nonprofits such as the Huntington Beach Assistance League, and local churches through donations.

A member of the Merdjanian family of jewelers always greets customers as they enter the store. They are jewelry experts in model-making, custom designing, diamond setting and all types of jewelry repair. Their work is done on the premises, and repairs are often made while customers wait. As a special service, one of the brothers is certified by the Gemology Institute of America as a gemologist and

diamond expert. He can give customers information regarding the grade of their gems and the market value of their jewelry. Written appraisals are also available for personal or insurance purposes.

Old world values of honesty and excellence of quality are precious gifts from the brothers to each and every customer. Along with these traditions come creative design and hand-crafted workmanship which are difficult to find. Unique designs start as simple sketches on paper which are then carved into wax models and finally cast in 14 karat gold. The final step before each creation is presented to the customer is setting the piece with beautiful stones. Each designer oversees the complete jewelry making process for every piece of custom jewelry. The brothers, who are true artisans, work closely together, each masters at their craft. Often the unusual shape of a gem is a determining factor in the creation of a particular design, making custom jewelry designs even more special.

Whether customers come in with their own design idea, or they choose from pieces which have already been created, Harry's Fine Jewelry is a place where almost any jewelry creation imagined is possible.

Tilly's Clothing & Shoes

The July 1987 opening of the Huntington Beach Tilly's Clothing & Shoes for Men, Ladies & Kids marked a turning point in the prosperity of the company. Owner Hezy Shaked credits Huntington Beach citizens with changing the direction and focus of the company. Their demand for quality clothing and cutting edge style forced Tilly's Clothing to re-evaluate the lines and types of clothes it carried to meet their needs.

Tilly's Clothing officers — (Left to right) Sam Mendelsohn, vice president; Hezy Shaked, CEO/ president; and Tilly Levine, head buyer

Learning to listen to its customers and following up with great service has put Tilly's Clothing in the enviable position of being a stable corporation with the ability to expand and grow into the 21st century. It did not start that way for the trend-setting chain.

In April of 1982, Hezy and his wife Tilly needed to support their family. They were looking for a new direction in which to grow and learn. With a $10,000 loan co-signed by a friend and without any formal training in fashion, they opened their first clothing store in Los Alamitos called "World of Jeans and Tops."

Shaked believed that the early 80s was an easy time to succeed in retail if a store carried the right brand names. Although interest rates were high, Tilly's Clothing did not operate on a line of credit or bank-related loans. The original loan had been paid off so that it was liberated from the normal constraints of money-related problems generally associated with small business.

Through trial and error, they found the clothing lines people were interested in wearing. Some of the fashions they carried at that time consisted of Jordache, OP and Stubbies. The new store was doing well except for one minor difficulty — the name.

"World of Jeans and Tops" gave customers the impression that it only carried jeans and t-shirts when, in fact, it included dresses, shoes and pants. It became necessary to change the name so people would understand what it sold. In 1984 with the opening of the second store in Westminster, the name was changed to Tilly's Clothing.

Part of the reason for the success Tilly's Clothing had in the 1980s came from lack of competition, but most of it came from the hard work that the Shakeds put into it.

Business not being without risk, Shaked saw potential in the Huntington Beach area and decided to take a big chance. The turning point came in 1987 when they doubled the size of the company by building the Huntington Beach store. It became the biggest store at 8,100 square feet. At that time the rent was very expensive, but Shaked saw great potential in the area.

Immediately upon opening, Tilly's Clothing made major changes in the type of merchandise purchased. Decisions were based on the clothes that sold and the demands of its customers.

At the time of the Huntington Beach store opening, competition was not a consideration. But as the end of the 80s descended, other clothing stores were launched in the area. Then came the 90s with its drastic change in fashion and concept.

Used clothing became accepted as a "new outfit" by the younger generation. Companies that changed with the times survived, others closed. Customers wanted different fashion lines and lower pricing and Tilly's Clothing reacted.

The company lowered prices, purchased the brands people requested and increased customer service. Tilly's Clothing kept prices lower than its competitors. Other than Levi's, fashion lines constantly were being updated and it reacted in response to customer requests. It carried the most current styles while responding quickly to the fickle fashion front. Keeping a wide range of selection in style, price and size became an important cornerstone of success. The real difference became service.

Tilly's Clothing trained the sales staff to respond to the customer, to be supportive, helpful and to listen to what the customer had to say. It employed more people on the sales floor than most other companies simply for

Front entrance to Tilly's
Clothing landmark
Huntington Beach store

the benefit of the customer. Service became the hallmark of the business and Tilly's Clothing rose from a few stores to an effective force in the market.

Employees follow guidelines and training programs developed over the past successful years. Tilly's Clothing encourages its employees to make their own decisions and to take more responsibility with the company's full support. With competition stronger and tougher, the employee is critical to the continued success of the company. Tilly's Clothing goal is to make sure that everybody who works for the company enjoys what they do and becomes successful.

Bottom line profit is not the motivating factor in the success of the company. Shaked's belief is that it is more important that every customer who walks in leaves satisfied because Tilly's Clothing has the best product for the best price.

Tilly's Clothing intends to keep on changing by listening to its customers. "And when you finish changing, change again," Shaked says. Tilly's Clothing believes in taking customer complaints and compliments to heart.

Profit has not been the incentive behind the success of Tilly's Clothing. It remains a practice of the company to support high school sports teams, charities and most fundraisers with a strong emphasis on educational donations. Not limiting itself to one city, the company contributes to pediatric AIDS charities, the Nicole Brown Foundation, the Ely Home and various women's shelters. Long range plans for the company include more charitable contributions in Huntington Beach and to be an integral part of more events.

Whether it's charitable donations, fashion shows or supporting education, Tilly's Clothing basic corporate philosophy lies in giving back to the community where it lives. Often, the donations are handled anonymously and in many cases it is a condition for the contribution. Over the years, Shaked finds that the more he helps people, the more he feels rewarded. To him the real meaning of charity comes from the goodness of the heart, not the tributes and testimonials.

Customers checking out the
vast range of styles and
clothing carried in the
Huntington Beach Store

For Tilly's Clothing the city of Huntington Beach holds a special place. The unique character of local residents helped it to achieve a successful milestone in its future direction. The company believes that without the city and its residents, it wouldn't be where it is today.

Loehmann's 5 Points Plaza

oehmann's 5 Points Plaza, a Huntington Beach landmark since 1962, is thriving under the management of Terranomics Development. It is one of those market places that evolves with the times, yet retains the flavor and charm reminiscent of a hidden bazaar of treasures. The shops and restaurants are there with appealing surprises ready to be discovered. It is the type of place discriminating shoppers seek and will drive miles to access. The Plaza has been somewhat remarkable by virtue of having five roads converge directly to this singular plot of land. Merritt and Ron Sher, owners of various plazas throughout California and Washington, feel a special nostalgia for Loehmann's 5 Points Plaza. It marks the beginning of their participation and interest in shopping center development that goes back to their father, Sydney Sher and his brother, Saul.

In 1958 Sydney and Saul Sher acquired an irregular piece of undeveloped land in Huntington Beach off of Beach Boulevard, where Main Street and Ellis Avenue converge at 18593 Main Street and started building. The far-sighted Shers knew that this was a time of incubation, the prelude to a burst of growth that would turn the quiet beach town into a booming community. Completion of the building project produced a Bank of America, an Alpha Beta Market, the W. T. Grant discount store, a Chevron Station and the Edward's Cinema.

Houses and people were replacing farmland and Orange Groves. The timing for the Plaza was right.

The 5 Points property ideally located in the center of the coastal building drew buyers who needed banking, grocery, and miscellaneous services. Young families gravitated to the 5 Points requiring more consumer amenities. The Plaza continued to grow with other merchants and restaurateurs opening their doors. The 5 Points shopping facility became so popular over a short span of time people would drive 70 miles to shop there.

Loehmann's 5 Points Plaza is not just a place to shop, according to owner Merritt Sher. It has history and tradition. Sher recalls how with his father's encouragement and backing, Mario Valenzuela, a young immigrant from Mexico, opened Mario's Mexican Restaurant. Valenzuela, over 28 years in business and now owner of two other family owned and operated restaurants, is still going strong. His daughters, Diana and Rose Linda along with his son Johnny grew up in the family enterprise, assisting in running Mario's and two other restaurants in different locations. Jack's Jewelry is another long time business. George Jack opened Jack's Jewelry in 1963 and even though he is in his late 70s, continues the operation. Today George Jack is teamed up with his daughter, Linda and together they serve patrons, many being second generation cus-

202

Ron and Merritt Sher, owners of Terranomics Development

Loehmann's 5 Points
Plaza today

tomers. Early locals recall taking their families shopping at the Plaza, stopping off at Jack's Surf Shop, catching a movie at Edward's Cinema, and concluding the evening with dinner at Mario's. The old Edward's Cinema is now home for the expanded Old Navy Store.

It was not all smooth sailing for 5 Points. Huge, enclosed malls springing up in the surrounding area during the late 1970s and 80s were tough competition for the smaller Plaza, and a period of decline hit the popular shopping spot. The original developers, Sydney and Saul were suffering from failing health in their declining years and in an effort to rescue the Plaza Merritt and Ron Sher took the helm in 1982. The younger Sher brothers brought in the award-winning San Francisco Architect Jacques de Brer to completely redesign the Plaza giving it new life. Additional extensive work was done in 1984 and 5 Points bounced back bigger and better than ever. Not only was attention paid to the structural design and layout, but also the parking facilities were designed with customer convenience in mind allowing ease of access to ample parking on the property. The motif is in keeping with the Huntington Beach image, with tall palm trees gracing the lot. Even though it is not on a main thoroughfare, people seek out the Plaza.

The Plaza remains in the Sher family. Its strong image and market position comes from the strength of the Sher's company, Terranomics Development, which manages, markets and leases the center. Terranomics Development provides these services for its various shopping centers throughout California. Ron Sher guides the financial and legal division of Terranomics Development from the Seattle, Washington office.

Terranomics orchestrates the advertising and promotional programs that are the backbone of Loehmann's 5 Points Plaza. Merritt Sher is assisted by a hand-picked management team who sees to the day to day operations in Huntington Beach. In keeping with the Sher willingness to give new businesses a push, it is not unusual for Terranomics Development to help fledgling ventures get a start. Terranomics is on a constant quest for businesses that are appealing to consumers.

Today, the Plaza is home to over 35 merchants and businesses with Loehmann's, Trader Joe's and Tilly's as its anchor stores. The burgeoning retailing family includes everything from imports to specialty foods. A variety of clothing retailers and discount fragrances to surfing duds line the walkway. Whether it's hair care, eye care, postal services and banking—all are a part of the scene. A medley of dining choices is conveniently at hand. The most particular of creative shoppers can find a large divergence of merchandise in one area.

Marketing 5 Points to visitors and residents is only part of the task. The changing marketplace is closely followed in anticipation of future consumer needs and the effort to bring in better stores is an ongoing responsibility. Terranomics Development works closely with the Huntington Beach Conference and Visitors Bureau, providing shopping incentives like discount coupon books and special promotions during seasonal events. Sher feels more is in store for the popular Shopping Plaza that is in constant growth and change. Its past and present success together with its future potential, affirm that Loehmann's 5 Points Plaza, under the management of Terranomics Development, will keep pace with the desires of the consumer.

Restaurants and Services

East Coast Bagel Co.
Hong Kong Express
Java City Bakery Cafe
Mario's Mexican
  Restaurant
Bank of America
Dr. Jitosho, Optometrist
E J 30 Minute Photo
Farm Boy
Five Points Cleaners
Main Stage Hair Salon
Mail Boxes, Etc.

203

List of Merchants

Accessory Plus
Bannister Shoes
Bath & Body Works
Bed, Bath & Beyond
Calico Corners
Converse Factory Store
Dell's Boutique
Hugo's Cigar Shoppe
Jack's Jewelers
Jessica McClintock
Company Store
Loehmann's
Mikasa Factory Store
Off the Wall Gallery
Old Navy
Party World
Pets Pets Pets
Pier 1 Imports
Quality Beauty Supply
SideKik Clothing
Styles
The Fragrance Shop
The Gap
Tilly's
Trader Joe's

Hilton Ocean Grand and Waterfront Beach Resorts

Nothing says "Welcome to Huntington Beach" like the luxury of The Hilton Waterfront Beach Resort. Since 1990, this four-diamond, award-winning resort has offered the community, tourists and business travelers a gracious place in which to relax, socialize or do business. The resort features a 12-story, 290-room tower, oceanfront conference rooms, fine restaurants and lounges, 12,000 square feet of ballroom space and an inviting Mediterranean-style ambience.

From the stately *porte cochere* to the dramatic oceanfront views, The Hilton Waterfront Beach Resort exudes casual elegance. In the skylit lobby, a dramatic rockscape frames a cascading water fountain accentuated by lush palms and colorful plants. Cool Terrazo tile and a dramatic marble staircase complete the lobby motif.

Porte cochere of Hilton Waterfront Beach Resort

Once guests step inside one of the luxurious guest rooms or suites, they gain a whole new outlook on elegance. Each room has a panoramic ocean view from a private lanai, while the concierge floor offers a private lounge with personal attention.

Ocean-view dining at The Hilton Waterfront Beach Resort ranges from the casual atmosphere of the Surf Hero Deli to the gourmet cuisine of The Palm Court Restaurant, which offers indoor and outdoor dining highlighted by ocean views in a tropical setting with palm trees and wall murals gracing the interior. The West Coast Club offers a comfortable, sophisticated place to unwind and enjoy its fireplace, library, boardroom and outdoor patio. Tropical drinks, classic cocktails and fine beverages from around the world are always available. And, of course, the lobby bar is the perfect spot to enjoy refreshments and gaze upon endless views of the Pacific Ocean.

Hilton Waterfront Beach Resort

The Hilton Waterfront Beach Resort can accommodate a variety of business-related events, from small meetings to large conferences and presentations. Eighteen meeting rooms offer flexible facilities with sweeping sea-view terraces presenting the perfect surroundings for receptions and cocktail hours. The 3,000-square-foot Pacific Room and the 2,500-square-foot Cielo Mare Ballroom each boast spectacular ocean vistas providing an elegant ambience benefiting the most formal gatherings. Eight ocean-view boardrooms create spectacular settings for meetings and seminars. For a truly impressive event, the Waterfront Ballroom offers luxurious accommodations for up to 600 guests.

With a focus on providing a superior customer experience, The Hilton Waterfront Beach Resort is a dynamic example of how Robert Mayer and Steve Bone guide a new and complex venture through each evolutionary stage. As the flagship of Waterfront Resorts, Inc., The Hilton Waterfront Beach Resort is the first phase of a 50-acre vacation resort in Huntington Beach that will set new standards in innovative development, land management and oceanfront luxury.

The 519-room Hilton Ocean Grand Resort is scheduled for completion in the year 2001. Designed in the understated Andalusian-style, the new resort will complement The Hilton Waterfront Beach Resort, and together the hotels will provide the ultimate in comfort and hospitality on the Southern California coast.

Guests arriving at the Ocean Grand Resort will view the ocean from the lobby across an elegant pool and courtyard. Each guestroom will reflect a sophisticated yet casually elegant style. Luxury amenities will prevail, and most rooms have fabulous ocean views from their private lanai. Twenty luxury corner suites, each 2,000

square feet, will have formal dining rooms which can be converted to private boardrooms for small corporate meetings. The hotel will also include three 3,000-square-foot magnificent presidential suites offering the finest amenities and luxury accommodations available anywhere on the California coast. These presidential suites will have unrestricted, panoramic ocean views from all rooms.

Dining experiences at the Ocean Grand Resort will range from the rich wood paneling and luxury furnishings of the lobby lounge to the fine cuisine and ocean views of the main restaurant, which offers dining in a comfortable dinner house setting. A second more casual restaurant will also be incorporated into the retail plaza, a unique variety of resort-oriented retail shops and accessory food and beverage outlets.

Amenities at the Ocean Grand Resort include the main pool courtyard, dominated by a large, softly curving lagoon-style pool, a surrounding deck and landscaped areas. A hot spa is located in a lowered area amidst tropical plants, while a recessed pool bar and grill creates a fun, relaxed setting for food and drinks. Additional courtyards with large lawns overlooking the ocean can be used for parties and functions.

Two tennis courts are set low into the site and heavily landscaped to keep them out of the guest room views, creating a special enjoyment of the sport. Tennis players and guests can enjoy an ocean-view patio nearby.

The Ocean Grand Resort will offer the largest and most scenic conference facility on the coast. The spacious 20,000-square-foot ocean view ballroom alone will accommodate up to 1,500 people for a banquet and will be adjoined by an ocean-view pre-function terrace. The conference center will also house two junior ballrooms of 6,300 and 3,400 square feet each as well as three boardrooms, an 11,000-square-foot dedicated exhibit hall and more than 12,000 square

Porte cochere at the Ocean Grand Resort

Ocean Grand Resort Function Courtyard

205

feet of additional meeting rooms. These meeting facilities surround a 15,000-square-foot outdoor function lawn, perfect for outdoor dining, weddings and special events.

The Oceanview Function Courtyard blends the activities of the adjacent meeting rooms, ballrooms, prefunction areas, retail uses, restaurants and hotel guests into a beautiful multipurpose outdoor space.

Overlooking the Function Courtyard will be an ocean-view retail plaza in the intimate European-style with fountains, fireplace, outdoor seating to enjoy the views while dining and 12,000 square feet of retail shopping.

The Ocean Grand Resort will also have a full-service 17,000-square-foot resort spa facility combining the newest developments in health and wellness from all over the world. The spa will be a living and learning center where activities stimulate the mind and body, where work and play are synergistic, and where health, inner exploration and enjoyment complement one another.

Together, Hilton Waterfront Ocean Grand and Waterfront Beach Resorts will be the premier beach destinations in Southern California, ensuring business and leisure travelers a luxury experience on the California coast.

Ocean Grand Resort retail plaza

Baci Italian Restaurant

An evening at Baci Italian Restaurant is like a vacation in Italy. Outside, the building is an attractive rectangle of bright coral stucco trimmed in green and flower boxes while inside, the walls are covered with trompe l'oeil murals of ancient and modern Italy, all hand-painted.

Angelo Juliano, owner and manager, acquired the restaurant in 1992 and has transformed it from a small mom and pop eatery into one of the 10 best restaurants in Orange County and winner of Southern California Restaurant Writer's Silver Award of Merit.

Hand-painted trompe l'oeil *murals cover the walls inside Baci.*

Juliano's restaurant career began when he was still a schoolboy in Rome. His older brother Antonio owned Hotel Sonne in Switzerland, where Angelo spent every summer vacation washing dishes, sweeping floors and waiting tables. Antonio sent him to culinary school at the Hotel Montana in Lucerne and to classes in England, Holland, Switzerland and France where Juliano acquired his skills as a chef and mastery of six languages.

For four years, Juliano worked for his brother and then in a variety of other restaurants as chef or manager. He immigrated to Bermuda where he was manager of an Italian restaurant and then ventured out on his own at the il Chianti where he fed dignitaries such as Queen Elizabeth and George Bush. After six years,

The unmistakable Baci Italian Restaurant

Bermuda became too confining so Juliano continued north to New York and Philadelphia (which were much too cold), and he eventually settled in Southern California. He worked as a chef in several restaurants, bought into a restaurant partnership, and finally, opened Baci where he has fulfilled his concept of what an Italian restaurant should be.

Juliano has expanded Baci's space from less than 2,000-square-feet to 5,000-square-feet. The restaurant can seat about 150 guests at one time. The cuisine is primarily Northern Italian but not exclusively so, and the menu is very extensive. Baci's boasts one of the largest dessert menus in the area.

Baci's has facilities for banquets, parties, all types of receptions and wedding dinners. On Wednesdays and Thursdays, a guitar player sings Neapolitan songs for the diners' enjoyment and on Friday and Saturday evenings, there is piano and flute entertainment and sometimes a harpist. On occasion the featured event is Italian night or even an opera night with vocalists from Opera Pacific and the Santa Fe Opera performing.

In the future, Juliano plans to expand his talents into the international marketplace with an industrial bakery that will produce Italian bread of all kinds. Although no name has been chosen, he is toying with the idea of calling it La Spigadoro (grain of wheat).

Juliano makes his home in Huntington Beach with his wife and daughter and hopes one day to sit on the City Council. "I'm a happy man," he smiles. "Huntington Beach has been very good to me, and I would like to help the people of this town in return."

Comfort Suites

omfort Suites prides itself on hospitality in the Southern California tradition. Located just off the 405 San Diego Freeway in Huntington Beach, the warm pink and green exterior reflects the warmth and friendliness the hotel offers to its corporate and leisure guests.

The hotel was built by owner Chandu Patel in 1987. Although it is individually owned and managed, it exists as a Comfort Suites hotel under the umbrella of Choice Hotels International, which has several different branches including Comfort Inns, Quality Inns, Quality Suites, Clarion Inns and Clarion Suites.

There are 102 suites in the hotel, all of which are designed as studio suites. The suites are spacious and comfortable, featuring a king-sized bed and a living area with a pull-out couch for either relaxing or an additional guest. All the suites have refrigerators and all have in-room coffee makers.

Comfort Suites offers its guests many amenities including a complimentary deluxe continental breakfast which is served every morning. There is an outdoor heated swimming pool and spa, and an exercise room. Meeting facilities are available in a 425-square-foot meeting room, with theater-style seating for 35 to 40 people. There are also valet/guest laundry facilities for those who need them.

The hotel is centrally located, just 11 miles from the John Wayne Airport, 30 miles from the Los Angeles Airport and only 10 miles from the Long Beach Airport. It is close to two major shopping malls, eight miles from Disneyland, eight miles from Knott's Berry Farm and only four miles from the famous Huntington Beach Pier and the Bolsa Chica Ecological Reserve.

Currently, 80 percent of the clientele consists of corporate clients who come to Huntington Beach for meetings or business, and in this manner, Comfort Suites plays an integral part in the commercial life of the city.

Manager Kent Patel (no relation to owner Chandu Patel) has managed Comfort Suites since 1991 and is also a Huntington Beach resident.

Comfort Suites prides itself on hospitality in the Southern California tradition.

As Manager Patel expresses it, "We strive to provide an exceptional quality of friendliness, professional service and etiquette, which we hope will linger fondly in the memories of our guests long after they have visited our Comfort Suites hotel."

Comfort Suites features comfortable and spacious suites.

207

Guests may enjoy a continental breakfast in Comfort Suites' attractive lobby.

Huntington Beach Beer Company

I n 1992, there were very few microbreweries in Orange County, and none in Huntington Beach. Canadian Peter Andriet decided to change that by opening the Huntington Beach Beer Company in the newly renovated downtown area on the corner of Main Street and Walnut. A combination restaurant and microbrewery, Huntington Beach Beer Co. has become one of the hotspots of Surf City, and was voted No.1 Best Beer and Micro Brewery in Orange County by the readers of the *Orange County Register* three years in a row...and counting. The secret? Great food, great beer and a great atmosphere.

Interior of Huntington Beach Beer Company

Andriet had spent several years in the construction industry, and didn't consider going into the brewery business until he and a buddy went on a fishing expedition to Colorado and visited a local microbrewery. The brewery idea appealed to Andriet, so he began to look for investors and scouted locations along the California coast for a place to start his own brewery. He chose Huntington Beach, which had just undergone a transformation from a sleepy surfing town to a bustling beach community. He selected a new structure that was reinforced with steel beams to hold the weight of the brewery tanks. Once the building was ready, Andriet hired a brew master, kitchen chef and management team, and opened for business. The Beer Co. has been a success from day one, thanks to some very tasty cuisine, a prime location with balconies open to the sun, a view of the pier and ocean and a terrific selection of beers and ales brewed onsite.

The brick building houses an all-wood interior, with hardwood and slate floors and oak trim surrounding the brewery, where the beers are created. The bar and brewery take up the back portion of the restaurant, with the brewing equipment and fermenters in plain view behind the bar. Floor-to-ceiling windows provide dazzling views of Catalina Island at sundown. The ambience is family friendly, and the extensive menu (over 50 items are listed) offers a wide variety of food, including creative appetizers such as Cajun lamb, beer battered steak fries and steamed clams. Pasta dishes include Cajun jambalaya and Surf City penne pasta, while the wood-fired brick oven pizzas range from buffalo chicken and fajita pizza to vegetarian. Brewery favorites including the H.B. burger, fish tacos, clam chowder, steak, a Cajun chicken sandwich and fine fish dishes round out the selections. There's even a menu just for kids.

And then, of course, there is the beer. The Huntington Beach Beer Company brews 10 different beers and a few special seasonal selections. Four to five selections are available at any given time, and are rotated on a regular basis. The restaurant typically goes through a batch of beer every two weeks. Two or three brewing days are scheduled each week. The style to be brewed depends on the season, and the available yeast. Darker beers are popular in winter, while the lighter pilsners and wheat beers are preferred during the warmer months. Popular concoctions include the Main St. Wheat, Huntington Beach Blonde, Bolsa Chica ESB, Black Gold Porter and the Pier Pale Ale. The Black Gold Porter won a bronze medal at the 1997 Great American Beer Festival, while the Pier Pale Ale received a silver medal at the 1994 Great American Beer Festival.

The Brewery holds beer appreciation nights once a month, where patrons can learn more about the history and brewing process of beer, and sample the latest batches. Special events such as cigar dinners have been very popular, and live entertainment features the music of local musicians. The brewery's Web site offers information on upcoming events and beers of the month.

The Huntington Beach Beer Company has proven to be so popular that Andriet has opened other locations in Newport Beach, Laguna Beach, Tustin and Westwood. Now those communities know what Huntington Beach has been experiencing for years — "great food, great beer, great atmosphere — and outstanding customer service."

Huntington Beach Dodge

What makes Huntington Beach Dodge unique among car dealerships is its very strong employee base. As owner Clay James explains his personal business philosophy, "If you take care of your employees, your employees will take care of the customers. Here at Huntington Beach Dodge, we really try to go out of our way to make sure our organization is responsive to our employees. We meet their needs, and they meet the dealership's needs and this trade-off has worked very successfully for us."

Huntington Beach Dodge has been a familiar sight along Beach Boulevard since the late 1960s, when there wasn't much else around and fog engulfed the whole area during the winter months. The dealership was originally owned by Howard Able who sold it about 10 years later. The company then went through several different ownership changes and was finally acquired by the well-known car dealer Cal Worthington in the early 1980s. Worthington ran the dealership until Chrysler Corporation purchased the assets in December of 1990. In August 1992, Clay James came on the scene and has been running it ever since.

James has a long history with the Chrysler Corporation. He began working for them when he graduated from USC in 1975 and worked for Chrysler for the next 17 years in various capacities. His last position before purchasing Huntington Beach Dodge was as Satellite Communications Director for Chrysler Corporation in Detroit. Although James enjoyed a successful career with Chrysler, he always wanted to be in the retail side of the business rather than on the wholesale side so when the opportunity presented itself in 1992, he jumped on it.

Born in Whittier, James moved out of the state with his family when he was only five years old. However, he returned to the Los Angeles area in 1973 and began his junior year of college at USC. After he graduated two years later, he remained in California working for Chrysler for the next 10 years. Following career opportunities, James then moved to Detroit where he remained for nine months, to Atlanta for the next three years and finally back to Detroit for another three years. Interestingly, Clay James' father also had a career with Chrysler Corporation.

Huntington Beach Dodge occupies an extensive lot nearly seven acres in size. When James bought the dealership in 1992, there were 37 employees. Today, the company boasts 120 employees. Many of the employees, especially in the parts department, the service director, several mechanics and several office staff have been with the dealership since the early days.

Under James' leadership, Huntington Beach Dodge now ranks 39th in national sales and fourth in the Los Angeles area, aptly demonstrating the success of his business philosophy and company leadership.

Huntington Beach Dodge is a familiar sight to Huntington Beach residents.

Huntington Beach Mall

"We Make Good Things Happen"

Since its grand opening in November 1966, Huntington Beach Mall (originally named Huntington Center), has played an integral role in the city. A sweeping redevelopment project undertaken by The Macerich Company will dramatically change the face of the center, ensuring that the property maintains that important role in the community well into the next century.

Looking back at the property's history, the original $20 million development was completed after four

The 63-acre site, opened on November 17, 1966, was recognized as Orange County's only enclosed mall with a year-round temperature of 72 degrees. It was also one of the earliest of its kind in the entire United States.

years of planning and construction on a site where bean and sugar beet fields once stood. A joint venture of the Huntington Beach Company and the Gordon L. MacDonald Corporation of Santa Barbara, Huntington Center was not only Orange County's only enclosed mall, but one of the earliest in the United States.

The two original anchor stores, The Broadway and Montgomery Ward, were joined by over 50 specialty shops. The property included an angled strip center and restaurant pad on the mall's perimeter, visible from the 405 San Diego Freeway. Inside, unique features such as imported Danish gas lamps added elegance to the facility. Amenities like contoured benches, telephones, drinking fountains and soft background music encouraged shoppers to extend their stay.

In the years that followed, the property served as a major employer and retail center, while hosting thousands of special events, including concerts, art shows, antique exhibits, food drives, gymnastics demonstrations and parades.

An initial expansion was completed in 1968, when JC Penney became the third anchor. In 1981, the mall experienced its first "facelift," with improved landscaping and the addition of two entertainment stage areas. Incorporated in this project were 405 Freeway off-ramp improvements to Center Avenue.

Huntington Center expanded again in 1986, with a two-story wing that included fourth anchor Mervyn's. A unique food court featured an innovative "Teflon" roof that gave customers the feeling of being outdoors in a pleasant tropical setting. Because much of the construction was done on difficult existing soil conditions, the entire enclosed mall is constructed atop a pile foundation featuring an expansion system that would reduce damage during an earthquake.

After reaching its peak with 109 stores in 1990, Huntington Center's popularity began to wane due to fierce competition from newer Orange County malls and changing trends of shoppers nationally. Recognizing the site's enormous potential, Santa Monica-based Macerich, a specialist in the redevelopment of regional retail properties, purchased the center in 1996. With a new vision, Macerich began to embark on a course to revitalize the property into an open-air shopping/entertainment experience that would better represent the outdoor lifestyle of Huntington Beach residents.

The redevelopment will include a 92,000-square-foot, 5,000-seat megaplex cinema with 18 screens, accompanied by sit-down family restaurants, and entertainment and specialty retail venues. Design features of the plan include lush landscaping, potted gardens, sparkling-interactive fountains and a play area in the courtyard. Children will have the opportunity to interact with a smaller fountain, sea-life topiaries and a beach-inspired sandbox.

The mall set a new trend in 1966 with its enclosed structure, and as the new millennium approaches, it will again play a major role in the lives of residents and the future of Huntington Beach. While the look and name will most certainly change, the rich history of this 63-acre parcel will not soon be forgotten.

The Huntington Shores Motel

Located across Pacific Coast Highway from the beach, and one block from the Huntington Beach pier, The Huntington Shores Motel caters to guests from the community, the nation and the world, providing moderately priced, comfortable accommodations in a friendly, caring atmosphere. Currently, there are 45 double queen and five king size rooms. The six kitchenettes are fully stocked, and every room offers an ocean or poolside view.

The first 12 rooms of this 50 room mini-resort were constructed in 1958 on the site of the Standard Oil Company/Chevron of America oil field. The formation of The Chevron Land and Development Corporation and The Huntington Beach Company provided the major impetus for development in the community. The Huntington Beach Company built The Huntington Shores Motel to bolster both tourism and local real estate development by providing comfortable beach front accommodations.

In 1963, The Huntington Shores Motel complex reached its current size. The additional rooms, large heated pool and the improved landscape design built guest loyalty. Many of the children whose families first stayed at The Huntington Shores Motel in the 1960s now bring their own children to enjoy the property. One couple has been celebrating their anniversary here for over 35 years. Since more than half of the motel's guests return year after year, a friendly family atmosphere has developed. It is not unusual to see two or three families get together and renew their acquaintance over a game of ping-pong, badminton or horseshoes.

Many grandparents who have family living in Huntington Beach stay at the motel especially over the winter holiday season. They find that families are always welcome to visit, and there are lots of ways to spend time with their grandchildren. The large comfortably heated swimming pool is a real favorite with this group, and hot dog and marshmallow roasts at the barbecue area run a close second.

Overseas guests think of the motel as their home away from home. They come here year after year for the clean comfortable rooms, friendly people and the great beach front location. The Huntington Shores Motel is listed with a star in *Foders International Travel Guide*.

The Huntington Shores Motel plays host to over 50 groups participating in beach events each year. These events, which range from three-man basketball tournaments to wave-running regattas, draw several million people to Huntington Beach each year. Most of these athletic events are staged on the beach right across the street from The Huntington Shores Motel. It provides both participants and spectators with moderately priced accommodations while in town for the events. For instance, both amateur and professional surfers love to stay at the motel when they are in town each summer to compete in the only rated surfing contest in the continental United States.

Other events held at the motel include church retreats, business company "play days," weddings, birthdays and family reunions. People especially enjoy the motel's conversation nooks on three acres of flower covered grounds. They find The Huntington Shores Motel a relaxing, moderately priced oasis where their group or family can get together to relax and renew their friendships.

The longtime managers of The Huntington Shores Motel, Pete and Leslie Holt, say "Come and stay with us. Enjoy the beach and all the motel's comforts. This is the best moderately priced beachfront mini-resort for families. It's the place for you to stay while enjoying Huntington Beach without emptying your pocketbook."

Mario's Restaurant

Mexican tile on the floor. Mariachi music over the loudspeaker. Delicious aromas of enchiladas, beans and salsa. Take it all in because you're in Mario's Restaurant.

Before it was Mario's, the restaurant was a small donut shop. Then it became a hamburger stand. Finally, in 1970, it was transformed into Mario's Restaurant. Mario Valenzuela had opened the restaurant in 1969 but because cash was tight, he could not afford to change the sign until 1970. In those days, there were very few other Mexican restaurants in the area. Diners craving the exotic flavors of Mexican cooking flocked to Mario's.

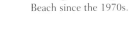
Mario's Restaurant has been thriving in Huntington Beach since the 1970s.

In its early days, Mario was owner, menu planner, chief cook and bottle washer, and his wife, Consuelo, waited tables. As their son and four daughters grew up, they took their turns helping out, either waiting tables, washing dishes, or doing whatever else needed doing. Some of the original employees are still with the restaurant today which adds to the overall nostalgic feeling.

The family's efforts, combined with a menu of basic Mexican dishes and the public's interest in experimenting with Mexican food, ensured Mario's of continued success. Mario learned his craft from his aunt who owned a small restaurant. He graduated to working at other restaurants and eventually became the chief at La Paz Mexican Restaurant where he remained for many years before opening Mario's.

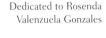
Dedicated to Rosenda Valenzuela Gonzales

Originally, the restaurant had only 10 booths and consisted of what is now the middle area of the building. Later, an addition to the back extended it considerably and a third addition, the sidewalk in the front and on the side became the bar and patio part of the restaurant, greatly expanded the seating capacity.

In 1975, Mario opened Mario's Restaurant #2, also in Huntington Beach, at Beach and Main. About five years later, he opened a delicatessen and liquor store, Mario's Mexican Deli and Liquor, located on Beach Boulevard between Slater and Warner in Huntington Beach. Recently, Mario has embarked on a new venture with a fourth establishment, Fiesta Maya, located next to Mario's Mexican Deli and Liquor. Mario, his wife Elia and two sons run the new restaurant.

When Mario's Restaurant opened its doors, the menus consisted of the basic traditional Mexican food. Although exotic in comparison with the other area restaurants, the recipes were tailored to suit the American taste, and the "heat" was turned down. Now there is more of an interest in and demand for the full scope of Mexican cuisine which includes spicier dishes that in the past would have been considered too daring. At Fiesta Maya, patrons will find a more contemporary exploration of the full range of Mexican cuisine, including a variety of seafood creations.

The Valenzuela family is a family with its roots deep in the city of Huntington Beach. When Mario immigrated from Torreon, Coahuila, Mexico in the early 1950s, he settled first in Santa Ana but soon made Huntington Beach his home, where the family remains. All seven of the Valenzuela children have gone through the Huntington Beach school system.

Today, although Mario still holds the reins, the second and even third generations of Valenzuelas are actively involved in the several Mario's Restaurants. Son, John Valenzuela runs the original Mario's and is assisted by family members. Diana Valenzuela runs Mario's #2 and is assisted by family members, her sister Rosie and her nephews.

The Valenzuela family plans to expand its horizons with additional restaurants in the future. However, they are currently in no rush. They want to continue serving the many patrons who have been loyal to the restaurant since its beginning. They intend to maintain the family atmosphere which they feel has been the basis for their success, along with the delicious food.

Mother's Market & Kitchen

Since 1978, Mother's Market and Kitchen has been "manifesting truth, beauty and goodness in the context of a natural foods store." From soup to nuts and everything in between, its shelves are stocked with products to nurture mind, body and soul — while trying to treat Mother Earth with kindness and dignity.

A tour through Mother's Huntington Beach location is a treat for the senses. Out front is a vast selection of herbs and plants which are organically grown, often from heirloom seeds. Inside, one can see rows of colorful, locally or organically grown vegetables and fruits, bins bursting with bulk grains, nuts, seeds and dried fruits, and a large selection of books and magazines. Bakery-fresh breads come in a variety of flavors and textures, while fragrant aromatherapy oils and lotions call attention to an abundant bodycare department. Additionally, a juice bar squeezes juices from fresh produce, not concentrates, which include carrots, mixed veggies, fruits and shots of wheat grass.

Mother's was chosen by the *Orange County Register* as the "Best Health Food Store in Orange County" and the restaurant was chosen as one of the "Top Value" restaurants in Orange County by the prestigious Zagat Survey in 1998. It's no surprise, since Mother's Kitchen offers one of the finest selections of vegetarian cuisine with recipes from all over the world. The freshest ingredients are used and organic produce is included whenever possible.

Breakfast is served all day using cage-free eggs, tofu entrees, homebaked corn bread, biscuits and flapjacks served with pure maple syrup. Lunch and dinner selections include hearty, satisfying soups reminiscent of home, meatless entrees from oriental stir fry to lentil nut loaf, and South-of-the-border items fit for a Mexican fiesta. The chef's daily specials add variety to the menu and the coffee and espresso is brewed with organic coffee beans which are grown without herbicides or chemical fertilizers. For those without the luxury of sitting down to a meal, the deli is overflowing with delicious takeout items.

Corn muffins and biscuits are baked fresh daily in Mother's kitchen.

Mother's seeks companies manufacturing beauty products with no mineral oils or animal testing and food items made with no artificial ingredients, colorings or preservatives. Mother's is proud to have the reputation as having the largest selection of discounted vitamins, herbs and sports nutritional supplements in Orange County.

Today, Mother's has expanded from 2,600 square feet to 15,000 square feet in the original Costa Mesa store which opened in 1978. Additionally, a 10,000-square-foot store, opened in 1984, and is situated on one of Huntington Beach's main boulevards, and the 10,000-square-foot Irvine store opened in 1996.

Mother's Market and Kitchen, however, is more than just a store. For the past 20 years, many loyal fans consider Mother's a second home. They enjoy being able to eat and shop for food at the same place, and the knowledgeable and friendly staff at Mother's Market and Kitchen is committed to providing healthy, delicious cuisine and environmentally responsible products.

Mother's Huntington Beach store is situated on one of the city's busiest boulevards.

Old World Village

Old World Village, nestled between the 405 freeway and Goldenwest College, has always been synonymous with Oktoberfest. Over the years thousands have witnessed the pulsating beat of oom-pah-pah bands direct from Germany, the cheers and laughter of dachshund races, as well as the bizarre but delightful ritual of the "chicken dance." The aroma of freshly baked rolls, bread and European pastries fill the air. German specialties such as sauerkraut, bratwurst, sauerbraten, potato pancakes and apple strudel delight guests daily. Overflowing mugs of ice-cold European beer and shots of Jaegermeister top it all off. Visitors flock to Old World during the months of September and October to participate in the festivities. This Bavarian village was designed, however, to be enjoyed every month of the year.

(Both Photos) Old World, a quaint European village where shopkeepers live above their stores

Josef Bischof, a German developer, came to this country in 1952 and dreamed of bringing with him a piece of his homeland to share. After finding acreage available in Huntington Beach, his dream was to become a reality. He and his wife, Dolores, built 50 homes above 50 shops in the traditional Bavarian style. They imported lanterns to light the way along the cobble stone streets. They left space on the building's walls for 70 vibrant murals depicting scenes from 18 European countries. They built a church for worship, a hall for gatherings and wedding receptions, restaurants and a motel so that visitors can come to Orange County and stay in Europe at the same time. The shops were filled with a variety of products and services from crystal, collectibles and clocks to Birkenstocks, health foods and German groceries. Balconies filled with flower boxes marked the finishing touches and a sun clock was perfectly placed along the side of the town hall building. With every detail complete, September 1978 marked the first annual Oktoberfest in Huntington Beach.

Today, Old World Village is alive and bustling with activity year round. Each January the new year begins with a birthday celebration for Grandmama Elly, Dolores' mother. She was born in Wiesbaden, Germany on January 18, 1895! She came to this country in 1929 and lived next door to Josef and Dolores until she passed away on June 10, 1998. She was 103 and a half years old. One Sunday in May is devoted to "Maifest" with German bands and folk dancers. A maypole has been erected to depict all the ingredients for a wonderful life, including hearty food and a cozy home. The second Sunday of July marks German Heritage Day when the music keeps the toes tapping, the beer flows and the food is free for the first 500 visitors. The middle of August is the Plum Festival with delicious fresh-baked goods made with sweet juicy plums. There is even a festival featuring sauerkraut prepared a variety of ways from roasting with pork to baking into sweet moist cakes. Any time of the year Old World Village is host to countless fund-raisers, weddings and business meetings.

Dolores and Josef still reside on the property at Old World, along with their children Cindy and Bern, Bern's wife Barbara and grandson Markus. Today the Bischof family work to create new ideas for future festivals while keeping with steadfast traditions. Together they invite one and all to experience the heart of Europe in the center of Surf City.

The Park Bench Cafe

The Park Bench Cafe in Huntington Beach City Park is a charming rest stop for park visitors and for their dogs. Unique not only to Huntington Beach but to Southern California as a whole, a congenial atmosphere prevails where families, children and pets are all welcome.

Owners Michael and Christie Bartusick took over the cafe in 1988 although it has been in the park since 1974. Originally a walkup stand for cold drinks and ice cream, the Bartusicks offered to buy the restaurant, and it has been growing ever since, from 30 seats to 160, inside and outside.

The Bartusicks knew they wanted to focus on a family atmosphere and to promote a healthy menu, but right from the beginning, people walking their dogs by the lake began stopping for water or to sit with their dogs while enjoying something to eat. As Michael Bartusick recalls, "At first we were unsure what to do, but then we realized it was part of what we wanted to create." By 1990, people were coming specifically to bring their dogs. At first an outside water table with bowls for dogs was erected. Then, between 1990 and 1993, a menu of Canine Cuisine was created. The offerings include such items as Hound Dog Heaven (a juicy hamburger), Chilly Paws (a scoop of vanilla ice cream) and Doggie Kibble, among other things. Also available are dog toys, dog mats and dog parties, including dog birthday parties.

The people menu is quite extensive for a small cafe, including a wide variety of breakfast items for those enjoying the park on a sunny spring or summer morning. In keeping with the Bartusicks focus on healthy items, four kinds of burgers are available made of beef, garden, turkey or chicken and all are prepared in a variety of ways.

The Bartusicks are Huntington Beach residents, and the whole family is involved in The Park Bench Cafe. Michael's mother, Bernice Avalos donates her recipes, baking skills and many hours of time and his sister, Kashka Warden, also puts in some waitressing hours.

On Friday and Saturday evenings, people and pooches can enjoy acoustic guitar and occasionally harp entertainment while savoring their culinary treats.

In the future, The Park Bench Cafe expects to be offering a line of dog bakery items and canine activities such as agility training and competitions.

"The Park Bench Cafe has been good for us," commented Michael Bartusick. "Every business needs a niche, and this is ours. It's a getaway where people come to relax, to enjoy an open environment. There are very few places like this in Southern California and serving the dogs is an added benefit for us and our public."

215

Most patrons of The Park Bench Cafe enjoy their meals at the umbrella-topped outside tables.

Sugar Shack

Patrick and Mary Williams drove to California with dreams of their future together and a bag of potatoes in the car. At the time they were unaware that, as restaurant owners, they would be buying thousands of bags of potatoes and serving them up to hundreds of hungry diners daily.

In the early 1950s, following Patrick's tour with the U.S. Marines, the couple bought a home and settled in Huntington Beach. Patrick drove a truck and worked in the oil fields while Mary worked in real estate, filled

The Sugar Shack, established in 1967, feeds hundreds daily with home-style food, huge portions and prices that roll back more than a decade.

in at a local convenience store and worked for the post office. They were also raising their six children, Patti, Michele, Jeanie, Pam, Matt and Cindy.

Walking down Main Street one day in 1967, Mary noticed a small cafe named Joyce's Pantry with a "For Sale" sign in the window. Mary reasoned that working in a restaurant would be a good way for her children to learn responsibility, a strong work ethic, the feeling of having a little money in their pockets and interacting with and being kind to people. She inquired within, the price was right and she bought the building and the restaurant. Patrick changed the name to the "Sugar Shack," after one of his favorite hit songs.

The Williams kids didn't just work in the restaurant, they ran it. Mary kept her job with the post office and offered help only when necessary. In the small kitchen, the kids prepared home-style meals with instruction from an older lady named Elaine Tineley. The limited menu included meat loaf, daily specials, and steak and eggs for $1.50. As their parents taught them, the kids gave 120 percent effort. Patti and Michele, being the oldest, fulfilled every job from cooking and serving to cleaning and taking out the garbage.

"It was frustrating," Michele says, "Patti and I put our tips in the register so it looked like the restaurant made more at the end of the day." Michele cooked at the Sugar Shack in the mornings and then went to a second job at Dennys in the evening. It was rough in the beginning but Patrick and Mary's kids were raised to never give up and they persisted, slowly establishing the restaurant's reputation.

Most of the Williams kids have since left the family business, opting for marriage and careers in other locales. Michele, however, made the decision to stay. Following her parents' retirement to Northern California in 1978, she and her husband Tim — also her childhood sweetheart — took over the restaurant's operations. Accommodating a large, loyal patronage, they expanded next door and added the first outside dining area in the city. In addition to her own children, Holly, Ryan and Timmy, Michele has employed her nieces and nephews, as well as all the kids in her neighborhood, keeping with her parents' original reasons for buying the restaurant. "The kids are almost ready to run it themselves," she says.

Each day at the Sugar Shack, all walks of life gather — businessmen, surfers, retirees, tourists and even the local homeless population — to share great food, conversation and Michele's bright smile. Everyone is treated and fed well. Deeply religious, she says "You never know when you're serving Jesus or an angel in disguise. There's a special feeling here."

Sunline-Electric Chair

When the Spice Girls are on television, take a good look at their outfits. Check out the wild clothing and incredible shoes. Most people may not be able to sing like the Spice Girls, but they can definitely dress like them if they make a visit to Sunline-Electric Chair in Huntington Beach.

Sunline-Electric Chair is a retail store catering to the alternative clothing and accessories market. Its merchandise might be startling, but the Sunline story is the story of a successful business operation.

In 1980, Abdul Memon opened Sunline Surf Boards at 111 Main Street. He was not a surfer himself, but he was a shrewd businessman. The shop carried Sunline Surf Boards and the whole spectrum of surfing accessories and clothing. The boards were manufactured for Sunline at a plant in Huntington Beach, and the business boasted a top surfing team and a top knee boarders team, all Top 10 NSSA rated.

Upstairs was a small boutique which stocked women's clothing, bikinis and other beachwear. All of the clothing was out on the edge of the surfing industry fashions, and the customer was guaranteed to find the crazier shorts and pants. Seeing the growing punk-rock movement and realizing that there was nowhere in Orange County to meet the demand of the scene, Memon opened The Electric Chair in a very small half address shop in the first block of Main Street. In a few years, the two businesses were combined into one location at 127 Main Street where they remained for several years.

The hard-core punk rock scene was in full bloom at this time and as a result, The Electric Chair kept growing. In 1990, both businesses were moved again to the current address, and the surf products were phased

out entirely. However, part of the original name was preserved to keep its surfing roots, and the business became Sunline-Electric Chair.

Sunline-Electric Chair is a family owned and operated business. The Memon family grew up in Huntington Beach and Abdul's son Mohammed (Moe) Memon has worked in the store since he was 10 years old and he now runs the mail order business for the store. Sister Shirley and Uncle Saeed can also be found working in the shop.

In addition to a whole line of clothing from normal street wear to nightclub wear for men and women, accessory items such as body piercing and henna temporary tattoos are available at Sunline. Extreme fashions such as fetish clothing (chain bras and panties, leather and latex) are available. In the shoe department, customers can choose from a huge selection of Dr. Martens and Creepers, the largest variety available in Orange County, as well as a whole line of women's shoes. To accessorize, products by Ape Leather and many other companies can be found.

Sunline Electric Chair's customers are primarily high school students, but many of its original customers have remained loyal, so in some cases, there are three generations of buyers frequenting the shop.

The business is expanding into a wholesale clothing line which will include the actual manufacturing of its own line of items. But whether made by Sunline or by one of the many alternative clothing brands in the store, no matter what a customer's looking for, it will probably be found at Sunline-Electric Chair.

Sunline-Electric Chair is a "must visit" attraction of downtown Huntington Beach.

No matter how wild an item, it can be found at Sunline-Electric Chair.

Professions

Artists, photographers, electricians, engineers, newspaper and realty organizations provide essential services to Huntington Beach.

The Huntington House Photography Studio

For Paul Thompson, what began as a dream more than 15 years ago, is now a Huntington Beach landmark. After photographing weddings for 10 years, first out of a converted garage and later from a residential building, Thompson decided to build a photography studio of his own, from the ground up. In 1987, The Huntington House was born.

While some photography studios feel more like a retail store, walking into The Huntington House is like walking into a familiar living room. The elegant three-story Cape Cod-style building that houses Thompson's studio is comfortably appointed to look and feel like a well-furnished home. Situated in the heart of Huntington Beach, the 3,500-square-foot studio is a unique reflection of both the photographer's personality and the quality of the portraits he creates.

Virtually every wall of Huntington House is covered with eye-catching and award-winning photographs. Individuals, families, newlyweds and children, all captured in poses that are at once intimate and inviting. These portraits, like fine works of art, seem to draw the viewer in. It is this unique style that has earned Thompson such acclaim throughout the years, including a video profile done by Kodak called "Image is Everything," which was viewed worldwide and serves as a training tool at numerous how-to seminars.

In addition to offering many of the comforts of home, The Huntington House also offers state-of-the-art electronic imaging which allows customers to view their pictures within minutes, not days, of their session. The images are presented in a private viewing room on a large-screen video monitor, allowing selections to be made the same day. This electronic previewing system saves valuable time for customers, and for the studio as well. "Everyone is busy today, we all want an immediate response. Photography is no different," says Thompson. "Our studio seems to make life easier for everyone."

The Huntington House also uses digital technology, a relatively new technique in photography today, and one that is becoming increasingly popular. This process makes it possible for the photographer to manipulate images once they've been photographed, allowing for such special effects as moving a head from one frame to another. This technique is also used for photo restoration, a growing part of the studio's business.

The studio's business comes from weddings and portraits. When not done in the studio, Thompson's portrait sessions frequently take place at nearby Huntington Beach, a beautiful backdrop which conveys California's more casual approach to portrait photography. While the standard look of many family portraits features the subjects in stiff, unnatural poses, Thompson's portraits have a certain relaxed look about them, whether the subjects are decked out in formal wear or dressed down in casual jeans and tee shirts.

Thompson's initial goal is to make people feel comfortable. He accomplishes that by listening to their needs and spending time getting to know them, so that the images he captures on film convey not just their physical likeness, but their personalities as well. This does not mean that Thompson's subjects are not posed, however. Posing them to look as if they are not posed is an art in itself, an art Thompson has surely mastered. When asked, he says he prefers a casual, happy style of pho-

tography that best reflects the more laid back Southern California lifestyle.

Many people delay taking their family portraits for one reason or another, while others make a big production of having them done, only to wait many years before scheduling another sitting. Thompson is a firm believer that family portraits should be updated yearly, and as a husband, son and father, has kept a yearly record of his own family's growth throughout the years. One of his most striking works is a family portrait which hangs in his office. It is a multigenerational gathering celebrating his parent's 50th wedding anniversary, which was displayed at Epcott Center in 1990. He has also kept a photographic history of each of his children from birth through young adulthood, capturing their images in a combination of head shots and full-length poses that document both the subtle and dramatic changes each child has gone through year by year. Many of these shots, along with hundreds of others, are displayed in albums in the studio's lobby, offering customers the opportunity to browse at their leisure and find inspiration for their own portrait goals.

When planning a family portrait, the biggest question that arises is usually what to wear. The philosophy at Huntington House is that the clothing you wear should be comfortable, it should make you feel good,

and it should harmonize with the color scheme of your home, or at least the room in which you plan to display the portrait. Thompson says the portrait should look like a work of art and complement the home. He adds that in recent years he has seen a trend toward

portraits in general, and wall portraits in particular, replacing posters and paintings as acceptable wall decor.

Paul Thompson is an in-demand lecturer and speaker who enjoys helping beginning photographers get started in the business. In response to numerous questions about his expertise in wedding photography, Thompson produced "The Complete Guide to Wedding Photography," a two-volume video set which uses a real wedding as well as studio demonstrations to illustrate why Thompson is one of the nation's most successful wedding photographers. The video series has been widely acclaimed as one of the most authoritative instructional videos on the market, noted for its excellent direction and production. In addition to the full wedding and reception, the video also includes romantic outdoor photographs, studio sessions, equipment demonstrations and personal tips from Thompson.

Brides-to-be will appreciate The Huntington House bridal packet, which offers everything from information on marriage licenses and hints for ordering wedding invitations, to makeup tips and suggestions for planning a successful honeymoon. The comprehensive pack, which naturally also includes information on wedding photography, is just another way Thompson brings a more personal

touch to everything he does. "Customer service is a key in this business," he explains. "Friendliness, enthusiasm and a genuine commitment to quality are very important to me."

The Huntington House remains on the cutting-edge of the industry, offering all of the current trends and styles in photography, including the new Photo Journalistic look, which is becoming increasingly popular for wedding portraits. Other in-demand techniques include "The Orchid" watercolor technique, in which a printed image is scanned into a computer, manipulated and then re-printed on 100 percent rag paper to look like an original watercolor; "The Bronze" sepia tone, in which an image is captured on black and white negative film and then printed on color photographic paper; and "The Rose" Polaroid manipulation, a hand-manipulated image on Polaroid film which is scanned into a computer then manipulated and printed to look like a Monet painting.

The Huntington House is committed to giving back to the community it serves, and is very actively involved in local fund-raisers. They are listed in the Orange County Department of Education's book entitled *Successful Fundraising*, as one of the top 12 fund-raisers in Orange County. Many of the studio's efforts benefit local elementary schools and private organiza-

tions, offering complimentary portrait sessions to those who make a donation to worthy causes.

Paul Thompson is a Master Craftsman Photographer awarded from The Professional Photographers of America for Photographic Excellence. The Huntington House is the only studio in the nation to be featured by Eastman Kodak for a second time on their Business and Marketing Practices, Portraits of Success for 1994. In 1996, Thompson was selected by Kodak as one of 25 photographers in the nation to be a part of Kodak's Pro-Team. His studio has also had numerous images used for greeting card companies and advertisements, and has won awards for photographic excellence at the Orange County Fair. He recently returned from Japan after giving a seminar to 250 Japanese photographers on "Western Weddings." Paul Thompson's Huntington House is a photography studio known for excellence far and wide, and will continue its dedication to quality for years to come.

Brar Electrical Systems, Inc.

When Harnek ("Harry") Brar first became involved with large electrical equipment, people were located in the communications building monitoring the equipment. Now, there is a computer and a few staff members who can observe the status of the equipment right on the computer screen. This is the wave of the future, and Harry Brar is riding the wave by retrofitting the old equipment and updating it for the 21st century.

The Brar family, Lisa, Genevieve, Paul and Harry, is the heart and soul of Brar Electrical Systems, Inc.

Brar came to the United States in 1963 from his native state of Punjab in India to study, but he remained and received his bachelor of science degree in electrical engineering from California State University at Los Angeles in 1968. Three years later he became a U.S. citizen.

From college, Brar went to work for Westinghouse Electric Corporation in its engineering service department. As a project and lead engineer, he was responsible for the analyzing and solving of technical problems on low, medium and high voltage electrical equipment produced by major manufacturers. He became an expert in all areas of the engineering department.

When he saw that Westinghouse was phasing out this area, he took it as an opportunity to establish his own business, and in April 1982, Brar Electrical Systems, Inc. opened its doors. Originally the company was located in Fountain Valley, but after two years, it moved to Huntington Beach and has been at its current location ever since. Many of Westinghouse's customers followed Harry Brar when they had electrical needs because they had known and worked with him and because such service was no longer available from Westinghouse.

Brar Electrical Systems, Inc. is available on a 24-hour-a-day emergency call-out basis to assist its industrial and commercial customers in maintaining the continuous operation of crucial electrical systems. It services, tests and installs large circuit breakers and switches for high voltage operations at Standard Oil Refinery, Texaco Refinery, various hospitals, including Kaiser Hospital and a wide variety of industrial plants

and commercial buildings. It also does work for the U.S. Navy and Citicorp.

Some of Brar's major customers are the telecommunications industry, Pacific Bell, AT&T and GTE. Brar does infrared scanning for Pac Bell, looking for hotspots and problem areas. It does electrical installation, testing and servicing on the large electrical telephone equipment, including the circuit breakers. Brar oversees the transfer system so if Edison power fails, the diesel generators (which are the size of an office) automatically start up so the dial tone is never lost. There are 500 to 600 locations of such systems which Brar services.

The Brar family...makes it a special point to use the services of Huntington Beach-based businesses for the needs of its company.

"After many years of servicing this equipment, you get very familiar with the system and sometimes a problem called in to us in the middle of the night can be resolved over the telephone just by me asking the caller where he is standing and then telling him, turn to your left, there's a breaker over there. Push the red button, and it should go okay," relates Harry Brar.

Among the service capabilities of Brar Electrical Systems, Inc. are circuit breaker testing and repairs, static retrofit circuit breakers, protective relay calibration, yearly maintenance contracts, acceptance tests, cable high-pot testing, ground fault relay system testing, power system analysis, start up services and trouble shooting. It specializes in doing infra-scan thermographic surveys which is a modern way of detecting loose, corroded or high impedance connections. This process can locate hot spots before they develop into electrical fires and cause extensive equipment damage.

The whole Brar family, Harry, wife Genevieve, son Paul and daughter Lisa, provides the administration for the business. Genevieve, who is the daughter of Omer and Guadalupe Deen, early pioneers of the Imperial Valley, met Harry at Imperial Valley College, and they were married in September, 1968. Paul and Lisa Brar both received their bachelor's degrees with honors from University of California at Irvine.

In addition to the family, Brar maintains a staff of highly trained engineers, electricians and technicians who are thoroughly trained in maintenance inspection techniques and repairs using the most advanced design test equipment for field testing, instrument repair and calibration. When a service call comes in, an appointment is scheduled and a technician sent out.

"We service installations from as far north as Santa Barbara, all the way south to the Mexican border, east to Nevada; in short, all of Southern California," explained Genevieve Brar.

Harry Brar is a senior member of the Institute of Electrical and Electronics Engineers, Inc., and Brar Electrical Systems, Inc. is active in the Huntington Beach Chamber of Commerce. The Brar family, which has made Huntington Beach its home for the past 10 years, makes it a special point to use the services of Huntington Beach-based businesses for the needs of its company.

"We service installations from as far north as Santa Barbara, all the way south to the Mexican border, east to Nevada; in short, all of Southern California."

Currently, Brar Electrical Systems, Inc. is moving heavily into telecommunications work and the upgrading of systems to match the increasingly complex computer technology. The company has a commitment to excellence which has brought them considerable success in their 17 years in business, and they expect it to continue to do so.

(Below) Brar Electrical Systems, Inc. has been headquartered in Huntington Beach since 1984.

225

Sonos Models, Inc.

If one day you should happen to have a tremendously bright idea while at your favorite eatery and you sketched that idea on a paper napkin, you could take that napkin to Carl TenBrink, owner of Sonos Models, Inc., and he would turn it into a product. If your idea didn't even make it to the napkin stage, you could simply describe it to TenBrink, and his company would come up with the initial concept ideation and develop it all the way through to a functioning prototype or limited production. To you it would be phenomenal but to Sonos it would be their job — full product development.

Sonos produces a mind-boggling variety of products from medical to toys to automotive to consumer electronics to three-dimensional sculpting of figurines. Essentially, Sonos can produce anything that might be seen in stores such as Fry's Computers, Toys "R" Us or Circuit City. As one walks around its plant in Huntington Beach, California, one might see staff engaged in concept and creation of toys for the Star Wars movie prequel, working on a full-size concept Cadillac Voyage for General Motors, designing or sculpting action figures or designing a laparoscopic device for invasive surgery.

TenBrink has been involved in turning bright ideas into reality as far back as he can remember. Growing up in Battle Creek, Michigan, he made use of the tremendous array of tools in his father's antique car restoration workshop to create a model railroad world on the family pingpong table. He ended up with over 100 square feet of train layout with mountains, working lights, rocks which when turned would move the cranes and other rocks which would open and close the crossing gates. He made all kinds of items and entered them in city contests.

After high school graduation, TenBrink attended Kellogg Community College, as an art major, later transferring to Manchester, Indiana, which had a study-abroad program, something TenBrink had always wanted to do. He spent his senior year in Barcelona, Spain where he studied in an art conservatory that was built in a 13th-century Gothic hospital. TenBrink was fascinated by the flying buttresses and arched ceilings. He also took classes at the University of Barcelona in order to learn the language, culture and history of Spain.

When TenBrink returned home, he faced the task of turning his education into a career. Although he had worked throughout school in the field of graphics, he was amazed that on showing a picture of his train layout to a prospective employer, he was promptly hired to work in a model-shop department. He remained at the company for a year and then took off with a fellow employee to see what the rest of the United States had to offer in the way of job opportunities. They wound up in Los Alamitos, California where they received an offer of one job for one of them for a month. They countered with two jobs for two weeks and were hired. Eventually the two weeks turned into three months and finally into a year before TenBrink was ready to move on.

The next step in TenBrink's career was sheer magic. In 1983, he received a call from an engineer he knew from his former employment. A computer prototype was needed at Eagle Computers in Irvine. However, when TenBrink showed up to meet the boss, he was told it was needed in two days and since that wasn't really enough time, they would wait and try him out on another occasion. Not to be put off, TenBrink grabbed a copy of the blueprints and dashed home to go into business for himself, something he had long dreamed of. He spent the next 48 hours naming his fledgling company Sonos (because the first product he had ever designed was a case for music cassettes and "sono" in Spanish means sound or musical note), designing his business cards and working on the prototype. Bright and early in the morning, TenBrink, dressed in his best business suit, picked up his new business cards from the printer and headed over to Eagle Computers. When he arrived, all was in turmoil because the designer who had actually been given the project two weeks earlier had failed to show. The vice president of engineering was at wits' end without a product to show the bigwigs who had flown in for the presentation. Like Superman, TenBrink produced the prototype and saved the day. When it was time for him to leave Eagle Computers, not only was a check waiting for the new Sonos Models, Inc., but also three new projects. He was in business in a big way.

At first TenBrink ran Sonos from his garage but after a year, he had outgrown that facility (and the city was looking askance at him running a business in a residential neighborhood). He leased half a unit of a business facility. In another year, Sonos outgrew that also so it moved again, this time taking up a full unit. After three years in business and after completion of one of Sonos' biggest projects, the Cadillac Voyage, a full-size concept car for General Motors, TenBrink obtained a small business loan and purchased the current quarters in Huntington Beach.

Sonos' client list is an impressive who's who of the product world including Disney, Mazda, General Motors, Xerox, California Medical, Laparomed, Jet Propulsion Laboratories and Harmon-Kardon Stereo. For these clients it has produced home entertainment systems, home office automation, computers, printers, and laparoscopic and surgical devices (to name a few). In the automotive arena, Sonos has produced 5th scale, 4th scale, 3rd scale and full-size interiors and exteriors. A big project was a 40-foot by 40-foot scale model for Euro Disneyland in France.

One newer area for Sonos is the Sculpting Studio where the products are such items as action figures and premiums. The Studio produces anything figural which is human, animal or organic in nature as opposed to a telephone or a stereo. Sonos has sculpted everything from a human likeness to animated figures, the likes of

Disney, Hanna-Barbara and Warner Brothers. Clients include Mattel Toys, Tyco, Tonka, Hasbro and virtually all of the major toy companies.

TenBrink envisions a new area of endeavor for Sonos, which is inventing products for other companies instead of the other way around. In this case, Sonos originates the initial concept, develops the product and licenses the concept. But whether Sonos originates the concept or a client brings a new idea to it, its work philosophy remains focused on understanding the whole marketing concept and who the consumer is for any product. As TenBrink expresses it, "We strive to exceed the clients' expectations and bring more to the product than they originally thought possible."

AM/PM Property Management

On August 10, 1982, Susan Harris opened the smallest "office" in Orange County. Her office was a post office box. Harris met customers in a variety of locales, including clients' rental properties, private homes and restaurants. Harris gave up the post office box long ago. She built a viable property management company using her talent, skill and professionalism.

AM/PM President and Chief Executive Susan Harris

After earning a bachelor's degree from Ohio State University in 1967, Harris taught elementary school in Ohio and California. In 1972 she began her real estate career and worked as a realtor for several large organizations.

By 1982, Harris was ready for an enterprise of her own. With the help of her young daughter Bridgett, she started AM/PM Property Management. Her first office was the downstairs bedroom closet. Within a short time, business grew and soon AM/PM Property Management moved to an office building on Beach Boulevard. The company incorporated in 1985 and they expanded into a larger space on Gothard Street where they conduct business today.

Licensed by the California Department of Real Estate, AM/PM Property Management offers its clients a wide array of services. The company represents buyers and sellers in real estate transactions, property management of homes, apartments, condominiums and management of homeowner associations. The company earned the respect of its clients and other realtors.

Investment property owners choose from a variety of services that include: collecting rents, maintaining accurate property records, coordinating repairs, obtaining bids for major repairs, preparing legal notices, disbursing funds to owners and preparing checks for property expenses. Their comprehensive tenant screening includes credit check by computer, verification of employment, banking, social security number, driver's license information, check for unlawful detainer (eviction) and they talk with current and prior landlords. Property owners receive monthly financial reports that are easy to read and a quarterly newsletter. The most important service the Harris's provide their clients is peace of mind. With all the details of building management taken care of, property owners have time to enjoy and profit from their rental property rather than worrying about their investments.

Qualified applicants find excellent housing. The AM/PM team provides daily "Hot Sheets" of information on available property and their rental information line is accessible 24 hours a day by phone. They inspect property on a regular basis and respond quickly to repair requests. Harris' philosophy for rental property is, "If the property is not good enough for us to live in, it is not acceptable for our residents."

Working with homeowner associations they interface with the board of directors, collect receivables, disburse expenses, coordinate maintenance, prepare board packages and attend board meetings.

Their office is OPEN Monday through Saturday, which enables owners and residents to speak directly with a management representative. And best of all...when clients call, they talk to a live person rather than an automated system. They are "on call" to respond to an emergency 24 hours a day, seven days a week.

Because of the personal touches she and the team provide, Harris says, "Many of our clients are now friends as well as business associates." It is not a surprise that 90 percent of their new business is referral.

Harris takes delight when one of their tenants uses their service to purchase their first home, outgrows that house, purchases a new home and places the original property with their management. "What a thrill that is!" she says.

The business has a firm commitment of building bridges within the community. Each October the team selects a project for the upcoming holiday season. Prior years' endeavors include a food drive for the homeless, collecting household necessities for shelters for battered women and a scholarship fund to support educational needs. The Harris's agree, "That is the spirit driving our business."

As a business owner and a mother, Harris takes pride in her daughter's involvement in the business. Bridgett rejoined the team after college and created the team approach to management. Today, Bridgett serves as the office manager and one day she will take over the business.

Looking to the future, both mother and daughter are confident in further growth and expansion.

Susan Harris' daughter, Bridgett, who currently acts as office manager and will someday take over the company's operations.

Campbell Realtors

Over the last 42 years, Campbell Realtors has brokered millions of dollars worth of real estate. In fact, the family operated firm has been helping people buy and sell homes longer than almost all other Orange County real estate companies. Scot Campbell is the second-generation proprietor of the firm and has been a Huntington Beach resident since 1973.

"I have witnessed many changes within Orange County, but the changes have been especially positive within the City of Huntington Beach. I remember when a huge portion of downtown was vacant land. As a kid, I couldn't ride my bike down 21st or 22nd streets because of the numerous potholes. Now these streets are beautiful and lined with homes ranging from $350,000 to $800,000," recalls Scot Campbell of Campbell Realtors. Founded originally in Anaheim in 1957 by his dad, E. J. Campbell, the office is now nestled snugly in a tree-lined residential area in the heart of the city's downtown park area near the corner of Main Street and Palm Avenue. The building itself, formerly Farwell's Flower Shop, is well over 50 years old, and has been home to Campbell Realtors for the last eight years.

Campbell Realtors prides itself on providing extraordinary real estate services that clients can depend on for a lifetime; more than half its business is repeat clients and referrals. Campbell attributes the company's success more to a long list of satisfied clients than to millions of dollars spent on advertisements. Campbell is a licensed real estate broker and has been certified by the State of California to complete residential real estate appraisals. With over 12 years experience, his focus on quality has enabled him to negotiate and close over 300 transactions totaling nearly $70 million worth of real

estate, including houses, townhouses, condominiums, vacant land, commercial and income properties.

Campbell and his team of experts are structured in the very successful Super-Agent Organization design. Unlike conventional real estate firms, the design consistently provides clients with service seven days a week. Additionally, it allows the Campbell Team members to specialize in their areas of expertise. Campbell feels the design will enable his firm to continue helping even the busiest of clients with their housing needs as Huntington Beach continues to grow.

Campbell Realtors is visibly proud of its historically significant downtown office building. It was once on the outskirts of a sleepy oil town. Today it is lovingly maintained and valued for its unbeatable combination of frontage, signage and easy curbside parking. The location has become a gathering spot during the city's annual Fourth of July parade. While enjoying the nation's largest Fourth of July parade west of the Mississippi River, past and current clients enjoy attending the company's annual gathering to celebrate friendship and the American spirit.

Looking toward the future, Campbell Realtors has created an Internet Web site so clients can view color pictures of homes for sale and obtain general real estate information. In June of 1998, the first Campbell Realtors scholarship was offered to a graduating senior at Campbell's alma mater, Huntington Beach High School, continuing the firm's service to the community.

The phenomenal success of Campbell Realtors can also be attributed to the family's strong work ethic. And if you're wondering about Scot's dad, E. J., you can find him at the office on Sundays, unless of course, he's out showing homes.

229

HVN Environmental Service Co., Inc.

California is often referred to as a paradise, and HVN Environmental Service Company, Inc., of Huntington Beach is doing its part to keep the local environment close to the paradise it once was. Safeguarding and restoring the soil and groundwater to safe levels after the industrial contamination of earlier, less environmentally concerned years, is its business. Frank Hekimian Sr., the founding father, laid the foundation of HVN.

The three Hekimian sons implement their father's ideals. Frank Jr., is an attorney and the secretary of the corporation. Kenneth, a registered civil engineer who received his doctorate in environmental engineering from the University of Southern California, is West Coast manager as well as principal engineer and treasurer of the corporation. Philip is a consultant to the vitamin industry for R & D on natural products. A third generation of the Hekimian family, David and Lauren, is now preparing to guide the company into the new millennium.

Environmental compliance is a major issue in both federal and local government efforts to maintain public health. HVN assists small to medium California companies, the real estate industry, commercial and industrial developers as well as banks and other lending institutions in following the compliance codes set by environmental agencies.

Keeping California an ideal place to live, work and play...

According to Anton Markarian, general manager and manager of construction, and Maralyn Megurian, office manager, environmental assessment, evaluation and restoration is performed in phases. The first is Phase I — environmental site assessment. This initial phase takes a degree of detective work to discover the real estate history of the site. The discovery includes previous use of the land and what was on that land in preceding years, based on a physical examination of the site, aerial photography and governmental records. Phase II is a sub-surface investigation to determine the vertical and horizontal extent of the contamination. Phase III, the final phase, is environmental remediation — executing a plan of action that restores the land to acceptable levels of residual hydrocarbons. This is followed by a report to the environmental agencies that have jurisdiction over the particular site being restored.

HVN specializes in above-ground and below-ground fuel tank projects that incorporate soil and water assessment and monitoring for clients. The company also performs asbestos surveys and removal management if asbestos is present. HVN's clientele include the cities of Costa Mesa, Huntington Beach and Newport Beach, Interstate Brands, Lasco Bathware, Carl's Jr., La Mancha Development and Cal-Asia Development. With a staff of six full-time OSHA and California-credentialed employees, the company's growth continues in order to keep pace with demands placed on our habitat. Keeping California an ideal place to live, work and play is the mission of HVN Environmental Service Company, Inc., the vanguard of the future.

The HVN management team (left to right), Kenneth Hekimian, Maralyn Megurian and Anton Markarian

(Left to right) Frank Hekimian, Sr. pictured with his son, Kenneth

230

Jean R. Anderson Photography

n a world of corporate takeovers, mergers and franchises, it is refreshing to find people like Jean and Terry Anderson, owners of Jean R. Anderson Photography in Huntington Beach. The Andersons run their business out of their home. In a few short years, they have built a powerful reputation within the community for their personal commitment and individualized service.

A corporate photographer for over 10 years, Jean decided in June of 1995 to turn his knowledge and expertise into his own business. Together with wife Terry, they opened Jean R. Anderson Photography and set forth on a photographic adventure.

Since then, their success has spread mostly through word-of-mouth, referrals and repeat clients. "We've done some local advertising, but mostly it's just been one person telling another about our services," says Anderson.

Perhaps it is the personalized approach Jean and Terry take to their business, extending themselves to their clients in a way that seems to have gotten lost with so many other companies. "We travel to our clients," explains Anderson, "and take advantage of the beautiful scenes of Huntington Beach and surrounding environment." In other words, clients don't get dressed up and travel to a studio to have their photography needs met; Anderson travels to them. Whether it be a family portrait at home or at the beach, a company photo at the office, or a remembrance photo of a special event, Anderson attributes his "client-driven" philosophy for the company's outstanding reputation.

Since the company's inception, Jean R. Anderson Photography has been actively involved in capturing Huntington Beach's history as well. As a member of Huntington Beach Chamber of Commerce and Professional Photographers of Orange County, he offers time and services to many local events including Pierfest, Savoir Faire/Taste of Huntington Beach, Leukemia Society of Orange County Celebrity Waiter's Banquet and Fund Raiser, Eagle Scout ceremonies, Special Olympics, Table Top Trade Shows and the Hebrew Academy Awards Dinner. Anderson also provides stock photos of Huntington Beach scenes for brochures and public relations purposes.

A full-service photographer, Anderson specializes in putting people at ease in front of the camera. His casual, unassuming manner, strong work ethic and never-ending stream of creative approaches has earned the company an honored and respected place in the community and resulted in many visual keepsakes for future generations.

As the economy continues to prosper and the company's reputation continues to speak for itself, Anderson remarks: "Business booming? Let us capture your success!"

231

The Local News

Remember that old saying, "no news is good news?" In Huntington Beach, Dave Garofalo has a new one: "Good news is the Local News." Garofalo is the owner and publisher of *The Local News*, a bimonthly newspaper that focuses on positive news articles about people and activities in the community. While other area newspapers dwell on crime and politics, Garofalo prefers to write about who is doing what for whom instead of who is doing what *to* whom. Whether it's a guide to the Huntington Beach Fourth of July Parade, or an article on the Boys and Girls Club, *The Local News* stays true to its front-page ideal that "Community news is our only business."

Garofalo, a 30-year resident of Surf City, began publishing the Local News in 1992 after spending the two previous years as publisher of the *Huntington*

Dave Garofalo (standing),
(left to right) Nancy
Garofalo, daughter, Phyllis
Garofalo, Dave's mother and
Kevin Garofalo, son

Beach Independent, a small weekly paper that was purchased by the *Los Angeles Times*. While at *The Independent*, Garofalo used his broad business knowledge to increase the profitability of the paper before it was sold.

"Being a publisher does not mean being a journalist," says Garofalo. "You need a set of business experiences that can help move a major product through a number of phases, including making a profit."

Although Garofalo wrote for the now-defunct *Huntington Beach News* back in the early 1970s and had some experience writing and publishing while in high school and college, he never considered a career

in journalism. After an honorable discharge from the Marine Corps in 1969, Garofalo moved to Huntington Beach and secured employment with Union Carbide Corporation selling high-tech engineering products. In 1981, he formed his own corporation and traveled the world selling and promoting a variety of new high-tech products and services.

Because of his marketing and consulting experience, Garofalo began creating brochures, newsletters and mailers for various organizations, and he now produces over one million pieces of direct mail each year. He also publishes visitors guides for Huntington Beach and Orange County, and business directories for Huntington Beach, Westminster and Fountain Valley.

With his continuous focus on serving the community through his newspaper and volunteer work, Garofalo decided to run for public office. He was elected to the Huntington Beach City Council in 1994, and now spends much of his free time on council duties. He chairs the council subcommittee on economic planning and is scheduled to serve a one-year term as mayor during the year 2000.

Currently, Garofalo's community service work includes vice chairman for the Huntington Beach Conference and Visitors Bureau, board member of the Huntington Beach Chamber of Commerce and the Fountain Valley Chamber of Commerce, director for the Huntington Beach/Fountain Valley Boys and Girls Club, board member of the West Orange County Cancer Board and the Orange County Cancer Center, and membership in many other nonprofit/charity organizations.

Garofalo was also named the 1997 Small Businessman of the Year by the U.S. Small Business Administration, one of only four people in California to earn that title.

Garofalo's family includes his daughter, Nancy, and his son, Kevin, both of whom have expressed an interest in eventually taking over their father's business. For now, though, Garofalo is keeping busy running his newspaper and helping to run the city of Huntington Beach.

"The reward is just doing it," says Garofalo, who plans to be serving the community of Huntington Beach for a long time to come.

233

Quality of Life

Medical, media, educational and religious
institutions, as well as recreation-oriented companies,
contribute to the quality of life enjoyed by
Huntington Beach residents and visitors to the area.

Beach Physicians & Surgeons Medical Group

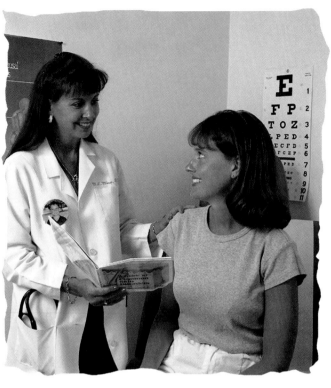

At Beach Physicians & Surgeons Medical Group, practicing good medicine involves more than high technology. The Group's founder, Dr. Arnold J. Brender, believes the best health care comes from people who care about others, a philosophy he puts into practice each and every day. A specialist in general family and sports medicine, Dr. Brender makes sure his patients are more than just medical charts and insurance forms by getting to know each one by name, and offering a listening ear and expert personalized care.

Mary Minar, D.O.

After working for medical groups in both Anaheim and Laguna Hills, Dr. Brender began his private practice in Huntington Beach in 1985. Several years later, as a commissioned captain for the Army National Guard, Dr. Brender was called to active duty in Turkey during the Gulf War. His practice suffered while he was away, and upon returning he began to seriously consider starting his own medical group. A short time later, he recruited partner Dr. David R. Bloom, and in January of 1991, Beach Physicians & Surgeons Medical Group was formed.

Today, the Group employs a multidisciplinary team which includes three full-time family practitioners, including Dr. Brender, Dr. Bloom, and the newest member of their team, Dr. Mary Minar. Other staff members include Nurse Practitioners, Physician

> *While medical science continues to make remarkable advances, some things never change, like a patient's desire to have a relationship with their doctor.*

Assistants and a Physical Therapy team. Some of the Group's services include complete wellness evaluations, body fat evaluations, exercise prescriptions, cancer screening and biopsies, international travel medicine, and cardiac stress testing. They also provide executive and employment physicals, sports evaluations and physical therapy. In addition, Dr. Brender is certified by the FAA as an aviation medical examiner to provide medical clearance for pilots.

Beach Physicians & Surgeons Medical Group offers its patients many private practice advantages, like same day appointment scheduling, an uncommon convenience in today's managed care environment. "I've seen a depersonalization of medical care in recent years," says Dr. Brender. "In my opinion, a small group can offer better care to individuals, and as physicians, we have to remember that we treat individuals, not the masses." He believes a small group allows more health care decisions to remain between the patient and the doctor, and says the challenge is to always remain centered on what a patient needs, not what a particular treatment is going to cost.

The group focuses on comprehensive care by offering a full range of services under one roof. Most testing, lab services and x-rays are done on the premises. Dr. Brender is a strong proponent of what he calls "wellness and prevention," encouraging patients to come in for screenings and evaluations to determine their major health risk factors. The evaluations look at family histories, lifestyle components and other factors that put people at risk for such conditions as cancer, heart disease and strokes. While Dr. Brender finds it is a challenge to get people to think about preventing illness when they are well, he says more education is a key to getting patients to understand the importance of preventive medicine. "It's a lot easier to prevent illness than it is to treat it," he explains.

Dr. Brender is actually a family doctor in more than one sense of the word. He comes from a family of physicians; both of his brothers are doctors. He says the impetus for forming the medical group was a dream his father had that all three sons would someday practice medicine together. Dr. Brender's brother, Dr. Elliot Brender, a surgeon and former chief of staff at Garden Grove Hospital, joined him at Beach Physicians & Surgeons Medical Group in 1993. His other brother is a general plastic and hand surgeon with a practice on the East Coast.

They are committed to providing a level of personal service and attention rarely found in larger group-care settings.

In Southern California, many people participate in athletic activities, and as one of the premier primary care sports medicine groups in Orange County, Beach Physicians & Surgeons Medical Group provides care for all levels of athletes, from high school and college levels to professional. Drs. Brender and Bloom have both served as team physicians; Dr. Brender for Golden West College and Dr. Bloom for Orange Coast College. Both doctors are also members of the American College of Sports Medicine and the American Medical Society for Sports Medicine.

As part of their continuing effort to provide more efficient care to their patients, Beach Physicians & Surgeons Medical Group recently implemented a major computer upgrade. The upgrade lets physicians access medical records, contact pharmacies and fill prescriptions, all with the push of a button. The new technology helps eliminate time-consuming paperwork and frees up more time for the staff to focus on their main priority: caring for patients.

Both Drs. Brender and Bloom are reserve officers and medical specialists for the Long Beach Police Department, and they recently applied with the Huntington Beach Police Department, as a part of their ongoing commitment to active community service. Beach Physicians also has extensive experience in pre-employment exams and in handling worker's comp injuries for various Huntington Beach employers.

Beach Physicians & Surgeons Medical Group is affiliated with Hoag Memorial Presbyterian Hospital, Huntington Beach Hospital, Fountain Valley Regional Hospital and Pacifica Community Hospital. They are also a preferred provider for most insurance plans, including HMO, PPO, EPO and POS.

While medical science continues to make remarkable advances, some things never change, like a patient's desire to have a relationship with their doctor. Beach Physicians & Surgeons Medical Group understands that simple desire, and has built a practice around providing more than just the most advanced medical care. They are committed to providing a level of personal service and attention rarely found in larger group-care settings. It is this caring attitude that makes them a first choice of individuals and families looking for something which in recent years has become almost obsolete: a good family doctor.

(Left) David R. Bloom, M.D.

(Right) Arnold J. Brender, M.D., medical director and founder of Beach Physicians & Surgeons Medical Group

Delma Corporation

As the dawn of a new millennium approaches, many changes lie in store for the population of the United States. Chief among these changes is a dramatic shift in the age range of the country's population — the U.S. Bureau of the Census reports that by the year 2000 people 65 years and older will represent about 13 percent of the population, and that by the year 2030 that figure will climb to 20 percent. These changes present a remarkable challenge to providers of senior housing health care. One company that is stepping up to these challenges, and in a unique and pioneering way, is Delma Corp.

Delma Corp. got its start in 1960 when a site in Huntington Beach was acquired. The following year the first convalescent hospital in Huntington Beach was built on that spot. With remarkable foresight, Robert Zinngrabe, the current chairman of Delma, began developing and expanding the site into the modern medical campus that it is today. Over the following

Success in Huntington Beach led to further opportunities for the company in other communities.

years the medical campus in Huntington Beach continued to grow, fueled by the success and essential rightness of the concept. In 1968 the corner property was acquired and developed into a doctor-owned medical office building, and in 1970 Zinngrabe and a group of local doctors joined together and expanded the original convalescent hospital into an acute general hospital, known as Pacifica Hospital. That same year, a new 143-bed Skilled Nursing Facility was developed adjacent to the hospital. Finally, in 1971 a connecting corridor was built which tied both buildings together. This was, however, only the start of the company's growth. In 1978 a new 161-unit assisted living facility was completed to be known as Huntington Terrace, and in 1983 construction was begun on Pacifica Tower, an 11-story medical office building connected to the hospital. Additionally, construction was completed on a 21,000-square-foot medical office building for doctors as well as conference building for the hospital.

Success in Huntington Beach led to further opportunities for the company in other communities. In 1985 Delma Corp. was awarded a contract by the city of Westminster to develop 312 senior apartments in the city's redevelopment area. The first building was completed in 1987 and the next two years saw the facility enjoy a remarkable occupancy

Pacifica Tower in Huntington Beach

rate. This led to the city's offer of a contiguous 1.4-acre site on which construction has already started on an 82-unit assisted living facility that will be completely integrated with the existing senior campus, creating the largest senior housing complex of its kind in Orange County.

Another tribute to the soundness of the company's vision is the Morro Bay facility. In 1969 the company seized the opportunity to develop a convalescent hospital there and construction commenced on a 65-bed Skilled Nursing Facility and an 88-bed Assisted Living facility in June of the following year. This project stands apart in that Delma received the first approval from the State of California to physically connect these two separately licensed facilities which shared a kitchen, activities room and offices. After the success of the initial endeavor an additional 80-bed Skilled Nursing Facility and 74-unit Assisted Living Facility were completed, while a further five acres of undeveloped land is already in the planning stages for future development.

An integral factor in the company's success and the foundation of Delma Corporation's vision is the concept of building a "Continuum of Care." This unique form of health care delivery represents a comprehensive and wide-ranging approach to the challenges of providing care and housing for seniors. Delma's singular approach to these challenges have led to its unprecedented success. The "Continuum of Care" model it has created offers almost every conceivable facet of health care and housing required by seniors today. Services include food, housekeeping, activities, medical assistance, transportation, pharmacy, assistance in choosing a physician, physical therapy, occupational rehabilitation, aquatic therapy programs, cardiovascular care, and mental health programs and wellness programs, among others. In short, every need is provided for, from basic residential services to advanced therapies for Alzheimer patients, all housed in one location. This philosophy virtually eliminates the need for residents to travel long distances for needed services.

One of the company's most important resources is its staff. Covering almost every field in the health care industry, extraordinary effort is made to keep employees versed in the latest developments in their fields. Ongoing training programs for all employees ensure

Founder Robert J. Zinngrabe (second from left) and executive officers

239

that this goal is met. In addition, the company has experienced personnel in development, marketing and operations to manage and guide current projects and plan for future ones. This attention to employee training and skills has been a key in the company's growth and unrivaled position as a provider if care and housing to seniors.

Delma Corp. has prospered by helping those under its care to prosper. No other company has done so much to integrate every aspect of care for seniors into one comprehensive package. The "Continuum of Care" philosophy has led to renown for the company, but more importantly, it has led to better living for the residents in Delma's various facilities. With unprecedented changes in store for America's population, the

> *An integral factor in the company's success and the foundation of Delma Corporation's vision is the concept of building a "Continuum of Care."*

company is uniquely positioned to meet those challenges. It is said that with age comes experience, and that can be said for companies as well. Since 1960 Delma Corp. has provided quality medical care and other services to its residents. This foundation of experience, coupled with an unparalleled staff and a deep and abiding knowledge of the needs of the elderly, will ensure that Delma continues to grow and age well along with the people it serves.

Huntington Beach City School District

The Huntington Beach City School District was established in 1905 and encompasses approximately 14 square miles within the city of Huntington Beach. It currently operates seven elementary schools and two middle schools serving over 6,400 students in grades kindergarten through eight. The district employs 325 certified teachers and administrators and 280 nonteaching staff.

The schools serving the Huntington Beach City School District are Ethel R. Dwyer Middle School on Palm Avenue, Isaac L. Sowers Middle School on Indianapolis Avenue, John H. Eader Elementary on Banning Avenue, Dr. Ralph E. Hawes Elementary School on Yellowstone Drive, William E. Kettler Elementary on Dorsett Drive, S.A. Moffett Elementary

Huntington Beach Elementary School, 1946

on Burlcrest Avenue, Joseph R. Perry Elementary on Harding Lane, John R. Peterson Elementary on Farnsworth Lane and Agnes L. Smith Elementary on 17th Street. Huntington Seacliff Elementary is set to open in September of 1999.

The educational philosophy of the Huntington Beach City School District emphasizes the achievement of basic skills, nurtures the dignity and worth of each student, promotes cultural, aesthetic and leisure pursuits, develops problem-solving competencies in each student and is committed to the development of effective citizens.

All courses of study are designed to prepare students for high school. Kindergarten through sixth grade areas of focus include reading, arithmetic, oral and written language, health, fine arts, physical education, science, social science, career education and computer literacy. Additional subjects at grades seven and eight include applied arts and foreign language. Outdoor education programs supplement the regular program, and provide an opportunity for ecological concepts to

be integrated in the teaching of established disciplines such as science, social studies and language arts.

The district believes that the arts offer significant opportunities for enrichment in all subjects and provides instruction in visual and performing arts. Throughout the year, students participate in visual arts, music, drama and dance. Many schools offer the "Meet the Masters" program, and selected student works are prominently displayed in the District Art Gallery. Plays, choral readings and musical presentations are given by students at monthly PTA meetings and other school events. The arts staff includes qualified community volunteers and district mentor teachers with special abilities in the visual and performing arts.

In accordance with the school board's philosophy to develop the special abilities of each student, the Huntington Beach City School District has provided a program in Gifted and Talented Education (GATE) for qualified students since 1971. Students in grades two through five are offered the option of a "cluster" program in their own school or the "magnet" program at Peterson Elementary School. The magnet program offers units of study beyond the regular curriculum. Students are grouped by grade level and receive differentiated instruction in all curricular areas. In the cluster program, students attend their neighborhood school and are grouped by grade level within a specific class.

Identified students in grades six, seven and eight are placed in the GATE language arts and social studies classes at both Dwyer and Sowers middle schools. Advanced skills are taught in research, science fiction, literature appreciation, speech and debate, study of comparative cultures and the Renaissance. Leadership abilities, critical thinking processes and sensitivity to the needs of others are emphasized throughout the program.

With exposure to a more sophisticated world through television, many of today's kindergarten children come to school ready for complex ideas and experiences. The district provides an Extended Day Kindergarten program that focuses on the development of basic skills, enrichment of ideas, and development of responsibility for themselves and their actions. This full-day program gives children an excellent start toward a satisfying and productive total school life by allowing time to build a child's self-concept, providing varied experiences, promoting a feeling of self-worth, and enabling children to leave kindergarten happily anticipating the next step and needing fewer adjustments upon entering first grade.

Other specially funded programs include the School Improvement Program, which encourages school improvement through a joint decision-making process within the school community; the Title I Program, established to assist students who may be "at risk" and/or who fail to demonstrate expected achievement at their grade level; the State Compensatory Education Program, which provides Economic Impact Aid for "at-risk" students who are underachieving academically, and gives additional support to students with limited English ability; and the Drug Abuse Resistance Education (DARE) and the Drug, Alcohol, Tobacco Education (DATE) program, which teach children in primary grades about drugs, how to solve everyday problems and to make sound, healthy decisions. The district also provides an English Language Learners (ELL) program designed to transition students as quickly as possible to English fluency. Students with special needs are offered alternatives that extend from the regular classroom to special full-day placements.

A full range of before- and after-school activities and sports programs provide a framework for children to develop their recreational skills and ideas. Many students also attend after-school music, art, math and science programs. Supervised instruction is provided in a variety of areas.

Teachers in the Huntington Beach City School district are extremely dedicated to each child's success. They are highly trained and experienced professionals who understand the complex stages of child development and who also set realistic and achievable academic and social goals. A mentor teacher program recognizes and

retains exemplary teachers in the profession by having them remain in the classroom and share their expertise with new and continuing teachers. Classified employees are a valuable support to students, the schools and the instructional program. Members include secretaries, clerks, library media technicians, custodians, maintenance workers, groundskeepers, bus drivers, food service workers and instructional aides.

Lunches and snacks for children in the Huntington Beach City School District are prepared daily, distributed from the central kitchen and delivered by truck to each school. The school district participates in the National School Lunch Program, which makes free or reduced-price lunches available to students who qualify.

Other programs within the Huntington Beach City School District include parent participation preschool, child care, back-to-school and open house nights, PTA/PTO/PTSA organizations, transportation services, an educational foundation, regular progress reports and tuition-free summer school.

Five of the Huntington Beach City School District schools have been designated as a "California Distinguished School": Dwyer Middle School, Eader Elementary, Hawes Elementary, Moffett Elementary and Smith Elementary. That honor is a reflection of the academic standards, ethical behavior and positive interpersonal communications taught within the district.

Huntington Beach City School District — proudly charting a course for success.

241

(Left Photo) Dwyer Middle School today

(Right Photo) Mike Case Science building at Dwyer Middle School

Huntington Beach Union High School District

The history of the Huntington Beach Union High School District dates back nearly 100 years, when Huntington Beach High School was founded in 1903 under the name Las Bolsas Union High School. It became known as "The School on Wheels" because it moved frequently and had a somewhat uncertain destiny. Originally planned for Los Alamitos, the school was abandoned after four days of classes because only one student appeared. A second try was made at Bolsa Avenue and Ward Street, followed by a move to Garden Grove. In 1905, the school moved again, this time to Wintersburg, where it was housed in an old armory building. At this time, the school colors of black and orange were chosen. In 1906, the school moved to the basement of an old Methodist campground auditorium in Huntington Beach, where it remained until the completion of its first permanent building on its present site in 1908.

The early years of the one-school district were full of legal struggles, including bond measures that were often declared illegal. A law was passed changing the name of the school to the Huntington Beach Union High School, and the Huntington Beach Company donated land for the school's permanent site at Main and Utica.

By 1909, enrollment at the school had reached 68 students. That number increased by 75 students in 1912 when the school trustees purchased a two-ton truck to bus students in from surrounding cities. By 1919, enrollment was up to 364 students. In 1926, a distinctive new school was built that featured the current auditorium and clock tower, which was dedicated in 1987 as an historic landmark.

Enrollment climbed to 637 in 1933, and to 950 in 1950. The Huntington Beach High School remained the only school in the district until 1959, when 50 acres of land in Westminster was purchased for a second high school. When the housing boom of the 1960s hit the county and school enrollment began to rapidly increase, the district responded with the construction of Marina High School in 1963, Fountain Valley High School in 1966, Edison High School in 1969 and Ocean View High School in 1974.

The peak enrollment of the Huntington Beach Union High School District occurred in 1978 when the six schools housed 21,193 students by utilizing 10-period days and eight portable classrooms. Fountain Valley High School was recognized as the largest school west of the Mississippi with an enrollment in excess of 4,300 students. In fact, all the schools except Ocean View were in excess of 4,000 students.

In the 1980s and early 1990s, the district was hit with a rapid enrollment decline as young families grew older and fewer students were in the county to attend high school. The problems associated with high enrollment numbers were replaced by dwindling finances, program reductions and staff layoffs. Recently, though, the enrollment numbers have stabilized as more young families move into the area and former high school students have their own school-age children.

During the past decade, the district has maintained a strong commitment to education which has provided a rich tradition of athletic and educational success for students. The district has been praised by *Newsweek* magazine and *The Los Angeles Times* for its commitment to academic excellence. SAT and ACT scores at all six schools are above the national average.

As the Huntington Beach Union High School District approaches the new millennium, the district's mission is to educate all students by ensuring a relevant and focused educational program which develops responsible, productive and creative individuals with a potential for leadership.

Each high school within the district has its own unique programs and services.

Edison High School, a 1995 California Distinguished School, is known for its academic competition team, which has won a number of national championships. The school's Model United Nations Program is also a national champion, while the school's athletic teams have been regional, state and individual winners in sports as varied as varsity football and girl's field hockey.

Fountain Valley High School offers a wide range of learning options, from music to a 24-sport, award-winning

HB High School, 1984 — The clock tower is now a historic landmark.

of science-related areas of study. Business, electronics, manufacturing and marketing are all career paths available at Marina. The school also boasts the C.I.F. state champions in girl's volleyball.

Ocean View High School was awarded the state's Distinguished School award in 1992. Ocean View is one of only six high schools in the county to offer the prestigious "International Baccalaureate" diploma program, which provides an internationally recognized series of courses in basic and high level skills. A popular Business Academy links students to business mentors, job shadowing opportunities and even employment.

Westminster High School was a California Distinguished School in 1992, and was named a National Blue Ribbon School in 1993. The school is considered a leading-edge school, and offers exposure to careers that focus on critical technologies of the 21st century. The Health Sciences Career Academy combines academic with hands-on training to prepare students for careers in health care, while the Teachers Academy trains students to become bilingual instructors. A five-acre farm teaches students the principles of horticulture, floriculture, and animal and veterinary science. A majority of the teachers within the Huntington Beach Union High School District have advanced degrees, one reason that a high percentage of parents believe that the district is doing a good job of educating students and helping them develop into responsible, productive citizens. The Huntington Beach Union High School District — preparing today's students for the world of tomorrow.

athletic program. The School-to-Career program helps students prepare for future careers by linking academics and job training. Advanced placement classes afford students the opportunity to earn college credit for upper division class work, while the school's sports legacy includes league and division titles in football, basketball, baseball and other seasonal sports.

Huntington Beach High School was a 1994 California Distinguished School. A Model United Nations program has won numerous awards, and the school's surf team has been named National Championship Surf Team five times since 1990s. A fully equipped television studio is available for students to prepare for broadcasting careers, while the on-site School for the Performing Arts provides a wide variety of options for students in music, theater, drama and dance. Students can also learn computer programming at six computer labs.

A Distinguished School Award recipient, Marina High School has a multimedia lab, a writing lab and an industrial arts technology lab. A high percentage of Marina students go on to four-year colleges, and the school has high SAT and PSAT scores. The school has 12 science classrooms and eight laboratory classrooms, providing a strong academic environment for a variety

Girls P.E. class inside the HB High School gymnasium, late 1920s

243

Huntington Central Park Equestrian Center

Just off Goldenwest Street, two miles from the Pacific Ocean, you will find 25 acres of a completely different universe from the world of business and commerce. Turn in at the sign which reads "Huntington Central Park Equestrian Center," drive up the short driveway, park and get out. You will be amazed at what you will see.

Perhaps a rider will be practicing Western-style riding in one arena while someone else is "posting" English-style in another. It is possible a rider will be working with her horse on dressage, which is the exhibition of a horse to show its obedience and deportment or a "ballet on horseback." As you walk down the pathway into the lower part of the Center, you may spot the farrier (blacksmith) shoeing a horse. People in dusty jeans and boots can be spotted up and down the pathways. You certainly will see many, many horses and many happy people engaged in activities with them.

One of the largest equestrian facilities in Orange County, Huntington Central Park Equestrian Center dates back to the 1950s when there were numerous private stables in the area as well as Rex Reynold's stables, known as Rex's Rental Stables. However, by the early 1980s, horses were seen by builders and developers as a liability and efforts were being made to eliminate them from the area. Huntington Beach was no different, and since the city still owned the land the stables were

standing on, it appeared equestrian activities were doomed. However, determined horse lovers united to save their sport in Huntington Beach, and one group which was especially effective was ETI, Equestrian Trails, Inc., Coral #100, a national organization to safeguard equestrian interests. They lobbied the City Council for land to be set aside for stables and trails, persuaded horse lovers to enter the political arena and eventually won the battle resulting in the preservation of the area for equestrian purposes.

The city of Huntington Beach took bids from individuals interested in building an equestrian facility, eventually awarding the project to Eddie Milligan in 1982. Milligan went to work and built the center, primarily the upper level portion.

In 1986, Mary Harris Warren entered the picture. Mary had always loved horses and began riding at the age of eight. She herself is a champion rider and is especially famed for her jumping skills and beautiful jumpers. She was looking for a career at the time, and it didn't take long before Mary and her father, Bill Harris, bought a partnership interest in the Center with Milligan. By 1989, Mary and Bill became the sole owners and have remained so ever since.

The location of the Huntington Central Park Equestrian Center is designated as parkland and therefore cannot be developed. The area adjacent to the center is specified for estate housing where owners are permitted to have horses on their property. A system of trails has been constructed to meander through the area.

The Harris's have made considerable improvements during their tenure. Throughout the center, they have added a 24-stall riding school barn with tack store, three more riding arenas, 136 pipe corrals plus 15 additional wash racks. Horse equipment is sold at Steinberg's Tack and Feed.

Currently, the center staff consists of Mary, a foreman and about 11 others including stall cleaners and maintenance people.

The center sponsors riding shows throughout the year. Its biggest event is the G.T.E. Summer Classic. For this event,

244

Western-style riding as well as English is available at Huntington Central Park Equestrian Center.

the city allows the use of the park next to the center. Portable stalls for the horses are brought in, allowing an additional 400 horses to compete. The horses begin arriving on Monday of the second week of August and stay through the following Sunday. The shows consist of horse jumping at various levels of difficulty. Riding arenas are set up in the park where riders and spectators enjoy the competition on the grass. Giant white tents line the grass fields and spectators enjoy brunch while watching the competition. The show concludes with a high jump contest where the G.T.E. Show record is six feet nine inches. The G.T.E. Summer Classic Horse Show raises money for the Huntington Beach Art Center, supporting ongoing programs at the Art Center.

The center's riding school is open six days a week. Not only can eager riders learn Western and English style riding, they can also learn dressage. In addition, polo lessons are available. Polo teams have scrimmages every weekend, and there are tournaments about once a month for local and outside teams. Polo matches are

open to the public on Thursdays, Saturdays and Sundays for no charge. Lessons are also available.

There are several different trainers at the center, each providing horses for whatever kind of lessons are offered. The riding school has about 10 horses used for lessons and teaching English riding. There is a Western trainer who has about five horses available for lessons and another trainer who teaches English-style riding. There is also a trainer for dressage who uses a special dressage trained horse for lessons.

If you just want a pleasant weekend afternoon, you can join a one hour guided trail ride through the parks of Huntington Beach. If you are contemplating the purchase of a horse, you can lease a horse from the center while you are deciding on a purchase.

Mary and Bill have not only developed Huntington Central Park Equestrian Center, they have also developed a tremendous relationship with the city. It is their intention to do all they can to keep the world of horses part of the growth and expansion of the city of Huntington Beach.

The annual G.T.E. Summer Classic features a high jump contest. The current record is 6 feet 9 inches.

Oral & Maxillofacial Surgery
Dr. Ronald M. Kaminishi

Fishing and the lure of surfing first called Dr. Ronald Kaminishi to Huntington Beach during his youth, when he remembers the area as mostly farms and marshes. Then, in 1989, he and his partners opened the Oral & Maxillofacial Surgery Group in the Memorial Medical Center building in Huntington Beach.

Smiling and eating without pain or discomfort are activities that most people consider part of everyday living. Dr. Kaminishi is able to help people for which these activities are unpleasant or difficult.

Most people know their oral surgeon as someone who removes wisdom teeth. But, oral and maxillofacial surgery consists of a much broader scope of treatment. Correcting deformities of the face and jaws, treating infections and tumors, and fixing broken jaws and facial bones are just part of the treatment provided by the Oral & Maxillofacial Surgery Group. Additional services include treating diseases of the jaw joints (TMJ), treating facial pain disorders, placing dental implants, reconstructing the face and jaws with bone and synthetic implants, and cosmetic enhancement of

Dr. Ronald Kaminishi, maxillofacial surgeon, researcher, author and lecturer.
Photo by Heritage Photography

Dr. Kaminishi (right) performs arthroscopic surgery of the TMJ with assistant, as students watch.

the face. These are all areas included in the realm of the oral and maxillofacial surgeon.

In the area of education, the contributions by Dr. Kaminishi and his associates are many. Dental libraries across the country have numerous listings which include Dr. Kaminishi's name. Most of the articles and chapters he has written focus on TMJ arthroscopic surgery. They appear in dental journals, and are considered a part of most classic dental school textbooks.

Dr. Kaminishi understands and often defines the many roles of oral surgery as senior surgeon at the Oral & Maxillofacial Surgery Group, with partners Dr. David Hochwald, Dr. Michael Marshall and Dr. Peter Lam. His goal is to expand the limits and surgical boundaries of oral and maxillofacial surgery in order to treat disease more effectively and efficiently. Not only does Dr. Kaminishi perform surgery, he conducts research in his specialty and shares this information with his colleagues worldwide through lectures and scientific programs. He describes his practice as one of the most unique in the United States because it involves three distinct areas: surgery, research and education. In addition to surgery and research, Dr. Kaminishi is a clinical professor at USC Dental School, and has served as assistant professor at Loma Linda Dental School, Loma Linda Medical School and UCI Medical School.

Early in his career, together with his partner, Dr. Howard Davis, Dr. Kaminishi helped research and develop the field of orthognathic surgery, creating and perfecting surgical techniques, as well as developing new instrumentation necessary to perform this surgery. Orthognathic surgery is performed to correct jaws and faces which

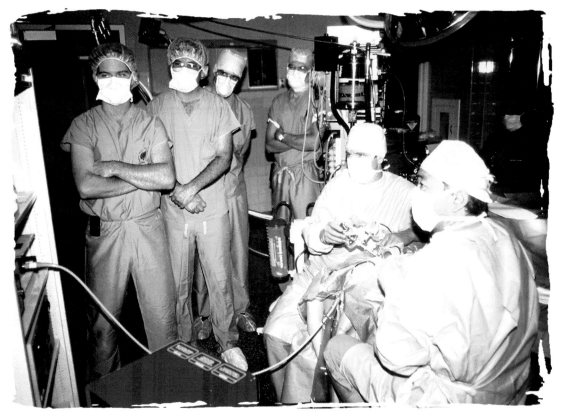

develop abnormally and impair eating, speaking and formation of normal facial expressions. It is the first true resolution available for people with these problems.

In 1985 Dr. Kaminishi traveled to Japan to work with Dr. Masatoshi Ohnishi, the originator of arthroscopic surgery for TMJ. This surgery is performed with a very small incision using a scope to look inside the temporomandibular joint. It was a major medical breakthrough in the surgery of human temporo-mandibular joints, allowing for significantly less pain and permanent debilitation. Dr. Kaminishi brought this information back to the United States, developing surgical protocols with his partner and the help of the USC Dental School Anatomy Department. He also worked with surgical instrument makers throughout the world in development of TMJ arthroscopic surgical instruments.

At a historic meeting held at Memorial Medical Center in Long Beach in July of 1986, Dr. Kaminishi and his partner, Dr. Christopher Davis, formally introduced TMJ arthroscopic surgery to the United States. After this historic introduction, arthroscopic surgery grew in popularity to the point where it is one of the most common modes of surgical treatment for TMJ. Even so, Dr. Kaminishi continues his research, endeavoring to enhance and improve this modern surgical technique.

Dental implants are another area gaining widespread recognition. After many years of development a system has been devised that works very effectively. For the first time, people who lose teeth have the option of a replacement that looks and functions almost as good or better than the original. With this new option it is possible to bite, chew or eat almost anything that a person with natural teeth would eat.

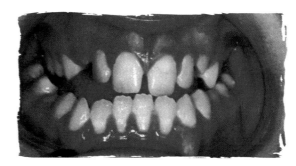

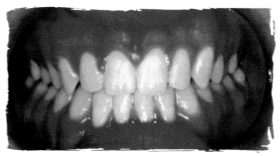

Working with his partners, Dr. Kaminishi continues to improve the techniques used and the results achieved by dental implants. Particularly important to the process of dental implants is his extensive experience in bone grafting procedures over 25 years. Preparation of the jaw with sufficient bone to place the dental implants is currently the area where research and education will result in improvements that will be most beneficial to patients.

The quest for new and more effective surgical advancements continues at the Oral & Maxillofacial Surgery Group through research, surgery and education. For Dr. Kaminishi there is always the vision of a more effective technique and another new surgical procedure waiting to be discovered.

247

(Left) This photo of a patient before surgery shows that her upper jaw is too small and her lower jaw is too big.

(Right) After surgery the patient's face has balance and ideal dental occlusion or bite. Her upper jaw was brought forward and her lower jaw was moved back. This surgery was combined with orthodontic treatment.

Orange Coast Memorial Medical Center

Orange Coast Memorial Medical Center is a testimonial to high standards. As a tribute to its quality, Orange Coast was recently awarded Accreditation with Commendation by the Joint Commission of Accreditation of Healthcare Organizations, an honor granted to fewer than five percent of the hospitals in the nation.

Established in 1996 as a nonprofit community hospital, Orange Coast Memorial Medical Center is the newest member of the Memorial Health Services family of hospitals which also includes Long Beach Memorial Medical Center, Saddleback Memorial Medical Center and Anaheim Memorial Medical Center. The extensive history and tradition of this institution is the foundation of its purpose, to set the standard of excellence in health care.

The hospital, originally built in 1986 as a 135-bed facility, was the brainchild of Dr. Robert Gumbiner, the founder of FHP. In 1992 an expansion of the facility added 95 beds to increase the total to its current 230-bed capacity.

When Gumbiner developed FHP, the system became the prototype for an integrated health care system. A visionary, Gumbiner strongly believed that hospitals should regard patients as special customers and cater to their specific needs, a belief carried on today. This revolutionary idea quickly replaced the more institutional, sterile hospitals of the past. Special attention was given to the exterior and interior design of the hospital giving it the atmosphere of a hotel rather than an infirmary.

Today, the college-like campus of Orange Coast Memorial continues to cater to the customer — the patient. Freeway close in the city of Fountain Valley, the hospital offers convenient and safe parking. To appeal to even the most discriminating tastes, the hospital employs a full-time executive chef offering catering and other hotel services. Extra attention is given to the cleanliness of the grounds, enhancing the hospital's appeal to patients and visitors. Wallpaper gives a warm ambience, and tasteful murals and paintings grace the walls. Patient rooms open onto private balconies providing a sense of openness and freedom, while electrical components are hidden from view. Vibrant plants and flowers accent corridors that are covered with soft-toned carpeting throughout the building. The exterior landscaping of trees, flowers, fountains and walkways enhance the architecture.

Dedicated to serving the health care needs of the residents of Fountain Valley, Huntington Beach and surrounding communities, Orange Coast Memorial is especially proud of its physicians and medical services. Crucial to its population, the 24-hour, full-service emergency center is conveniently located off the 405 freeway at Brookhurst and

An overview of Orange Coast Memorial Medical Center

248

Talbert. Its staff of board-certified physicians, expert in the field of emergency medicine, stands ready to handle any emergency — large or small.

Led by a team of the most prestigious physicians in the United States, The Memorial Care Breast Center at Orange Coast provides imaging, pathology, surgery, oncology and even a second-opinion service all under one roof, eliminating the need to travel miles from office to lab to hospital. In addition, every screening mammogram is read by two different radiologists, extensively experienced in breast-imaging and interpretation, and results are available in 24 hours. The Breast Center also offers support groups designed to educate and assist patients through stressful medical events.

The Women's and Children's Center at Orange Coast offers excellence in obstetrics, gynecology, infertility and pediatric care. It is also reassuring to know that the hospital has one of the finest Neonatal Intensive Care Units in the county for babies needing specialized care. A perfect choice for childbirth, Orange Coast Memorial Medical presents parents with a wide range of prenatal and postnatal education programs. Classes include childbirth preparation, breastfeeding, postpartum care, parenting and baby massage. The hospital also hosts an elegant Maternity Tea designed to familiarize new parents with maternity and pediatric units within the hospital.

For quality cosmetic surgery in a safe hospital setting, the Cosmetic Center is ready with the latest in procedures, including facelifts, tummy tucks, breast augmentation or reduction, eyelid surgery, liposuction and other body-contouring techniques. The center offers a spa-like atmosphere that pampers patients with private parking, private entrance and elegantly decorated private rooms.

Along with the expertise of its surgeons, Orange Coast Memorial also provides an exceptional array of surgical services including orthopedics, gynecology, neurology, podiatry, vascular, urology and surgical weight loss.

A leader in senior care, the hospital has always focused on the special needs of its older adults, whether it be streamlining cumbersome paperwork or taking extra time to explain an individual treatment plan. Baby boomers, soon to be part of the

largest population, have gained attention at the Orange Coast Memorial Medical Center, and physicians and staff are already addressing issues specific to an aging population. Currently, senior programs include flu shots, health screenings, fitness programs, health information and access to services such as home health care.

Future plans for Orange Coast Memorial include additional expansion and building to keep pace with the demand for quality medical services. Chief operating officer, Marcia Manker, is with the center to guide it into its future plans. The hospital boasts an expansion that includes more than six additional services including occupational health, psychiatry, neurology, cardiology, stroke prevention and complementary health care services.

Those who use the hospital do so with the confidence that it is a place for healing, health education and emotional sustenance. To this end, Orange Coast Memorial Medical Center continues in its pledge to better serve the individuals and families of the rapidly growing community they call home.

Rainbow After-School Care

Tay Norton, owner of Rainbow After-School Care, is a remarkable example of a single mother who solved her own day care problems by solving other people's day care problems. Today, she runs a thriving, licensed day care center for about 230 children and has to turn away 40-50 children every year.

In 1983, Tay found herself a single mom unable to find affordable, quality child care. Because she had always wanted to work with children, she decided to open a day care center herself. She entered into a partnership and her first endeavor, "Under the Rainbow," was a preschool center located in Seal Beach. Tay worked at the day care center in the morning, went home to be with her own school-age child and also cared for ten children in her home. At that time, there was little in the way of after-school care available. Word of her fine program got around, and her telephone started ringing off the wall. By this time, Tay's second child was two or three years old, and she wondered how she was going to expand care for both of their age groups.

In the spirit of "if you can't get it done, do it yourself," Tay presented a proposal to Ocean View School District to run an after-school care program in its facilities. Representatives of the District observed her preschool program and were so impressed they agreed to give her a chance. Initially, the Rainbow program was located at Marine View (which is now a middle school) but the following year, the program moved to Harbour View where it is today. Tay and her partner split their business, with

Tay and Robert Norton are the proud owners of Rainbow After-School Care.

Tay taking the after-school program and the other partner taking the preschool. By 1987, Rainbow After-School Care was firmly established.

Tay has carefully developed the philosophy of Rainbow After-School Care: "Our program at Rainbow encourages the development of a strong self-esteem

and feeling of competence. We believe a sense of accomplishment and self-worth can grow through a balance of structured play experiences, organized activities and free choice. All children are treated as individuals with warmth and acceptance. They are encouraged to communicate their feelings and verbally express themselves."

Rainbow opens its doors at 6:30 a.m. and stays open until 6:00 p.m, year around, closing only 10 days out of the year. The center is open during winter and spring breaks and on some holidays when Harbour View school is closed. Rainbow admits children in grades kindergarten through sixth grade but is currently testing a small, modular prekindergarten program for siblings of children already enrolled at Rainbow.

A wide variety of enrichment activities are offered, such as cooking, dancing, arts, crafts, math and science. Older children can take advantage of a homework period. Out on the playground, the children can choose from karaoke, organized games, skating, jumping rope, joining ball games and riding bikes. Experts are brought in to show reptiles and puppies. There are numerous field trips during the summer weeks, when the kids can enjoy water activities, bowling, roller skating and visits

Director Kristin Olson reads to an avid audience of children.

to museums. In short, a full and enriching array of age-appropriate activities is offered.

The program is designed in a "family style." During snack time, the ratio of teacher to students is one-to-nine and during homework time it is one-to-ten, both of which are very workable. The state legally requires a one-to-14 ratio, but Rainbow features a smaller grouping.

Rainbow leases classrooms at Harbour View and has access to a large, multipurpose room available for second through fifth grades in the afternoon when school is dismissed. Rainbow also uses Harbour View's outside areas and facilities after school. The Rainbow program is very portable. It puts things away when not in use, but when the time comes, out come the tables and chairs, toys and equipment.

There are currently 22 caring, enthusiastic staff members working at Rainbow After-School Care. Director Kristin Olson started with the center at the age of 19. She had planned to become an elementary teacher but since finishing her bachelor's degree has chosen to stay with Rainbow. Kristin's role has become an intricate part of this large day care center. Margery Armstrong, Tay's mother, has been a strong behind-the-scenes supporter both financially and educationally. Tay attributes her own positive attitude toward diverse situations to the tremendous inspiration from her mother and her own strong, Christian beliefs. Since her early days, Tay has married again, and husband Robert Norton is a very important part of the second-through fifth-grade program. Robert's consistent support and love for the children he works with has been a tremendous asset to their ever-growing enrollment. With Rainbow's increased enrollment, Assistant Director Michael Greenberg has been a welcome addition to Rainbow's team.

Tay has many dreams for the future. "We want to grow and would like to find a place in Huntington Beach that is an off-school site location where we have more opportunities to expand into other areas. Many parents have expressed interest in a program for infants and preschoolers. Also we're very aware of the need for after-school care for older children. Every year we send children on to middle school where there isn't an on-site after-school care program. We would also like to offer a place for this age group to come on Friday nights where there's supervision and organized activities. It would be a safe place to grow and be with friends." If her past record is any measure, Tay will make sure her dreams come true.

251

Tay's mother, Margery Armstrong, has been a supportive influence.

KOCE Television

In KOCE's more than two and one half decades of community service, it remains a civilizing, vital alternative to commercial television. The year 2000 will mark its 28th year of service to public television viewers throughout Southern California.

The station began modestly with a six hour per day schedule. By 1984, KOCE expanded its broadcast time to 16 hours per day with more than 50,000 hours of television for the residents of Orange County and it is among the top 17 most watched public television stations in America. Today, KOCE has over 3 million viewers in Southern California.

KOCE's mission is to be known as the communities' preeminent provider of education, information and culture, through a comprehensive broadcast schedule of quality television programs. The station also serves the educational need of Coastline Community, Golden West and Orange Coast colleges. KOCE invites local businesses and community residents to call them to find out how they can become involved in the support of their local public television station.

KOCE maintains a high level of public affairs broadcasts with exclusive local specials and series which meet unique needs in Orange County. "Real Orange," its weeknight news and lifestyle series for and about the people of Orange County, debuted in September, 1997. "HEAR & Now" on KOCE's Secondary Audio Program (SAP) channel, provides a unique reading service for the print impaired. The station also offers a wide range of public television pro-

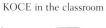
KOCE in the classroom

grams including "American Experience," "The Lawrence Welk Show," "Nova," "The Nightly Business Report," British comedies and National Geographic specials.

KOCE was involved with the city of Huntington Beach since its earliest days. It has televised live events, talent shows, the Huntington Beach Fourth of July Parade and the annual "GTE Summer Classic" equestrian event.

Over the years, KOCE has won hundreds of awards and honors for both local and national programming. Among these are Emmy Awards, Golden Mike Awards and Disneyland Community Service Awards.

Working in conjunction with Coastline Community College, KOCE annually broadcasts more than 1,500

hours of telecourse programs, enabling thousands of adults to earn college-level credit while viewing and studying in the convenience of their own homes. With its "Degree TV," KOCE boasts one of the largest formal adult-education schedules of any public television station in the United States.

Additionally, KOCE "Classroom K-12" instruction reaches more than one million California elementary and

secondary students, including over 400,000 students in Orange County. KOCE's Telecommunications of Orange County (TOC) offers specialized instruction for educators in Hyper Studio, using the Inernet, Web site design, grant writing and more.

Community service is also an important part of KOCE's mission, as a catalyst for community action and in generating partnerships between local businesses, foundations and nonprofit agencies. The Friends of KOCE, the station's community volunteer team, provide essential resources for KOCE's annual fund-raising campaigns and special events.

With many new discoveries in communications technology, public television and KOCE-TV will continue to chart a viable course on the information superhighway. The station's home pages can be found on the Internet with links to Coast District colleges, PBS television program home page and more. With the digital revolution in progress, KOCE is preparing for the opportunities and challenges ahead when television, computers and personal communications become integrated and interactive.

KOCE is poised for an exciting future — one in which it will be able to create and distribute even more civilizing, educational television than ever before.

California Rehabilitation & Sports Therapy

In what has since been called the "pop heard around the world," President Clinton (like an estimated 7,000 Americans each year) ruptured his quadriceps tendon — the connective tissue that binds the powerful muscles of the thigh to the kneecap — when he slipped on a dimly lit wooden step.

The accident, and subsequent media coverage of the president's orthopedic odyssey, illustrated the impact and importance of physical and rehabilitative therapy in the recovery process today. Once utilized to rehabilitate athletes, physical therapy methods are recommended by physicians for patients recovering from a variety of injuries.

Staffed by a team of physical therapists who are also Board Certified Orthopedic Specialists, the Huntington Beach-based California Rehabilitation & Sports Therapy center represents an innovative approach to "optimizing human performance in work, sport and daily life."

Founded by Alan E. Vogel in 1987, this multi-specialty rehabilitation service group offers "prehabilitative, rehabilitative, education and consultation services." The group specializes in orthopedic rehabilitation, including work environment assessment, sports medicine, occupational therapy, industrial rehabilitation, headache-facial pain therapy and advanced spine rehabilitation.

California Rehabilitation & Sports Therapy reports a high success rate with patients of all ages who have had multiple surgeries, failed experiences with rehabilitation at other clinics and complicated diagnoses. Vogel adds that the company's success is a direct result of his staff's "commitment to quality care and willingness to go the extra mile" for each patient.

Unlike many other rehabilitative centers across the state, California Rehabilitation & Sports Therapy is locally owned and managed by a trio of Board Certified Orthopedic Specialists. Although the state doesn't require continuing education, employees of this Huntington Beach-based firm mandates regular attendance at seminars and workshops to keep abreast of the latest technologies and innovative therapies.

Company founder Alan E. Vogel (left) credits the company's success to his staff's "commitment to quality care and willingness to go the extra mile" for each patient.

253

Another factor that sets this firm apart from its competition is the commitment of its founders to the community. When the Marina High School administration was having a hard time retaining the services of an athletic trainer, Vogel volunteered his services. The Huntington Beach School District, Water District and Robinwood Little League are among the local organizations to benefit from the group's commitment to the community.

"Our success really comes down to our commitment to quality care," says Vogel. "If you really are better clinically and you care, you'll see good results. For therapists, that's what it's all about. We get a lot of satisfaction from being able to offer our clients relief from pain and optimizing their function and performance with long-term results."

"There's a high rate of burnout in this industry. As a therapist, it's difficult to continue in this position if you aren't experiencing success with patients. That's why we are selective in hiring individuals who love what they do and are committed to offering their clients the very best care available."

Golden West College

Golden West College opened on September 12, 1966, and for over three decades it has been providing academic excellence and student success to the residents of Huntington Beach and the neighboring communities.

"We have educated a generation of students who have entered almost every profession and trade," said Golden West College President Dr. Kenneth Yglesias. "Many of our former students are sending their children to Golden West, and that's a testament to the excellence of Golden West College's commitment to providing the programs and classes that meet community needs. The success of our students is our purpose and our pride. With the observance of the accomplishments of the past 30 years comes the renewed commitment to our students for the new millennium."

Back when jackrabbits darted across dirt patches that had yet developed into lawns, Golden West was lauded by Time magazine for its use of high-tech equipment, such as slide projectors with integrated tape players.

These days, Golden West College students learn how to use and program the World Wide Web, build computers and make interactive CD-ROM presentations. They are training the next generation of police officers, nurses, architects, television producers, musicians and recording arts engineers.

Since opening, over 20,000 students have received associate in arts degrees. Countless others have earned certificates of achievement in career and technical

Students prepare to embark on new paths as they graduate from Golden West College. More than a quarter of GWC students continue their educations by earning bachelor's degrees from California State University or University of California campuses.

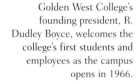

Golden West College's founding president, R. Dudley Boyce, welcomes the college's first students and employees as the campus opens in 1966.

fields. In all, more than half a million students have been served by Golden West College.

It doesn't stop at academics. Golden West College's 22 collegiate sports teams have won 28 state championships in the 1990s, double the total of the next closest college. Dominant in competition have been the "beach-sport teams": men's and women's water polo and men's and women's volleyball.

While much has changed in the 30-plus years since Golden West College opened its doors, one constant has marked the college's history: providing quality education for all in the community. In addition to learning a myriad of technical job skills, Golden West College students also can start work on their bachelor's degrees at a fraction of the price charged at both private and state-run universities.

Faculty members, most of whom hold master's or doctoral degrees, are dedicated to student success. The college's typically small classes, always taught by faculty, prepare students to meet their career and personal goals. Additionally, state-of-the-art equipment and facilities keep students on the cutting edge of employment trends in more than 60 career programs at Golden West College. Faculty members also build bonds with business and professional leaders to stay current with job training needs.

Golden West College's doors are open to the community for use of athletic facilities, for picnics on the college's spacious lawns and for art events such as theater and the world-renowned symphonic band. Golden West College is proud to be the home of the Pacific Coast Civic Light Opera.

With Golden West College just around the corner, the student's future is golden!

Huntington Beach Historical Society

n 1898, a young man and his wife moved to a town called Pacific City, bought land on an ancient Gabrielino Indian midden and built a family home. They farmed the 500 acres, planting lima beans, chili peppers, celery and sugar beets. William and Mary Juanita Newland, one of the founding families of Huntington Beach, raised 10 children, helped establish the Methodist Church, the local newspaper, bank and the first school.

Newland built a Midwestern two-story, nine-room farmhouse, representative of the Queen Anne Victorian style of architecture. After Mary Newland's death in 1952, employees of Signal Oil Co. lived there for the next 20 years.

On May 4, 1972, the Huntington Beach Junior Women's Club came to the aid of the Newland house by re-activating the Huntington Beach Historical Society. At that time its sole purpose became restoration of the house. In the next two years the house suffered repeated attacks of malicious vandalism, including loss of the fireplace mantle, doorknobs and chandeliers.

Soon after the society began work on the house, someone set fire to a mattress in the attic causing a hole in the roof. The water used to put out the fire and subsequent rains destroyed the lath and plaster walls. The project proved more frustrating than anyone had imagined.

Undaunted, the members pried off boards protecting the windows and stepped over broken glass to begin the massive undertaking. They trooped into the house armed with trash cans and shovels.

Residents of Huntington Beach banded together in a grand volunteer effort, involving over 200 people, to help in the historical society's maiden undertaking. The main sources of income were fund-raisers, donated labor and later, conceived by board members, sponsorship of individual rooms in the house. A brass plaque engraved with the donor's name hangs amidst the restored woodwork and replicated furnishings, each one a testament to the men and women who gave unselfishly of their time and money. Today, the Newland House Museum, the oldest house in Huntington Beach, rests on the bluff as a reminder of the city's interesting past.

With the success of the Newland House restoration, the society spends time identifying other historic buildings in the city. For preservation and acceptance into the historical register, older buildings need to be brought up to city and state safety codes and standards.

Many possible candidates for recognition have been destroyed due to lack of funding. One of the society's successes is the Boy Scout Cabin in Lake Park, which was recommended as a historical landmark.

The society has become a repository of old photographs, heirlooms, artifacts and period clothing, which are all exhibited at various times in the Newland House. Members record the oral histories of older residents for future generations to study. Ongoing projects include lectures and community meetings, an annual flag retirement ceremony, an old-timers tea and entry into the Fourth of July parade.

Standing watch over the cherished memories of the city's history, the society encourages citizens to volunteer their time and/or money to allow the extraordinary work to continue — preserve the past for future generations and support the society by becoming a lifetime member or a docent at the Newland House.

255

(Above) The Newland House, pictured here after the Huntington Beach Historical Society renovations, it is maintained by the Huntington Beach Historical Society. *Photo by Carl Clink, Huntington Beach Historical Society*

The Newland House, built in 1898 by William and Mary Newland, before the Huntington Beach Historical Society renovations

Huntington Beach Hospital

A dramatic transformation was taking place in the Huntington Beach landscape in 1967. The opening of Huntington Beach Hospital on April 2, then known as Huntington Beach Intercommunity Hospital, was part of this transformation from endless bean fields to an urban community. The city's first acute care hospital quickly became a center of community activity and has continued to fulfill a commitment by providing excellence in health care, community outreach and education programs.

Sherrill Dick, R.N., first ER Supervisor at this 24-hour emergency facility, recalls that she started in January of 1967 to get the hospital ready prior to opening in April. In 1997, on its 30th anniversary, the hospital was named one of the nation's top accredited hospitals by the Joint Commission on Accreditation of Healthcare Organizations (JCAHO). This seaside community hospital of 135 beds has achieved national status with the help of over 500 employees and 280 physicians. Today Sherrill Dick is still an important part of the staff, working weekends as house supervisor. As the years passed, many specialized centers joined the hospital campus, offering numerous areas of medical and surgical expertise. Today the hospital provides nationally recognized specialty and comprehensive health care treatment at one convenient location. These specialized centers include: The California Orthopaedic Center, The Center for Gastrointestinal Wellness, The California Pain Center, and The Southern California Nasal and Sinus Program. The California Orthopaedic Center provides an advanced, interactive approach to orthopaedic services. These four specialty programs establish the hospital as a resource for wellness and education. Additional special services include a comprehensive Occupational Medicine Program for injured workers, a Senior Friends Organization, men's and women's wellness programs and a free 24-hour physician referral and community education hot line.

Many young college students attending Golden West College or UCI have been grateful over the past three decades for a supportive hospital volunteer program, the Silver Anchor Auxiliary. The auxilary raises money for numerous medical scholarships, in addition to its primary function of performing various services for patients and hospital staff. One such scholarship, the Marian Meyers Scholarship, is awarded to a UCI medical student to honor a former volunteer who walked miles to work each Sunday while in her 70s.

As part of its outreach program, the hospital works closely with the Health Science Career Academy at Westminster High School and the Ocean View High School Business Academy. It provides lecturers, tours, mentors and summer internships for these programs, enriching the educational and vocational experiences of local students.

A variety of community education classes are offered at Huntington Beach Hospital: a Diabetes Education series; Heartsaver CPR training; Home Alone, to prepare young adolescents on home safety; and a Basics of Baby Sitting class to prepare teenage baby sitters to responsibly care for children. In addition, parents and volunteer coaches from youth sports programs learn about preventing injuries through Huntington Beach Hospital's Coaches Seminar.

Huntington Beach Hospital community involvement also includes over 1,800 area seniors who know how to make the most of their days. As part of the National Association of Senior Friends, they enjoy bowling, bridge, Tai Chi, mall walking, armchair aerobics, and trips in the U.S. and abroad.

The hospital has touched many lives. Former patients often recall receiving flowers and a personal note from the Hospital Administrator, as well as the special dedication and spirit of the physicians and staff. Known for its excellence of medical treatment and patient care with a caring touch, Huntington Beach Hospital has roots deep within the community.

Wycliffe Bible Translators

Under a hot July Southern California sun in 1971, prominent Orange County businessman Ralph E. Welch raised a New Guinea warrior's adz over his head and struck the hard-packed clay soil on the 4.7 acres of land at Beach and Adams. The occasion was the groundbreaking ceremony that marked the beginning of a new 120-foot by 140-foot three-story 60,000-square-foot building that was to house the international headquarters of Wycliffe Bible Translators.

Ralph and Rowena Welch, with their daughter and two sons, owned the property jointly. In recognition of Wycliffe's worldwide philanthropic ministry among the world's ethnic minority peoples, the Welch family members donated the choice piece of property that became 19891 Beach Boulevard.

Wycliffe's founder was William Cameron Townsend, who was born in Riverside County and grew up in Downey. In 1917 at age 21, Townsend took a break from his senior year at Occidental College and went to Guatemala, under the auspices of the Bible House of Los Angeles, as an itinerant Bible salesman. He soon realized that most of the ethnic minority peoples in Guatemala could not read or write their own distinctive languages since they were never written down. Nor could the vast majority of the people he met read the Spanish Bible and Scripture portions he was commissioned to try and sell.

Townsend remained in Guatemala and began to implement a most remarkable dream, a dream to translate the New Testament into the language of the Cakchiquel people and teach them to read and write in their own language.

Against all odds, but with the help of his Swedish wife, a missionary from Chicago whom he met and married in Guatemala, Townsend spent the next 15 years as an educator, Bible translator, literacy expert and more. He established a clinic and schools, including a Bible school to train Cakchiquel men to minister to their own people. After completing the Cakchiquel New Testament in 10 years, Townsend and his wife conducted extensive reading and literacy classes.

Townsend left Guatemala in 1932 with an even bigger dream, namely, to begin a school to train prospective Bible translators in linguistics and pioneer living. In 1934 he established "Camp Wycliffe" in Sulphur Springs, Arkansas, with two students.

Townsend's dream has grown into one of the most significant Bible translation, literacy and academic endeavors in the world with more than 6,000 members serving in 50 countries. Currently Wycliffe translators work in more than 1,000 languages worldwide and have helped to complete New Testament translations in more than 450 languages.

Wycliffe's first office was over a garage in Glendale, California, with one employee and 13 field members. In 1960 the office moved to Santa Ana. The Huntington Beach office opened its doors in 1974. Shortly after, it became Wycliffe's U.S. headquarters as the international headquarters opened in Dallas, Texas. In 1996 it was named George M. Cowan and Kenneth L. Watters Building in recognition of their outstanding leadership of Wycliffe Bible Translators.

The Huntington Beach office currently has 250 workers. The primary task of this home office is to help provide the resources — personnel, prayer and finances — to accomplish the primary ministry goals of the corporation.

Fumi Shioya

Above all else, Ezernet Inc. values people and desires to enhance and improve the human situation. To that end, the Oyamas wish to introduce Fumi Shioya of Huntington Beach, a woman whose life story is certain to bring hope to all who become acquainted with her.

Fumiko "Fumi" Shioya personifies the hope that comes through a life surrendered by faith to God. Fumi knows from her own experience the love and provision of the Almighty.

Crippled with cerebral palsy — brain damage caused by a lack of oxygen for several minutes after birth — Shioya has spent most of her life in a wheelchair, unable to walk, talk, speak or even feed herself.

What she has been able to do, however, is win the hearts of thousands of people with her deep and unshakable trust in God, whom she has seen supply her needs over and over again.

At the urging of a friend, Shioya enlisted the help of Lula Rampey of Garden Grove to research her life and put Fumi's words down in a book. The result is a moving autobiography entitled *Fumi — A Tool in the Hands of God*, which chronicles her birth in Anaheim to Japanese parents, Junji and Kikuye Shioya, the resulting cerebral palsy and the series of obstacles she was forced to face in subsequent years.

In 1942, her family was sent to a World War II internment camp for Japanese Americans after the attack on Pearl Harbor. After their release three years later, Fumi's mother entered a state mental institution where she died two years later. After her father succumbed to lung cancer in 1954, Fumi was left in the state's care.

She eventually moved to the Huntington Beach Convalescent Hospital, where she has spent the past 37 years of her life.

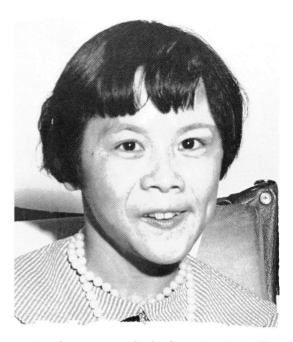

But these are merely the facts. Fumi's "real" story lies in her faith in God, the lives she has touched and the outpouring of love she receives from friends.

Fumi's parents chose at the beginning of her life to allow her as much freedom as they could, to demand from her as much as she could give. They nurtured in her a positive, accepting spirit and freed her from a life trapped in pity and bitterness. After they died, she trusted that God would continue to provide for her. And He has.

As she was moved from hospital to hospital, she could see God's hand at work, arranging for someone to be there who could provide for her special needs and foster her independent spirit. Although she had no source of income other than minimal state support, her physical needs have always been met in abundance, even to the provision of a motorized wheelchair, a small electric keyboard, and a special stylus and letterboard which allow her to communicate in both English and Spanish.

Her simple, profound trust that God loves her and that He will supply all her needs has been a moving testimony and source of encouragement to the many who know her personally and to the thousands who have met her through her book. Her example reminds people of what is truly important in life and bears witness to the love and faithfulness of God, who loves unconditionally and without limit.

Photo by Debbie Stock

Bibliography

Armor, Samuel. *History of Orange County, California, With Biographical Sketches*. Los Angeles Historical Record Company. 1911.

_____. *History of Orange County, California With Biographical Sketches*. Los Angeles Historical Record Company. 1921.

Ballman, Irana Freeman. *Westminster Colony 1969-1979*. Friis-Pioneer Press. Santa Ana, CA. 1983.

Bauer, Connie. *City of Huntington Beach Historical Notes*. City of Huntington Beach. 1975.

Bell, Horace. *On the Old West Coast; Being Further Reminiscences of a Ranger*. William Morrow and Co. New York, NY. c. 1930.

Biggs, Lt. Michael. *The First 80 Years: History of the Huntington Beach Police Department*. Huntington Beach, CA. 1989.

Bolsa Chica Conservancy. *Bolsa Chica Ecological Reserve Trail Guide*. Huntington Beach, CA. 1991.

Bolsa Chica Conservancy. *Sold: February 14, 1997*. Huntington Beach, CA. 1997

Boscana, Geronimo. *Chinigchinich: Historical Account of the Belief, Usages, Customs, and Extravagancies of This Mission of San Juan Capistrano*. First published in 1836. 1933 Edition. Fine Arts Press. Santa Ana, CA.

Brigandi, Phil. *Orange: The City Round the Plaza*. Heritage Media Corp. Encinitas, CA. 1998.

Brockway, Connie. *Huntington Beach History Notes*. City of Huntington Beach. Undated.

Cleland, Robert Glass. *Cattle On a Thousand Hills 1850-1880*. Huntington Library. San Marino, CA. 1969.

Cleland, Robert Glass. *From Wilderness to Empire: A History of California*. Alfred A. Knopf. New York, N.Y. 1959.

Colman, Fern Hill. "History of the Celery Industry." *Orange County History Series: Volume 3*. Orange County Historical Society. 1939.

_____. *Daily Evening Blade*. Santa Ana, CA. 1903-1908.

Friis, Leo J., *Orange County Through Four Centuries*. Pioneer Press. Santa Ana, CA. 1965.

Gallienne, William. *My Life Story*. Unpublished and undated.

Garcia, Mikel. "Federated Women's Clubs Through the Nation." *Proceedings of the Conference of Orange County History, 1988*. Orange County Historical Society and Chapman College. 1989.

Gleason, Duncan. *The Islands and Ports of California*. New York, N.Y. 1958.

Hall, Trowbridge. *California Trails: An Intimate Guide to the Old Missions*. McMillan Company. 1920.

Hallen-Gibson, Pamela. *The Golden Promise: An Illustrated History of Orange County*. Windsor Publications. 1986.

Hart, Louis Paul. "Huntington Beach." *The Arrowhead*. Industrial Department of the San Pedro, Los Angeles and Salt Lake Railroad, Los Angeles, CA. 1913.

Dumke, Glenn S. *The Boom of the Eighties in Southern California*. Huntington Library. San Marino, CA. 1944.

Henslick, Harry. *Huntington Beach: An Oral History*. Oral History Program, California State University Fullerton. Fullerton, CA. 1981.

Howard, Arline Huff. *Arline's Story: A Huntington Beach Story*. Unpublished. 1995.

Hunt, Rockwell D. *California Firsts*. Fearon Publishers. San Francisco. 1957.

_____. *Huntington Central Park*. City of Huntington Beach. 1974.

James, George Wharton. *In and Out of the Old Missions of California*. Little Brown, and Company. 1905.

Johnston, Bernice. *California's Gabrielino Indians*. Southwest Museum. Los Angeles, CA. 1962.

Jordan, Carol. *Tustin: City of Trees, An Illustrated History*. Heritage Media Corp., Encinitas, CA. 1996.

Kramer, Esther, and Keith Dixon. *A Hundred Years of Yesterday: A Centennial History of the People of Orange County and Their Communities*. Orange County Historical Commission and Orange County Register. (1988).

Lusignan, Paul. *Bolsa Chica Development*. Advisory Council on Historic Preservation. Western Office Review. Unpublished. (1994).

McCawley, William. *The First Angelinos: The Gabrielino Indians of Los Angeles*. Malki Museum Press. Morengo Indian Reservation, CA. 1996.

Meadows, Don. *Historic Place Names of Orange County*. Paisono Press Inc. Balboa Island, CA 1966.

Milkovitch, Barbara. *Influences of the Woman's Club on the Development of Orange County 1900-1930. Proceedings of the Conference of Orange County History 1988*. Orange County Historical Society and Chapman College. 1989.

_____. *Newland House Museum*. Huntington Beach Historical Society. 1987.

Newcomb, Rexford. *The Old Mission Churches and Historic Houses of California; Their History, Architecture, Art and Lore*. J. P. Lippincott and Company. 1925.

Orange County Genealogical Society. *Saddleback Ancestors*. Alladin Litho. and Art. Santa Ana, CA. 1969.

Person, Jerry. "A Look Back." Huntington Beach *Independent*. Huntington Beach, CA.

Pleasants, Adelina Brown *History of Orange County, California*. Los Angeles, CA. 1931.

Sanborn Insurance Company: *Sanborn Insurance Maps*. 1909, 1922, 1930.

Talbert, Thomas. *The Historical Volume and Reference Works...Orange County*. Whittier Historical Publishers. Whittier, CA. 1963.

Talbert, Thomas. *My Sixty Years in California*. Huntington Beach News: Huntington Beach, CA. 1952.

Thirtieth Street Architects. *Final Report of the Historic Resources Survey for the City of Huntington Beach*. Newport Beach, CA. July 1986.

Thirtieth Street Architects. *The Treasures in Your Community*. Huntington Beach Historical Society. 1986.

Wentworth, Alicia. *The Ultimate Challange*. Huntington Beach, CA. 1995.

_____. *City of Huntington Beach Miscellaneous Historical Data*. Huntington Beach, CA. 1979.

_____. *Orange County Historical Research Project No. 3105*. Works Progress Adminstration. Santa Ana, CA. 1937.

Wilson, John Albert. *History of Los Angeles County, California*. Thompson and West. Oakland, CA. 1880.

Index

264

265

267

Partners Index

270